Sanskrit Roots, Rote Learning and Cognates

Sanskrit Roots, Rote Learning and Cognates

Harry Nap

Table of Contents

Acknowledgments

Extensive usage of the following website.
"The Sanskrit Heritage Site" available at: https://sanskrit.inria.fr › DICO › index.en.html

Illustrations were taken from this alchemical text.
Georg von Welling
Opus mago-cabalisticum et theologicum : vom Uhrsprung und Erzeugung des Saltzes, dessen Natur und Eigenschafft, wie auch dessen Nutz und Gebrauch ... (1719)

Introduction

Standing on the shoulders of giants makes it much easier to survey the broad field of Sanskrit. Although Pāṇini (c. 500 BCE) codified the roots, William Dwight Whitney's (1885) "The Roots, Verb-Forms, and Primary Derivatives of the Sanskrit Language" has been the major influence regarding this collection of Sanskrit Roots. The main difference here is that the great majority of verb-forms has been paired down and the total number of roots is roughly double the original 800 roots that Whitney deemed to be genuine verbs[1]. In addition, the design is suitable for self-study.

The primary reason for creating this collection of 1610 Sanskrit roots is to facilitate the transition to direct engagement with Sanskrit texts. After having completed the required grammar, it will become apparent that when a beginning student is looking at a text next to nothing is recognised or understood. This is due (to a large extent) to a lack of vocabulary and the solution I propose involves, rather than merely acquiring vocabulary, obtaining the ability to "recognise patterns" within the Sanskrit text. Spotting patterns would be more a process of recognising the wide variety of forms that roots can generate instead of trying to directly cross-reference these with an English translation. Consequently, being able to make an "educated guess" with regard to lexical elements could transform the challenge of translating Sanskrit into something that becomes less bewildering and frustrating. Although rote learning is not really encouraged anymore, it arguably is instrumental for building up a frame of reference to make Sanskrit texts more accessible. To that purpose I would like to suggest a regime of memorising (at least) seven roots per day.[2] As 1610 roots might be excessive, memorising a lesser number is an option as well. A more detailed overview will follow later.

---

[1] According to Whitney more than half included in the list of approximately 2000 roots are fictitious and false roots presenting neither verb-forms nor derivatives.

[2] Roots are a linguistic sleight of hand as these are artificial constructs but they are convenient "shortcuts" for generating verbs, participles, nouns and the rest.

In principle, recognition and memorisation of Sanskrit roots will be easier if it is possible to find cognates in other European languages.[3] There exist in fact close relationships between Sanskrit and the rest of European languages but unfortunately these references often involve ancient forms of Avestan, Tocharian, Irish, Bulgarian etc. In order to facilitate memorisation, Latin and Greek cognates feature predominantly with a sprinkling of German, French and English. Mayrhofer (1992) and Pokorny (1959) are the main dictionaries that have been consulted for cross-referencing cognates.

The formation of "verb forms and derivatives" from the roots is a fairly regular and transparent process. It involves vowel gradation (ablaut), preverbs and suffixes that transform the root into a wide range of different forms. Following is a graphic and somewhat schematic overview that illustrates the variety of these formations. The grammar overview is merely given to highlight some aspects of this process. It would be best to consult a Sanskrit grammar for a comprehensive overview.

---

[3]   Cognates are sets of words that have the same origin as other words that have directly descended from an etymological ancestor of a parent language.

Word Formation

In a dictionary a verb is conventionally listed under its root using the √ symbol with all markers of voice, number, person, mood and tense removed. The root conveys the basic meaning of the verb. Verb conjugation in Sanskrit has the following characteristics.

Three voices: Active (parasmaipada) [P], Middle (ātmanepaida) [Ā] and Passive. Some roots are conjugated in both the active and middle voice (ubhayapada) [U].
Three numbers: Singular, Dual and Plural.
Three persons: First, Second and Third.
Four moods: the Indicative, Optative, Imperative and Conditional.
Five tenses: Present, Imperfect, Perfect, Aorist and Future.
In addition, there are present, perfect and future participles and one infinitive.

The present tense is different because, unlike the perfect, aorist and future tenses, it forms a special stem. The present stem of a verb is formed according to only one of the ten different classes. Unless verb endings are directly added to the root, roots will undergo some change. See for example √viś, 'to enter' where the vowel -a- is added after the stem.

Root	Stem	Ending	Full Form
√viś	viśa	ti	viśati 'he/she/it enters'

In the ten different classes there are four thematic classes and six athematic classes. In the thematic classes the vowel -a- is added whereas in the athematic classes affixes are added to the root either before (prefix), in the middle (infix) or at the end (suffix).
Vowel gradation or ablaut is a process that occurs frequently and refers to change in the vowel of a root when it undergoes grammatical transformations. √budh, 'to awaken' illustrates this change clearly. It is similar to the changes in the English verb to sing: 'sing, sang, sung'.

Root	Root	Stem	Ending	Full Form
√budh	bodh	bodha	ti	bodhati
zero grade	full grade	them. vowel	3 pers. sg.	'he/she/it awakens'

There are three grades for vowels: basic or zero grade (zg.), full grade (fg.) and lengthened grade (lg.). The basic grade refers to only the vowel itself, in the full grade (guṇa) an -a- is added and in the lengthened grade (vṛddhi) a long -ā- is added to it.

The four thematic classes show the following features:

1	√budh	bodhati	'he/she/it awakens'	zg. root, 3 sg. fg. + a
4	√tuṣ	tuṣyati	'he/she/it is satisfied'	zg. root, 3 sg. zg. + ya
6	√viś	viśati	'he/she/it enters'	zg. root, 3 sg. zg. + a
10	√cur	corayati	'he/she/it steals'	zg. root, 3 sg, fg. + aya

These are the six athematic classes:

2	√ad	atti	'he/she/it eats'	strong/weak forms, no affixes
3	√dā	dadāti	'he/she/it gives'	reduplication, strong/weak forms
5	√śak	śaknoti	'he/she/it is able'	root + no/nu
7	√yuj	yunakti	'he/she/it unites'	root + na/n
8	√tan	tanoti	'he/she/it spreads'	root + o/u
9	√krī	krīṇāti	'he/she/it buys'	root + nā/nī/n

The interplay of vowel gradation of the root combined with a multitude
of affixes can generate vast amounts of vocabulary that one can
nonetheless trace back without much effort to the original root.
Following is a graphic overview of the Primary Verbal Forms, Derived
Nominal Forms and Prefixed Root Forms of √kṛ 'do, make'.

Primary Verbal Forms

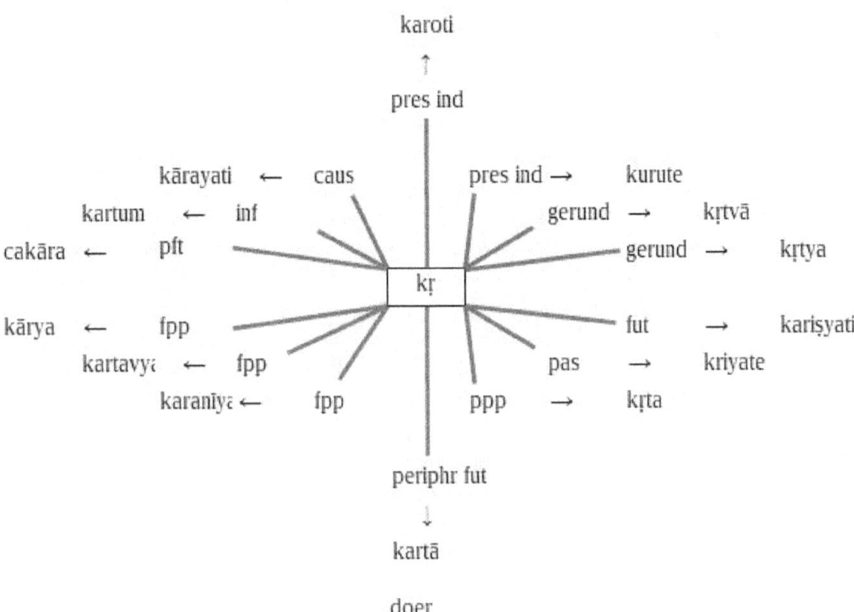

The abbreviations written in full: 'pres ind' - present indicative, 'fut' –
future, 'pas' – passive, 'ppp' – passive past participle, 'periphr fut' –
periphrastic future, 'fpp' – future past participle, 'pft' – perfect. 'inf' –
infinitive, 'caus' – causative. The causative kārayati - 'he/she/it causes
to do' together with desideratives, intensives and denominatives form
the so-called secondary conjugations.
In addition, [pft] relates to the 'perfect' tense that is occasionally listed
when verbs don't display a present tense.
'?' is sometimes listed when the etymology of a verb is disputed.

Derived Nominal Forms

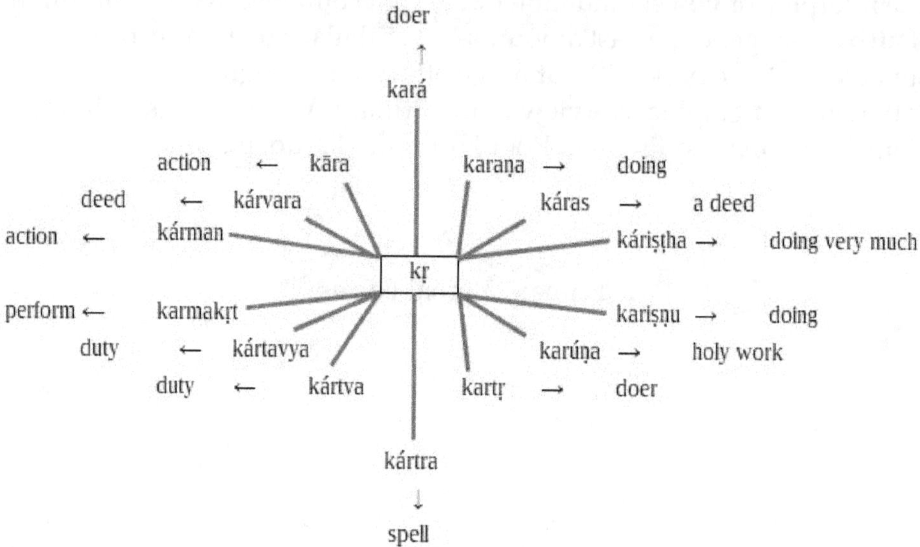

There are large numbers of suffixes: a, ā, ana, as, tas, nas, sas, is, us, i, ī, ti, ni ani, an, tu, nu, tha, thu, yu, ma, mi, man, van, vana, vara, ant, vāṅs, māna, āna, ta, na, u, ū, uka, aka, tṛ, in, īyas, iṣṭha, tra, ka, ya, ra, la, va, ri, ru, vi, snu, sna, tnu, sa, asi, abha and others.[4]

---

[4] Whitney 1146 Sanskrit Grammar

Prefixed Root Forms

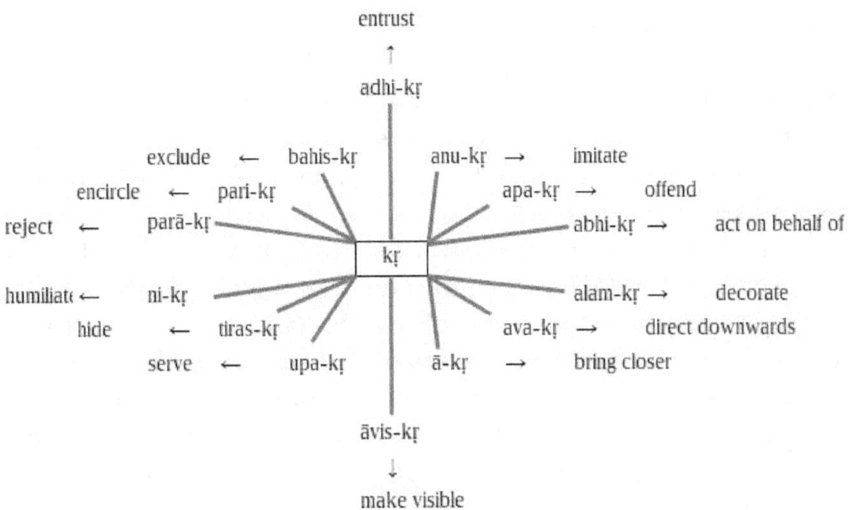

ati	beyond, over	āvis	openly, manifestly
adhi	above, besides	tiras	apart, secretly
anu	after, along, alongside	ni	down, in, into
antar	interior, within	nis	out, forth
apa	down, off, back	pari	roundabout, around
api	unto, close upon or on	parā	away, forth
abhi	to, towards, into, over	puras	before, first
alam	suitably, readily	pra	forward, onward, forth
ava	off, away, down	prati	back to, reversed
ud	up, upwards, upon, on	bahis	outwards, outside
upa	towards, near to, with	vi	apart, asunder, away, out
ā	near, near to, towards	sam	along, with, together

The use of alam, āvis, tiras, puras and bahis is decidedly more restricted.
It is possible to have two (or more) prepositions or preverbs "stacked" to
a single verb root such as upa-sam-yuj, 'to furnish with'.

How to Use This Text

The basic feature of Sanskrit Roots, Rote Learning and Cognates is one set of seven Sanskrit verb roots per unit. Each individual root shows the form in Devanagari, the transliteration in IAST (International Alphabet of Sanskrit Transliteration), the third person singular of the present indicative of the verb, an English translation, possible cognates mainly in Greek and Latin (367 in total) and often an adjective or a noun of the verb root. In addition, the number and the voice(s) will be listed. There is also an occasional 'W' (814 in total) referring to what Whitney considers a genuine root and '!' marking the root as high frequency (485 in total). At the end of each unit the seven roots are listed once more in order to facilitate rote learning. There are 23 units per chapter amounting to 161 roots. In total there are 10 chapters bringing the total number of roots to 1610. Underneath is a partial representation of what this looks like showing only the last root and recapitulation for study purposes.

210	क्र				204	[1P]	knath
[5U]	√kṛ				205	[4P]	knas
W	kṛṇoti	kṛṇute			206	[9U]	knu
English	do, make				207	[1Ā]	knūy
Latin	creo	create			208	[1P]	kmar
Greek	∅			!	209	[8U]	kṛ
Sanskrit	kárman	action		!	210	[5U]	kṛ

The major advantage of using a fixed schedule of seven roots is that it becomes much easier to organise a study workload and to allocate time. Also, one can make a choice to study 1600, 800 or around 500 roots as not everyone might feel inclined to memorise all 1610.

If a schedule of one unit per day (seven roots) is maintained it will take about seven and a half months to cover all 1610 roots. It is, of course, possible to vary this and to do this in half the time when 14 roots per day are covered. Alternatively, one could consider learning only the Whitney roots (W) and finish these 800 roots in nearly four months' time. The high frequency roots of 485 (!) would take about three months provided that a regime of seven roots per day is maintained.

An effective way to memorise something is to use associations that make the material more vivid. Association refers to relating material to a familiar context. Metaphors, analogies, examples, rewording, comparing and contrasting are ways to transform new material into something that is more meaningful. Occasionally, Sanskrit roots resemble slang or colloquial speech or something completely fortuitous like √car – 'move'. The use of cognates could make the process easier, provided that the language is familiar. In this case the Latin carrus – 'wagon' and the Greek πέλομαι – 'stir' has been employed. The Sanskrit adjective cara – 'moving' could also be associated with 'dear, precious, beloved' in Romance languages which would add another layer of association.

The verbs can be either memorised through direct association with the root like √kṛ - kṛṇoti, kṛṇute or, more abstractly, by working out the class 5 structure (root + no/nu). At the end of each chapter is a list of the 161 roots that were previously covered. Although perhaps somewhat tedious, it is absolutely necessary to make the effort to test the retention rate of the previously memorized material. The verbs that proved to be 'elusive', should be revisited again. This is a segment of how this would look like.

204	knath
205	knas
206	knu
207	knūy
208	kmar
209	kṛ
210	kṛ

If memorisation of certain verb roots proves particularly challenging, one could use a variation of the Loci System. Also known as a Memory Palace, it is a mnemonic device where items that are to be remembered are associated with specific locations. As the order of each unit of seven roots is fixed, it would be straightforward to relate each position within the unit to rooms in a mansion. Each room will have its own attributes and characteristics making it easier to add more associations to a particular root.

CELLAR	204	[1P]	knath	knathati		hurt
LIVINGROOM	205	[4P]	knas	knasyati		shine
KITCHEN	206	[9U]	knu	knunāti	knunīte	sound
SALON	207	[1Ā]	knūy	knūyate		be wet, stink
BOUDOIR	208	[1P]	kmar	kmarati		be fraudulent
OFFICE	209	[8U]	kṛ	karoti	kurute	do, make
NURSERY	210	[5U]	kṛ	kṛṇoti	kṛṇute	do, make

These are some of the additional associations that could be used to make root verbs easier to memorise. An important point is to treat the seven roots as a unit and to emphasise their respective positions. √knath – knathati – hurt comes in first position and will therefore have associations that are related to a cellar. Obviously, a cellar would be without windows so the colour is BLACK. There might be an overwhelming smell like leather or something smoky and DARK. The floor could well be made of compacted EARTH and, matching the oppressive atmosphere, a heavy metal like LEAD might be appropriate. Any taste will be BITTER. The meaning of √knath – hurt can also be quite easily associated with a dungeon or torture chamber where unspeakable acts take place. Alternatively, √kmar – be crooked, fraudulent could be linked without too much fuss to a woman's private dressing room: "The wealthy geriatric visited Kmar's BOUDOIR". In this instance, Kmar would be a personal name and although having a "wealthy geriatric" is not entirely necessary it makes √kmar more memorable. The other rooms in the mansion have their own, distinct attributes that can be used to facilitate the memorisation process. The following schedule illustrates these particular associations.
Smelling the verbs -and tasting or seeing them- can aid recollection, especially when two or more roots are the same.

ROOM	ELEMENT	TASTE	SIGHT	SMELL	METAL
CELLAR	EARTH	BITTER	BLACK	DARK	LEAD
LIVINGROOM	WOOD	SAVOURY	BROWN	CEDAR	TIN
KITCHEN	FIRE	SHARP	RED	SPICY	IRON
SALON	SUN	SWEET-SOUR	YELLOW	CITRUS	GOLD
BOUDOIR	METAL	SWEET	GREEN	ROSY	COPPER
OFFICE	WATER	SOUR	BLUE	MOSSY	MERCURY
NURSERY	MOON	SALTY	WHITE	NIGHT-FLORAL	SILVER

Concluding Remarks

The rationale behind memorising roots is the fact that they are the key to word formations in Sanskrit. The process of word formation is consistent and transparent and therefore spotting these patterns -pattern recognition- will be a practical first step in dealing with Sanskrit texts. It should be pointed out, however, that there are various additional aspects that should be taken into consideration.

Many roots have a semantic range that is truly prodigious. The full spectrum of a set of meanings sometimes covers more than a page of a dictionary. The meaning of a root listed here could be only one within a range of many other meanings so a one-to-one correspondence is unlikely.

As mentioned previously, the number of roots presented here is double of what Whitney considered to be genuine roots. There are numerous made-up roots to account for nouns such as √hal – plough, probably invented as a source for hala 'a plough'. Many others are either reduplications (dhīdhī)- or stem forms (ūrṇu[5]). These fictitious roots have been included nonetheless because they often refer to useful vocabulary. (The Whitney roots have been marked with "W" in the text) To use frequency as a criterion for learning and memorising is up to a point an efficient method. The problem is that it quickly reaches a plateau, like an inverted triangle, after which still relevant vocabulary falls outside of the range. When using the 'Sanskrit Word Frequency Tool' to search for verbs specifically, one can see the following comment: "535186 occurrences of 6945 unique words in 190 texts by 99 authors on 32 subjects".[6]

---

[5] Burrow, T (1955), The Sanskrit Language, p. 289

[6] https://www.sanskritdictionary.com/frequency/

The results are ranked in order of frequency with √kṛ - 'make, do' in first place, √vac – 'speak, say' in second and √bhū – 'to be, become' in third place, etc. Out of a collection of 2000 verbs, 373 have been selected and 485 have been listed as there are multiple forms of the same root. The majority of the 2000 verbs consist of preverbs (prefixes) and a root which have not been considered here. (The frequency roots have been marked with "!" in the text)

Cognates listed in Monier-Williams[7] have been used occasionally but the great majority has been cross-referenced with Mayerhofer and Pokorny. At times, there seems to be rather fierce disagreement about the etymology of roots, especially when there is a great deal unclear about the origins. Interpretations could be modified at a later stage but in any event the results of these current efforts (hopefully) will lessen the burden of memorisation.

It is evident that the general level of knowledge of classical languages in previous centuries greatly surpasses that of our present times and it was then not surprising that the similarity of both vocabulary and grammar of Sanskrit and of Greek and Latin was noted by European scholars by the end of the eighteenth century. This discovery has given impetus to an intense scientific study of languages of the Indo-European family with the objective to identify relationships between these languages and to arrive at a reconstructed "initial" language. Geographically, this is an area extending from "Iceland and Ireland in the West across Europe and Asia Minor-where Hittite was spoken-through Iran to the northern half of the Indian subcontinent".[8]

Old Avestan -together with Young Avestan and Old Persian- is part of the Iranian branch of the Indo-European languages. The "Gathas", Old Avestan hymns that are part of the Zoroastrian tradition, share strong linguistic similarities with the Rigveda. Its grammar and lexicon are largely similar to that of Vedic Sanskrit which points towards a comparable date: second half of the second millennium B.C. These shared linguistic characteristics of so many languages in time and space must surely be a source of endless fascination.

---

[7] Monier-Williams (1899), A Sanskrit-English Dictionary

[8] Watkins, Calvert (1995), How to Kill a Dragon

In addition to its vast and varied literature, Sanskrit is of great interest due to its antiquity and its geographical reach as part of the Indo-European family. The latter aspect is particularly appealing as it provides something of a (tenuous) linguistic link or bond in an otherwise fractured space. When Montesquieu (1689-1755) asked the frankly outrageous question in his "Persian Letters" (1721): "Sir is Persian? That's something extraordinary! How can one be Persian?"[9] The two Persian travellers, Usbek and Rica, could have answered in the following manner: "It might be possible that, after having carefully considered the matter, we are less different than it seems and have more in common than you might think as we all share in a common linguistic heritage."

---

[9] "Ah ! ah ! monsieur est Persan ?C'est une chose bien extraordinaire ! Comment peut-on être Persan ?" Persian letter 30

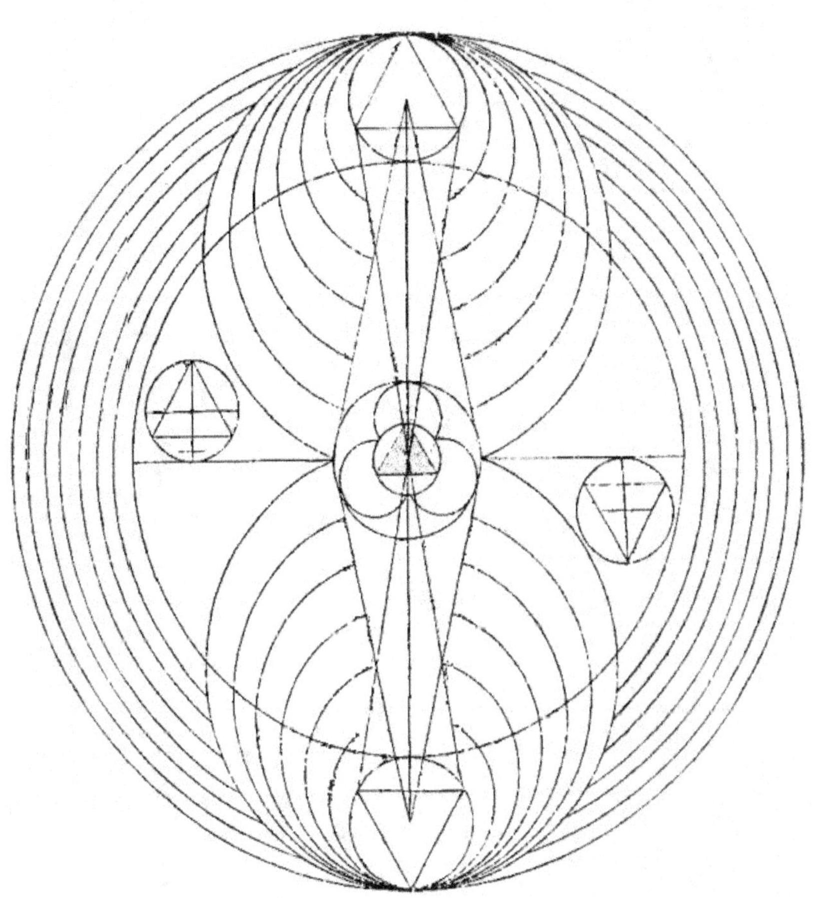

1	अंश्			2	अंह्	
[10U]	√aṃś			[1Ā]	√aṃh	
	aṃśayati	aṃśayate			aṃhate	
English	divide			English	go	
Latin	Ø			Latin	Ø	
Greek	ὄγκος	weight		Greek	Ø	
Sanskrit	aṃśa	share		Sanskrit	Ø	

3	अंह्			4	अंह्	
[10P]	√aṃh			[10U]	√aṃh	
	aṃhayati			W	?	
English	send, speak			English	strangle	
Latin	Ø			Latin	angustus	narrow
Greek	Ø			Greek	ἄγχω	choke
Sanskrit	Ø			German	Angst	fear

5	अक्			6	अक्ष्	
[1P]	√ak			[1P]	√akṣ	
	akati			W	akṣati	
English	move	tortuously		English	attain	
Latin	angulus	angle		Latin	axis	axle
Greek	ἀγκών	elbow		Greek	ἄξων	axle
English	angle			German	Achse	axle

7	अक्ष्					
[5U]	√akṣ			1	[10U]	aṃś
W	akṣṇoti	akṣṇute		2	[1Ā]	aṃh
English	mutilate			3	[10P]	aṃh
Latin	axis	axle		4	[10U]	aṃh
Greek	ἄξων	axle		5	[1P]	ak
German	Achse	axle		6	[1P]	akṣ
				7	[5U]	aks

8	अग्		9	अघ्	
[1P]	√ag		[10P]	√agh	
	agati			aghayati	
English	move	tortuously	English	sin	
Latin	Ø		Latin	ἄχος	distress
Greek	Ø		Greek	ango	distress
Sanskrit	ag	snake	German	Angst	fear

10	अङ्क्		11	अङ्क्	
[1Ā]	√aṅk		[10P]	√aṅk	
	aṅkate			aṅkayati	
English	move in a	curve	English	move in a	curve
Latin	uncus	hook	Latin	uncus	hook
Greek	ὄγκος	bend, curve	Greek	ὄγκος	curve
German	Angel	fishing rod	German	Angel	f. rod

12	अङ्ग्		13	अङ्घ्	
[1P]	√aṅg		[1Ā]	√aṅgh	
W	aṅgati			aṅghate	
English	go		English	go	
Latin	Ø		Latin	Ø	
Greek	ἄγγελος	messenger	Greek	ἄγγελος	mess.
Sanskrit	aṅgana	yard	Sanskrit	Ø	

14	अज्		8	[1P]	ag
[1U]	√aj		9	[10P]	agh
W	ajati	ajate	10	[1Ā]	aṅk
English	drive		11	[10P]	aṅk
Latin	ago	do	12	[1P]	aṅg
Greek	αγω	lead	13	[1Ā]	aṅgh
Sanskrit	ajá	a drove	14	[1U]	aj

15	अञ्च्	
[1P]	√añc	
W	añcati	
English	bend	
Latin	uncus	hook
Greek	ἀγκών	elbow
Sanskrit	añca	curling hair

16	अञ्च्	
[1U]	√añc	
W	acati	añcate
English	bend	
Latin	uncus	hook
Greek	ἀγκών	elbow
Sanskrit	añca	curling h.

17	अञ्ज्	
[7U]	√añj	
W	anakti	aṅkte
English	anoint	
Latin	ungo	anoint
Greek	Ø	
Sanskrit	añjana	ointment

18	अड्	
[1P]	√aḍ	
	aḍati	
English	exert	
Latin	Ø	
Greek	Ø	
Sanskrit	Ø	

19	अड्ड्	
[1P]	√aḍḍ	
	aḍḍati	
English	join	
Latin	Ø	
Greek	Ø	
Sanskrit	aḍḍana	a shield

20	अट्	
[1P]	√aṭ	
W	aṭati	
English	wander	
Latin	annus	year
Greek	ἀλάομαι	roaming
Sanskrit	aṭana	roaming

21	अट्ट्	
[1Ā]	√aṭṭ	
	aṭṭate	
English	exceed	
Latin	Ø	
Greek	Ø	
Sanskrit	aṭṭa	tower

!	15	[1P]	añc
!	16	[1U]	añc
!	17	[7U]	añj
	18	[1P]	aḍ
	19	[1P]	aḍḍ
!	20	[1P]	aṭ
	21	[1Ā]	aṭṭ

22	अट्ट्			23	अठ्	
[10P]	√aṭṭ			[1U]	√aṭh	
	aṭṭayati				aṭhati	aṭhate
English	diminish			English	go	
Latin	Ø			Latin	Ø	
Greek	Ø			Greek	Ø	
Sanskrit	aṭṭa	watch-tower		Sanskrit	Ø	

24	अण्ठ्			25	अद्	
[1Ā]	√aṇṭh			[2P]	√ad	
	aṇṭhate			W	atti	
English	go, move			English	eat	
Latin	Ø			Latin	edō	eat
Greek	Ø			Greek	ἔδω	eat
Sanskrit	Ø			German	essen	eat

26	अन्			27	अन्त्	
[2P]	√an			[1P]	√ant	
W	aniti				antati	
English	breathe			English	bind	
Latin	animus	soul		Latin	Ø	
Greek	ἄνεμος	wind		Greek	Ø	
French	âme	soul		Sanskrit	ánta	end

28	अभ्र्			22	[10P]	aṭṭ
[1P]	√abhr			23	[1U]	aṭh
	abhrati			24	[1Ā]	aṇṭh
English	err		!	25	[2P]	ad
Latin	Ø			26	[2P]	an
Greek	Ø			27	[1P]	ant
Sanskrit	Ø			28	[1P]	abhr

29	अम्			30	अम्ब्	
[1P]	√am			[1U]	√amb	
	amati				ambati	ambate
English	hurt			English	go,	sound
Latin	amō(?)	love		Latin	Ø	
Greek	ἀνίη	infliction		Greek	Ø	
Sanskrit	ámīvā	sickness		Sanskrit	Ø	

31	अर्घ्			32	अर्च्	
[1P]	√argh			[1P]	√arc, ṛc	
W	arghati			W	arcati	
English	value			English	praise	
Latin	Ø			Latin	Ø	
Greek	Ø			Greek	Ø	
Sanskrit	argha	value, price		Sanskrit	arcā	worship

33	अर्ज्			34	अर्थ्	
[1U]	√arj			[10Ā]	√arth	
	arjati	arjate		W	arthayate	
English	procure, go			English	request	
Latin	Ø			Latin	Ø	
Greek	Ø			Greek	Ø	
Sanskrit	arjana	gain		Sanskrit	arthanā	request

35	अर्द्			29	[1P]	am
[1P]	√ard			30	[1U]	amb
W	ardati			31	[1P]	argh
English	hurt		!	32	[1P]	arc, ṛc
Latin	Ø			33	[1U]	arj
Greek	Ø			34	[10Ā]	arth
Sanskrit	ardanī	destroyer		35	[1P]	ard

36	अर्ब्			37	अर्व्	
[1P]	√arb	[1P]		[1P]	√arv	
	arbati				arvati	
English	hurt	English		English	hurt	
Latin	Ø	Latin		Latin	Ø	
Greek	Ø	Greek		Greek	Ø	
Sanskrit	Ø	Sanskrit		Sanskrit	Ø	

38	अर्ह्			39	अल्	
[1U]	√arh			[1P]	√al	
W	arhati	arhate			alati	
English	deserve			English	adorn	
Latin	Ø			Latin	Ø	
Greek	ἀλφεῖν	precious		Greek	Ø	
Sanskrit	arhat	worthy		Sanskrit	Ø	

40	अव्			41	अश्	
[1U]	√av			[5Ā]	√aś	
W	avati			W	aśnute	
English	favour			English	arrive at	
Latin	aveo	desire		Latin	Ø	
Greek	ἄïτας	friend		Greek	Ø	
Sanskrit	avana	favour		Sanskrit	aśana	reaching

42	अश्			36	[1P]	arb
[9U]	√aś			37	[1P]	arv
W	aśnāti	aśnīte	!	38	[1U]	arh
English	eat			39	[1P]	al
Latin	esca	food	!	40	[1U]	av
Greek	ἄκυλος	acorn, food	!	41	[5Ā]	aś
Sanskrit	aśana	meal	!	42	[9U]	aś

43	अष्			44	अस्	
[1U]	√aṣ			[2P]	√as	
	aṣati	aṣate		W	asti	
English	go, shine,	receive		English	be	
Latin	Ø			Latin	est	is
Greek	Ø			Greek	ἐστί	is
Sanskrit	Ø			Sanskrit	ásu	breath

45	अस्			46	अह्	
[4P]	√as			[pft]	√ah	
W	asyati			W	āha	
English	throw			English	say	
Latin	Ø			Latin	aiō	say
Greek	Ø			Greek	Ø	
Sanskrit	asanā	missile		English	adage	

47	आप्			48	आस्	
[5P]	√āp			[2Ā]	√ās	
W	āpnoti			W	āste	
English	obtain			English	sit	
Latin	apiscor	reach		Latin	Ø	
Greek	Ø			Greek	ησται	sit
Sanskrit	āptí	attainment		Sanskrit	āsana	seat

49	इ		!	43	[1U]	aṣ
[2U]	√i		!	44	[2P]	as
W	eti	ite	!	45	[4P]	as
English	go		!	46	[pft]	ah
Latin	eō	go	!	47	[5P]	āp
Greek	εἶμι	go	!	48	[2Ā]	ās
Sanskrit	áyana	path	!	49	[2U]	i

50	इ			51	इख्	
[1U]	√i			[1P]	√ikh	
W	ayati	ayate			ekhati	
English	go			English	go, move	
Latin	eō	go		Latin	∅	
Greek	εἶμι	go		Greek	∅	
Sanskrit	áyana	path		Sanskrit	∅	

52	इङ्			53	इन्	
[1P]	√iṅg			[5P]	√in	
W	iṅgati			W	inoti	
English	go, move			English	drive	lead
Latin	∅			Latin	∅	
Greek	∅			Greek	∅	
Sanskrit	iṅgā	mobile		Sanskrit	∅	

54	इन्ध्			55	इन्व्	
[7Ā]	√indh			[1P]	√inv	
W	inddhe			W	invati	
English	kindle			English	drive	
Latin	aestus	heat, fire		Latin	∅	
Greek	αἴθω	kindle, light		Greek	∅	
English	oast	kiln		Sanskrit	inva	pervading

56	इल्			50	[1U]	i
[6P]	√il			51	[1P]	ikh
W	ilati		!	52	[1P]	iṅg
English	keep still			53	[5P]	in
Latin	∅		!	54	[7Ā]	indh
Greek	∅			55	[1P]	inv
Sanskrit	∅			56	[6P]	il

57	इष्			58	इष्	
[6U]	√iṣ			[4P]	√iṣ	
W	icchati	icchate		W	iṣyati	
English	desire			English	send	
Latin	Ø			Latin	irā	anger
English	ask			Greek	οῖμα	urge
Sanskrit	icchā	wish		Sanskrit	iṣaṇyā	impulse

59	ईक्ष्			60	ईङ्ख्	
[1Ā]	√īkṣ			[1P]	√iṅkh	
W	īkṣate			W	iṅkhati	
English	see			English	swing	
Latin	Ø			Latin	Ø	
Greek	Ø			Greek	Ø	
Sanskrit	īkṣaṇa	aspect		Sanskrit	iṅkhaya	moving

61	ईज्			62	ईञ्ज्	
[1P]	√ij			[1P]	√iñj	
	ījati			W	iñjati	
English	go, blame			English	go, blame	
Latin	Ø			Latin	Ø	
Greek	Ø			Greek	Ø	
Sanskrit	Ø			Sanskrit	Ø	

63	ईड्		!	57	[6U]	iṣ
[2Ā]	√īḍ		!	58	[4P]	iṣ
	īṭṭe		!	59	[1Ā]	īkṣ
English	praise			60	[1P]	iṅkh
Latin	Ø			61	[1P]	ij
Greek	Ø			62	[1P]	iñj
Sanskrit	īḍā	praise	!	63	[2Ā]	īḍ

64	ईर्			65	ईर्ष्य्	
[2Ā]	√īr			[1P]	√īrṣy	
W	īrte			W	īrṣyati	
English	set in	motion		English	envy	
Latin	orior	arise		Latin	Ø	
Greek	ὄρνυμι	urge on		Greek	Ø	
Sanskrit	īra	wind		Sanskrit	īrṣya	jealous

66	ईश्			67	ईष्	
[2Ā]	√īś			[1Ā]	√īṣ	
W	īṣṭe			W	īṣate	
English	own			English	flee from	
Latin	Ø			Latin	Ø	
Greek	Ø			Greek	Ø	
German	eigen	own		Sanskrit	īṣaṇā	haste

68	ईह्			69	उक्ष्	
[1Ā]	√īh			[6P]	√ukṣ	
W	īhate			W	ukṣati	
English	attempt			English	sprinkle	
Latin	Ø			Latin	ūveo	drink freely
Greek	Ø			Greek	Ø	
Sanskrit	īhā	effort		Sanskrit	ukṣaṇa	consecrating

70	उख्			64	[2Ā]	īr
[1P]	√ukh			65	[1P]	īrṣy
	okhati		!	66	[2Ā]	īś
English	go, move			67	[1Ā]	īṣ
Latin	Ø		!	68	[1Ā]	īh
Greek	Ø		!	69	[6P]	ukṣ
German	Ø			70	[1P]	ukh

71	उङ्ख्			72	उच्	
[6P]	√uṅkh			[4P]	√uc	
	uṅkhati			W	ucyati	
English	go, move			English	be pleased	
Latin	Ø			Latin	Ø	
Greek	Ø			Greek	Ø	
Sanskrit	Ø			Sanskrit	ucitā	pleasurable

73	उछ्			74	उज्झ्	
[1P]	√uch			[6P]	√ujjh	
	ucchati			W	ujjhati	
English	finish			English	abandon	
Latin	Ø			Latin	Ø	
Greek	Ø			Greek	Ø	
Sanskrit	Ø			Sanskrit	ujjhitā	abandoned

75	उञ्छ्			76	उध्रस्	
[1P]	√uñch			[9P]	√udhras	
W	uñchati				udhrasnāti	
English	glean			English	glean	
Latin	Ø			Latin	Ø	
Greek	Ø			Greek	Ø	
Sanskrit	uñcha	gleaning		Sanskrit	Ø	

77	उध्रस्			71	[6P]	uṅkh
[10U]	√udhras		!	72	[4P]	uc
	udhrāsayati	udhrāsayate		73	[1P]	uch
English	glean			74	[6P]	ujjh
Latin	Ø			75	[1P]	uñch
Greek	Ø			76	[9P]	udhras
Sanskrit	Ø			77	[10U]	udhras

78	उन्द्			79	उब्ज्	
[7P]	√und			[6P]	√ubj	
W	unatti				ubjáti	
English	moisten			English	subdue	
Latin	unda	wave		Latin	Ø	
Greek	Ø			Greek	Ø	
French	onde	wave		Sanskrit	Ø	

80	उभ्			81	उभ्	
[9P]	√ubh			[6P]	√ubh	
	ubhnāti				ubhati	
English	hurt, kill			English	cover	
Latin	Ø			Latin	Ø	
Greek	Ø			Greek	Ø	
Sanskrit	Ø			Sanskrit	Ø	

82	उम्भ			83	उठ्	
[9P]	√umbh			[1P]	√uṭh	
W	ubhnāti				oṭhati	
English	confine			English	strike	knock down
Latin	Ø			Latin	Ø	
Greek	Ø			Greek	Ø	
Sanskrit	Ø			Sanskrit	Ø	

84	उष्			78	[7P]	und
[1P]	√uṣ			79	[6P]	ubj
	oṣati			80	[9P]	ubh
English	burn			81	[6P]	ubh
Latin	ustus	burnt		82	[9P]	umbh
Greek	εὕω	singe		83	[1P]	uṭh
Sanskrit	uṣṇá	hot !		84	[1P]	uṣ

85	ऊर्ज्			86	ऊर्द्	
[1Ā]	√ūrj			[1P]	√ūrd	
	ūrjayate				ūrdate	
English	be strong			English	measure,	play
Latin	vergō	bend, turn		Latin	Ø	
Greek	οργαω	desire		Greek	Ø	
Sanskrit	ūrj	strength		Sanskrit	ūrda	cheerful

87	ऊर्णु			88	ऊर्व्	
[1U]	√ūrṇu			[1P]	√ūrv	
	ūrṇoti	ūrṇute			ūrvati	
English	cover			English	kill, hurt	
Latin	Ø			Latin	Ø	
Greek	Ø			Greek	Ø	
Sanskrit	Ø			Sanskrit	Ø	

89	ऊय्			90	ऊष्	
[1Ā]	√ūy			[1P]	√ūṣ	
	ūyate			W	ūṣati	
English	weave			English	be sick	
Latin	Ø			Latin	Ø	
Greek	Ø			Greek	Ø	
Sanskrit	Ø			Sanskrit	Ø	

91	ऊह्			85	[1Ā]	ūrj
[1U]	√ūh			86	[1P]	ūrd
W	ūhati	ūhate		87	[1U]	ūrṇu
English	remove,	push		88	[1P]	ūrv
Latin	Ø			89	[1Ā]	ūy
Greek	ωθέω	shove		90	[1P]	ūṣ
Sanskrit	ūha	removing	!	91	[1U]	ūh

92	ऊह्		93	ऋ	
[1P]	√ūh		[1P]	√ṛ	
W	ohati		W	ṛcchati	
English	reason,	infer	English	go, send	
Latin	Ø		Latin	orior	rise, get up
Greek	εὔχομαι	declare	Greek	ὄρνῡμῐ	set upon
Sanskrit	ūhana	reasoning	Sanskrit	ṛtá	afflicted by

94	ऋच्		95	ऋज्	
[1P]	√ṛc		[1U]	√ṛj	
W	arcati		W	arjati	arjate
English	praise		English	direct,	stretch
Latin	Ø		Latin	rectus	straight
Greek	Ø		Greek	ἄρχω	rule
Sanskrit	ṛcas	verses	Sanskrit	ṛjú	straight

96	ऋध्		97	ऋध्	
[4P]	√ṛdh		[5P]	√ṛdh	
W	ṛdhyati		W	ṛdhnoti	
English	thrive		English	thrive	
Latin	Ø		Latin	Ø	
Greek	ἄλθετο	be cured	Greek	ἄλθετο	be cured
Sanskrit	ṛddha	wealthy	Sanskrit	ṛddha	wealthy

98	ऋण्		!	92	[1P]	ūh
[8U]	√ṛṇ			93	[1P]	ṛ
	ṛṇoti	ṛṇute		94	[1P]	ṛc
English	go, move			95	[1U]	ṛj
Latin	Ø		!	96	[4P]	ṛdh
Greek	Ø		!	97	[5P]	ṛdh
Sanskrit	ṛṇā	fugitive		98	[8U]	ṛṇ

99	ऋण्			100	ऋफ्	
[8U]	√ṛṇ			[6P]	√ṛph	
	arṇoti	arṇute			ṛphati	
English	go, move			English	hurt, kill	
Latin	Ø			Latin	Ø	
Greek	Ø			Greek	Ø	
Sanskrit	ṛṇā	fugitive		Sanskrit	Ø	

101	ऋष्			102	ऋष्	
[1P]	√ṛṣ			[6P]	√ṛṣ	
W	arṣati			W	ṛṣati	
English	stream,	spread		English	rush,	push
Latin	Ø			Latin	Ø	
Greek	Ø			Greek	Ø	
Sanskrit	ṛṣi	poet		Sanskrit	ṛṣṭa	pushed

103	एज्			104	एध्	
[1P]	√ej			[1Ā]	√edh	
W	ejati			W	edhate	
English	stir			English	thrive	
Latin	Ø			Latin	Ø	
Greek	Ø			Greek	Ø	
Sanskrit	ejana	tremor		Sanskrit	edhas	prosperity

105	एष्			99	[8U]	ṛṇ
[1U]	√eṣ			100	[6P]	ṛph
	eṣati	eṣate		101	[1P]	ṛṣ
English	go, move			102	[6P]	ṛṣ
Latin	Ø			103	[1P]	ej
Greek	Ø	!		104	[1Ā]	edh
Sanskrit	eṣa	running		105	[1U]	eṣ

106	ओख्		107	ओण्	
[1P]	√okh		[1P]	√oṇ	
	okhati			oṇati	
English	be dry		English	remove	
Latin	Ø		Latin	Ø	
Greek	Ø		Greek	Ø	
Sanskrit	Ø		Sanskrit	Ø	

108	ओलण्ड्		109	ओलण्ड्	
[1P]	√olaṇḍ		[8P]	√olaṇḍ	
	olaṇḍati			olaṇḍayati	
English	throw out		English	throw out	
Latin	Ø		Latin	Ø	
Greek	Ø		Greek	Ø	
Sanskrit	Ø		Sanskrit	Ø	

110	कक्		111	कख्	
[1A]	√kak		[1P]	√kakh	
	kakate			kakhati	
English	be unsteady	proud	English	laugh	
Latin	Ø		Latin	cachinnare	cackle
Greek	Ø		Greek	Ø	
Sanskrit	Ø		Sanskrit	Ø	

112	कग्		106	[1P]	okh
[1P]	√kag		107	[1P]	oṇ
	kagati		108	[1P]	olaṇḍ
English	act, perform		109	[8P]	olaṇḍ
Latin	Ø		110	[1Ā]	kak
Greek	Ø		111	[1P]	kakh
Sanskrit	Ø		112	[1P]	kag

113	कच्			114	कच्	
[1P]	√kac			114	कच्	
	kacati			[1Ā]	√kac	
English	sound, cry				kacate	
Latin	Ø			English	bind,	fetter
Greek	Ø			Latin	Ø	
Sanskrit	Ø			Greek	Ø	

115	कञ्च्			116	कट्	
[1Ā]	√kañc			[1P]	√kaṭ	
W	kañcate				kaṭati	
English	bind			English	go	
Latin	cingō	circle, gird		Latin	Ø	
Greek	Ø			Greek	Ø	
French	ceinture	belt		Sanskrit	Ø	

117	कट्			118	कठ्	
[1P]	√kaṭ			[1P]	√kaṭh	
	kaṭati				kaṭhati	
English	rain,	surround		English	live in	distress
Latin	Ø			Latin	Ø	
Greek	Ø			Greek	Ø	
Sanskrit	Ø			Sanskrit	kaṭha	distress

119	कण्			113	[1P]	kac
[1P]	√kaṇ			114	[1Ā]	kac
W	kaṇati			115	[1Ā]	kañc
English	shrink			116	[1P]	kaṭ
Latin	Ø			117	[1P]	kaṭ
Greek	Ø			118	[1P]	kaṭh
Sanskrit	kaṇa	grain		119	[1P]	kaṇ

120	कन्			121	कण्ड्	
[pft]	√kan			[10P]	√kaṇḍ	
	cākana				kaṇḍayati	
English	be satisfied			English	winnow	
Latin	Ø			Latin	Ø	
Greek	καίνυμαι	surpass		Greek	Ø	
Sanskrit	cánas	delight		Sanskrit	kaṇḍana	winnowing

122	कङ्क्			123	कण्ठ्	
[1Ā]	√kaṅk			[1U]	√kaṇṭh	
	kaṅkate				kaṇṭhati	kaṇṭhate
English	go, walking			English	mourn,	desire
Latin	Ø			Latin	Ø	
Greek	Ø			Greek	Ø	
Sanskrit	kaṅkā	sandal		Sanskrit	Ø	

124	कण्ठ्			125	कन्द्	
[10P]	√kaṇṭh			[1P]	√kand	
	kaṇṭhayati				kandati	
English	mourn,	desire		English	cry	
Latin	Ø			Latin	Ø	
Greek	Ø			Greek	Ø	
Sanskrit	Ø			Sanskrit	Ø	

126	कन्द्			120	[pft]	kan
[1Ā]	√kand			121	[10P]	kaṇḍ
	kandate			122	[1Ā]	kaṅk
English	be confounded			123	[1U]	kaṇṭh
Latin	Ø			124	[10P]	kaṇṭh
Greek	Ø			125	[1P]	kand
Sanskrit	Ø			126	[1Ā]	kand

127	कड्			128	कड्	
[1P]	√kaḍ			[6P]	√kaḍ	
	kaḍati				kaḍati	
English	be confused			English	eat	
Latin	Ø			Latin	Ø	
Greek	Ø			Greek	Ø	
Sanskrit	Ø			Sanskrit	Ø	

129	कत्र्			130	कत्थ्	
[10P]	√katr			[1Ā]	√katth	
	katrayati			W	katthate	
English	loosen,	slacken		English	boast	
Latin	Ø			Latin	Ø	
Greek	Ø			Greek	Ø	
Sanskrit	Ø			Sanskrit	katthana	boasting

131	कथ्			132	कद्	
[10P]	√kath			[1Ā]	√kad	
W	kathayati				kadate	
English	say, tell			English	be	confused
Latin	Ø			Latin	Ø	
Greek	Ø			Greek	Ø	
English	quote			Sanskrit	Ø	

133	कड्ड्			127	[1P]	kaḍ
[1P]	√kaḍḍ			128	[6P]	kaḍ
	kaḍḍati			129	[10P]	katr
English	be hard,	rough	!	130	[1Ā]	katth
Latin	Ø		!	131	[10P]	kath
Greek	Ø			132	[1Ā]	kad
Sanskrit	Ø			133	[1P]	kaḍḍ

134	कब्	
[1Ā]	√kab	
	kabate	
English	colour,	praise
Latin	Ø	
Greek	Ø	
Sanskrit	Ø	

135	कम्	
pft	√kam	
W	cakame	
English	love	
Latin	comis	kind
Greek	Ø	
Sanskrit	kamana	desirable

136	कम्प्	
[1Ā]	√kamp	
W	kampate	
English	tremble	
Latin	Ø	
Greek	Ø	
Sanskrit	kampana	trembling

137	कम्ब्	
[1P]	√kamb	[1P]
	kambati	
English	go, move	English
Latin	Ø	Latin
Greek	Ø	Greek
Sanskrit	Ø	Sanskrit

138	कल्	
[1Ā]	√kal	
	kalate	
English	sound,	count
Latin	calculo	calculate
Greek	Ø	
Sanskrit	Ø	

139	कल्	
[1P]	√kal	
	kalayati	
English	incite,	carry
Latin	celer	fast
Greek	κέλλω	drive on
Sanskrit	Ø	

140	कल्	
[10U]	√kal	
W	kalayati	kalayate
English	drive,	produce
Latin	Ø	
Greek	Ø	
Sanskrit	kalana	making

	134	[1Ā]	kab
!	135	pft	kam
!	136	[1Ā]	kamp
	137	[1P]	kamb
	138	[1Ā]	kal
	139	[1P]	kal
	140	[10U]	kal

141	कल्ल्			142	कश्	
[1Ā]	√kall			[1P]	√kaś	
	kallate				kaśati	
English	be mute			English	go, move	
Latin	Ø			Latin	Ø	
Greek	Ø			Greek	Ø	
Sanskrit	kalla	deaf		Sanskrit	Ø	

143	कष्			144	कर्ज्	
[1U]	√kaṣ			[1P]	√karj	
W	kaṣati	kaṣate			karjati	
English	scratch			English	to pain,	torment
Latin	Ø			Latin	Ø	
Greek	Ø			Greek	Ø	
Sanskrit	kaṣṭá	hardship		Sanskrit	Ø	

145	कर्ण्			146	कर्त्र्	
[10P]	√karṇ			[10P]	√kartr	
	karṇayati				kartrayati	
English	pierce, bore			English	unloose,	remove
Latin	Ø			Latin	Ø	
Greek	Ø			Greek	Ø	
Sanskrit	Ø			Sanskrit	Ø	

147	कर्द्			141	[1Ā]	kall
[1P]	√kard			142	[1P]	kaś
	kardati			143	[1U]	kaṣ
English	rumble			144	[1P]	karj
Latin	Ø			145	[10P]	karṇ
Greek	Ø			146	[10P]	kartr
Sanskrit	Ø			147	[1P]	kard

148	कर्ब्			149	कर्व्	
[1P]	√karb			[1P]	√karv	
	karbati				karvati	
English	go, move			English	proud,	boast
Latin	Ø			Latin	Ø	
Greek	Ø			Greek	Ø	
Sanskrit	Ø			Sanskrit	Ø	

150	कव्			151	कव्	
[1Ā]	√kav			[10U]	√kav	
	kavate				kāvayati	kāvayate
English	describe,	praise		English	compose	
Latin	Ø			Latin	Ø	
Greek	Ø			Greek	Ø	
Sanskrit	kāvya	poetry		Sanskrit	kāvya	poetry

152	कंस्			153	कस्	
[2Ā]	√kaṃs			[1P]	√kas	
	kaṃste				kasati	
English	go,	command		English	go, move	
Latin	Ø			Latin	Ø	
Greek	Ø			Greek	Ø	
Sanskrit	Ø			Sanskrit	Ø	

154	काङ्क्ष्			148	[1P]	karb
[1U]	√kāṅkṣ			149	[1P]	karv
W	kāṅkṣati	kāṅkṣate		150	[1Ā]	kav
English	desire			151	[10U]	kav
Latin	Ø			152	[2Ā]	kaṃs
Greek	Ø			153	[1P]	kas
Sanskrit	kāṅkṣā	wish, desire	!	154	[1U]	kāṅkṣ

155	काश्			156	कास्	
[1Ā]	√kāś			[1Ā]	√kās	
W	kāśate			W	kāsate	
English	appear			English	cough	
Latin	Ø			Latin	Ø	
Greek	τέκμωρ	sign, token		Greek	Ø	
Sanskrit	kāśi	shining		Sanskrit	kāsajit	remov cough

157	किट्			158	किष्क्	
[1P]	√kiṭ			[10Ā]	√kiṣk	
	keṭati				kiṣkayate	
English	go,	approach		English	injure,	kill
Latin	Ø			Latin	Ø	
Greek	Ø			Greek	Ø	
Sanskrit	Ø			Sanskrit	Ø	

159	किल्			160	किल्	
[6P]	√kil			[10P]	√kil	
W	kilati			W	kelayati	
English	become white,	play		English	send,	throw
Latin	Ø			Latin	Ø	
Greek	Ø			Greek	Ø	
Sanskrit	kila	play		Sanskrit	kila	play

161	कीट्		!	155	[1Ā]	kāś
[10P]	√kīṭ		!	156	[1Ā]	kās
	kīṭayati			157	[1P]	kiṭ
English	tinge,	colour		158	[10Ā]	kiṣk
Latin	Ø			159	[6P]	kil
Greek	Ø			160	[10P]	kil
Sanskrit	Ø			161	[10P]	kīṭ

1	aṃś	41	aś	81	ubh	121	kaṇḍ
2	aṃh	42	aś	82	umbh	122	kaṅk
3	aṃh	43	aṣ	83	uṭh	123	kaṇṭh
4	aṃh	44	as	84	uṣ	124	kaṇṭh
5	ak	45	as	85	ūrj	125	kand
6	akṣ	46	ah	86	ūrd	126	kand
7	akṣ	47	āp	87	ūrṇu	127	kaḍ
8	ag	48	ās	88	ūrv	128	kaḍ
9	agh	49	i	89	ūy	129	katr
10	aṅk	50	i	90	ūṣ	130	katth
11	aṅk	51	ikh	91	ūh	131	kath
12	aṅg	52	iṅg	92	ūh	132	kad
13	aṅgh	53	in	93	ṛ	133	kaḍḍ
14	aj	54	idh	94	ṛc	134	kab
15	añc	55	inv	95	ṛj	135	kam
16	añc	56	il	96	ṛdh	136	kamp
17	añj	57	iṣ	97	ṛdh	137	kamb
18	aḍ	58	iṣ	98	ṛṇ	138	kal
19	aḍḍ	59	īkṣ	99	ṛṇ	139	kal
20	aṭ	60	īṅkh	100	ṛph	140	kal
21	aṭṭ	61	īj	101	ṛṣ	141	kall
22	aṭṭ	62	īñj	102	ṛṣ	142	kaś
23	aṭh	63	īd	103	ej	143	kaṣ
24	aṇṭh	64	īr	104	edh	144	karj
25	ad	65	īrṣy	105	eṣ	145	karṇ
26	an	66	īś	106	okh	146	kartr
27	ant	67	īṣ	107	oṇ	147	kard
28	abhr	68	īh	108	olaṇḍ	148	karb
29	am	69	ukṣ	109	olaṇḍ	149	karv
30	amb	70	ukh	110	kak	150	kav
31	argh	71	uṅkh	111	kakh	151	kav
32	arc	72	uc	112	kag	152	kaṃs
33	arj	73	uch	113	kac	153	kas
34	arth	74	ujjh	114	kac	154	kāṅkṣ
35	ard	75	uñch	115	kañc	155	kāś
36	arb	76	udhras	116	kaṭ	156	kās
37	arh	77	udhras	117	kaṭ	157	kiṭ
38	arv	78	und	118	kaṭh	158	kiṣk
39	al	79	ubj	119	kaṇ	159	kil
40	av	80	ubh	120	kan	160	kil
						161	kīṭ

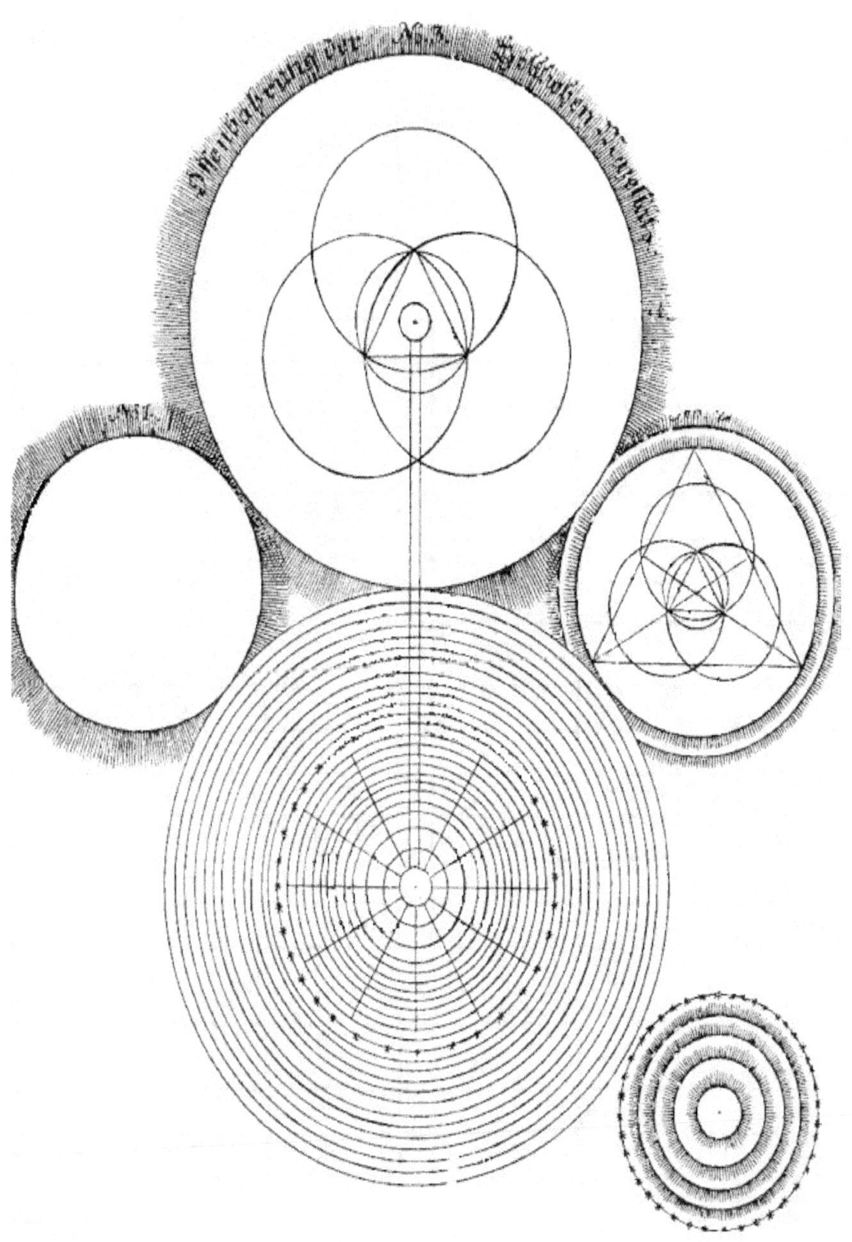

162	कीर्त्			163	कील्	
[10P]	√kīrt			[1P]	√kīl	
W	kīrtayati			W	kīlati	
English	mention			English	bind	
Latin	Ø			Latin	Ø	
Greek	Ø			Greek	Ø	
Sanskrit	kīrtana	mentioning		Sanskrit	kīla	pillar

164	कुक्			165	कुच्	
[1Ā]	√kuk			[6P]	√kuc	
	kokate			W	kucati	
English	take, accept			English	shrink,	curl
Latin	Ø			Latin	Ø	
Greek	Ø			Greek	Ø	
Sanskrit	Ø			Sanskrit	Ø	

166	कुज्			167	कुज्	
[1P]	√kuj			[6P]	√kuj	
	kojati				kujati	
English	steal			English	be crooked	
Latin	Ø			Latin	Ø	
Greek	Ø			Greek	Ø	
Sanskrit	Ø			Sanskrit	Ø	

168	कुञ्च्			162	[10P]	kīrt
[1Ā]	√kuñc			163	[1P]	kīl
W	kuñcate			164	[1Ā]	kuk
English	bend			165	[6P]	kuc
Latin	Ø			166	[1P]	kuj
Greek	Ø			167	[6P]	kuj
Sanskrit	kuñcana	contraction	!	168	[1Ā]	kuñc

169	कुट्			170	कुट्ट्	
[6P]	√kuṭ			[10P]	√kuṭṭ	
W	kuṭita			W	kuṭṭayati	
English	be bent			English	crush	
Latin	Ø			Latin	Ø	
Greek	Ø			Greek	Ø	
Sanskrit	Ø			Sanskrit	Ø	

171	कुड्			172	कुण्	
[6P]	√kuḍ			[6P]	√kuṇ	
	kuḍati				kuṇati	
English	act as a	child		English	sound,	aid
Latin	Ø			Latin	cano	sing
Greek	Ø			Greek	Ø	
Sanskrit	Ø			Sanskrit	Ø	

173	कुण्			174	कुण्ठ्	
[10P]	√kuṇ			[1P]	√kuṇṭh	
	kuṇayati			W	kuṇṭhati	
English	converse with,	invite		English	mutilated	blunted
Latin	cano	sing		Latin	Ø	
Greek	Ø			Greek	Ø	
Sanskrit	Ø			Sanskrit	kuṇṭha	blunt

175	कुण्ठ्			169	[6P]	kuṭ
[10P]	√kuṇṭh			170	[10P]	kuṭṭ
	kuṇṭhayati			171	[6P]	kuḍ
English	cover,	conceal		172	[6P]	kuṇ
Latin	Ø			173	[10P]	kuṇ
Greek	Ø			174	[1P]	kuṇṭh
Sanskrit	Ø			175	[10P]	kuṇṭh

176	कुण्ड्			177	कुण्ड्	
[1Ā]	√kuṇḍ			[1P]	√kuṇḍ	
W	kuṇḍate			W	kuṇḍati	
English	burn			English	mutilate	
Latin	Ø			Latin	Ø	
Greek	Ø			Greek	Ø	
Sanskrit	Ø			Sanskrit	Ø	

178	कुत्स्			179	कुथ्	
[10U]	√kuts			[4P]	√kuth	
W	kutsayati	kutsayate			kuthyati	
English	blame			English	stink	
Latin	Ø			Latin	Ø	
Greek	Ø			Greek	Ø	
Sanskrit	kutsā	abuse		Sanskrit	Ø	

180	कुद्			181	कुन्थ्	
180	कुद्			[1P]	√kunth	
[10P]	√kud			W	kunthati	
	kodayati			English	wound	
English	tell a lie			Latin	Ø	
Latin	Ø			Greek	Ø	
Greek	Ø			Sanskrit	Ø	

182	कुप्			176	[1Ā]	kuṇḍ
[4P]	√kup			177	[1P]	kuṇḍ
W	kupyati			178	[10U]	kuts
English	be angry			179	[4P]	kuth
Latin	cupio	desire		180	[10P]	kud
Greek	Ø			181	[1P]	kunth
Sanskrit	kopa	rage	!	182	[6P]	kup

183	कुम्ब्			184	कुम्ब्	
[10P]	√kumb			[6P]	√kumb	
	kumbayati				kumbati	
English	cover			English	cover	
Latin	Ø			Latin	Ø	
Greek	Ø			Greek	Ø	
Sanskrit	Ø			Sanskrit	Ø	

185	कुर्			186	कुल्	
[6P]	√kur			[1P]	√kul	
	kurati			W	kolati	
English	utter a	sound		English	accumulate	
Latin	Ø			Latin	Ø	
Greek	Ø			Greek	Ø	
Sanskrit	Ø			Sanskrit	kúla	family

187	कुश्			188	कुंश्	
[6P]	√kuś			[1P]	√kuṃś	
	kuśyati				kuṃśati	
English	embrace,	enfold		English	speak,	shine
Latin	Ø			Latin	Ø	
Greek	Ø			Greek	Ø	
Sanskrit	Ø			Sanskrit	Ø	

189	कुंश्			183	[10P]	kumb
[10P]	√kuṃś			184	[6P]	kumb
	kuṃśayati			185	[6P]	kur
English	speak, shine			186	[1P]	kul
Latin	Ø			187	[6P]	kuś
Greek	Ø			188	[1P]	kuṃś
Sanskrit	Ø			189	[10P]	kuṃś

190	कुष्			191	कुष्	
[9P]	√kuṣ			[6P]	√kuṣ	
W	kuṣṇāti			W	kuṣati	
English	tear	asunder		English	gnaw,	nibble
Latin	Ø			Latin	Ø	
Greek	Ø			Greek	Ø	
Sanskrit	Ø			Sanskrit	Ø	

192	कुह्			193	केप्	
[10Ā]	√kuh			[1Ā]	√kep	
	kuhayate				kepate	
English	surprise,	deceive		English	shake,	tremble
Latin	Ø			Latin	Ø	
Greek	Ø			Greek	Ø	
Sanskrit	kuhaka	rogue		Sanskrit	kepi	shaking

194	केल्			195	कू	
[1P]	√kel			[6Ā]	√kū	
	kelati			W	kuvate	
English	shake, be	frolicsome		English	cry, hum	
Latin	Ø			Latin	Ø	
Greek	Ø			Greek	κωκῡ́ω	shriek
Sanskrit	keli	play		Sanskrit	Ø	

196	कूज्			190	[9P]	kuṣ
[1P]	√kūj			191	[6P]	kuṣ
W	kūjati			192	[10Ā]	kuh
English	hum			193	[1Ā]	kep
Latin	Ø			194	[1P]	kel
Greek	Ø			195	[6Ā]	kū
Sanskrit	Ø		!	196	[1P]	kūj

197	कूड्		198	कूड्	
[6P]	√kūḍ		[10P]	√kūḍ	
	kūḍati			kūḍayati	
English	eat, graze		English	burn,	scorch
Latin	Ø		Latin	Ø	
Greek	Ø		Greek	Ø	
Sanskrit	Ø		Sanskrit	Ø	

199	कूट्		200	कूट्	
[10P]	√kūṭ		[10Ā]	√kūṭ	
	kūṭayati			kūṭayate	
English	burn,	advise	English	avoid	giving
Latin	Ø		Latin	Ø	
Greek	Ø		Greek	Ø	
Sanskrit	Ø		Sanskrit	Ø	

201	कूर्द्		202	कूर्द्	
[1P]	√kūrd		[1Ā]	√kūrd	
	kūrdati			kūrdate	
English	leap, jump		English	play	
Latin	Ø		Latin	Ø	
Greek	κραδάω	swing	Greek	κόρδαξ	dance of the
Sanskrit	kūrda	a jump	Sanskrit	Ø	old Comedy

203	कै		197	[6P]	kūḍ
[1P]	√kai		198	[10P]	kūḍ
	kāyati		199	[10P]	kūṭ
English	sound		200	[10Ā]	kūṭ
Latin	Ø		201	[1P]	kūrd
Greek	Ø		202	[1Ā]	kūrd
Sanskrit	Ø		203	[1P]	kai

204	क्रथ्			205	क्रस्	
[1P]	√knath			[4P]	√knas	
	knathati				knasyati	
English	hurt			English	be crooked,	shine
Latin	Ø			Latin	Ø	
Greek	Ø			Greek	Ø	
Sanskrit	Ø			Sanskrit	knasa	shining

206	क्नु			207	क्नूय्	
[9U]	√knu			207	क्नूय्	
	knunāti	knunīte		[1Ā]	√knūy	
English	sound				knūyate	
Latin	Ø			English	be wet,	stink
Greek	Ø			Latin	Ø	
Sanskrit	Ø			Greek	Ø	

208	क्मर्			209	कृ	
[1P]	√kmar			[8U]	√kṛ	
	kmarati			W	karoti	kurute
English	be fraudulent			English	do, make	
Latin	Ø			Latin	creo	create
Greek	Ø			Greek	Ø	
Sanskrit	Ø			Sanskrit	kārya	work

210	कृ			204	[1P]	knath
[5U]	√kṛ			205	[4P]	knas
W	kṛṇoti	kṛṇute		206	[9U]	knu
English	do, make			207	[1Ā]	knūy
Latin	creo	create		208	[1P]	kmar
Greek	Ø	!		209	[8U]	kṛ
Sanskrit	kárman	action	!	210	[5U]	kṛ

211	कृत्			212	कृप्	
[6P]	√kṛt			[1P]	√kṛp	
W	kṛntati			W	kṛpate	
English	cut			English	lament	
Latin	culter	knife		Latin	crepo	crack
French	couteau	knife		Greek	Ø	
Sanskrit	kartanī	scissors		Sanskrit	kṛpā	pity

213	कृश्			214	कृष्	
[4P]	√kṛś			[1U]	√kṛṣ	
W	kṛśyati			W	karṣati	karṣate
English	be lean			English	drag,	plough
Latin	cracēns	slender		Latin	Ø	
French	gracile	slim		Greek	Ø	
Sanskrit	kṛśa	thin		Sanskrit	kṛṣi	farming

215	कॄ			216	कॢप्	
[6U]	√kṝ			[1Ā]	√kḷp	
W	kirati	kirate		W	kalpate	
English	scatter			English	be regulated	
Latin	Ø			Latin	Ø	
Greek	Ø			Greek	Ø	
Sanskrit	kārin	scattering		Sanskrit	kḷpta	arranged

217	क्रथ्		!	211	[6P]	kṛt
[1P]	√krath			212	[1P]	kṛp
	krathati			213	[4P]	kṛś
English	hurt, kill		!	214	[1U]	kṛṣ
Latin	Ø			215	[6U]	kṝ
Greek	Ø			216	[1Ā]	kḷp
Sanskrit	Ø			217	[1P]	krath

218	क्रन्द्			219	क्रप्	
[1P]	√krand			[1Ā]	√krap	
W	krandati				krapate	
English	cry out			English	pity	
Latin	Ø			Latin	Ø	
Greek	Ø			Greek	Ø	
Sanskrit	krandas	battle-cry		Sanskrit	kṛpā	pity

220	क्रम्			221	क्री	
[1U]	√kram			[9U]	√krī	
W	krāmati	kramate		W	krīṇāti	krīṇīte
English	stride			English	buy	
Latin	Ø			Latin	Ø	
English	increment			Greek	πρίαμαι	buy
Sanskrit	kramatas	gradually		Sanskrit	krāyaka	trader

222	क्रीड्			223	क्रुञ्च्	
[1U]	√krīḍ			[1P]	√kruñc	
W	krīḍati	krīḍate		W	kruñcati	
English	play			English	curve	
Latin	Ø			Latin	Ø	
Greek	Ø			Greek	Ø	
Sanskrit	krīḍā	sport		Sanskrit	kruñca	curlew

224	क्रुध्		!	218	[1P]	krand
[4U]	√krudh			219	[1Ā]	krap
W	krudhyati	krudhyate	!	220	[1U]	kram
English	be angry		!	221	[9U]	krī
Latin	Ø		!	222	[1U]	krīḍ
Greek	Ø			223	[1P]	kruñc
Sanskrit	krodha	anger	!	224	[4U]	krudh

225	क्रुश्			226	क्लथ्	
[1P]	√kruś			[1P]	√klath	
W	krośati				klathati	
English	cry out			English	hurt, kill	
Latin	crocito	croak		Latin	Ø	
Greek	Ø			Greek	Ø	
Sanskrit	krośa	cry		Sanskrit	Ø	

227	क्लन्द्			228	क्लम्	
[1P]	√kland			[4P]	√klam	
	klandati			W	klāmyati	
English	sound,	lament		English	be weary	
Latin	Ø			Latin	Ø	
Greek	Ø			Greek	Ø	
Sanskrit	klanda	crying		Sanskrit	klānta	tired

229	क्लव्			230	क्लिद्	
[1A]	√klav			[4P]	√klid	
W	klavate			W	klidyati	
English	be fearful			English	be wet	
Latin	Ø			Latin	Ø	
Greek	Ø			Greek	Ø	
Sanskrit	klavita	stammered		Sanskrit	klinna	moistened

231	क्लिन्द्					
[1U]	√klind			!	225	[1P]	kruś
	klindati	klindate			226	[1P]	klath
English	lament				227	[1P]	kland
Latin	Ø			!	228	[4P]	klam
Greek	Ø				229	[1A]	klav
Sanskrit	Ø			!	230	[4P]	klid
					231	[1U]	klind

232	क्लिश्			233	क्लिश्	
[4P]	√kliś			[9P]	√kliś	
W	kliśyati			W	kliśnāti	
English	torment			English	torment	
Latin	Ø			Latin	Ø	
Greek	Ø			Greek	Ø	
Sanskrit	kleśa	pain		Sanskrit	kliṣṭa	distressed

234	क्लीब्			235	क्लीब्	
[1Ā]	√klīb			[10Ā]	√klīb	
	klibate				klībayate	
English	be impotent			English	be unmanly	
Latin	Ø			Latin	Ø	
Greek	Ø			Greek	Ø	
Sanskrit	klība	impotent		Sanskrit	klībatā	impotence

236	क्लु			237	क्लेश्	
[1Ā]	√klu			[1Ā]	√kleś	
	klavate				kleśate	
English	move			English	speak	inarticulately
Latin	Ø			Latin	Ø	
Greek	Ø			Greek	Ø	
Sanskrit	Ø			Sanskrit	Ø	

238	क्रण्		!	232	[4P]	kliś
[1P]	√kvaṇ		!	233	[9P]	kliś
W	kvaṇati			234	[1Ā]	klīb
English	sound			235	[10Ā]	klīb
Latin	Ø			236	[1Ā]	klu
Greek	Ø			237	[1Ā]	kleś
Sanskrit	kvaṇa	sound	!	238	[1P]	kvaṇ

239	क्रथ्			240	क्षज्	
[1P]	√kvath			[1Ā]	√kṣaj	
W	kvathati				kṣajate	
English	boil			English	go,	approach
Latin	cāseus	cheese		Latin	Ø	
Greek	Ø			Greek	Ø	
Sanskrit	kvatha	decoction		Sanskrit	Ø	

241	क्षज्			242	क्षद्	
[10P]	√kṣaj			[1Ā]	√kṣad	
	kṣañjayati			W	kṣadate	
English	live in pain,	want		English	cut,	divide
Latin	Ø			Latin	Ø	
Greek	Ø			Greek	Ø	
Sanskrit	Ø			Sanskrit	kṣadman	carving knife

243	क्षन्			244	क्षप्	
[8P]	√kṣan			[1U]	√kṣap	
W	kṣaṇoti			W	kṣapati	kṣapate
English	wound			English	abstinent	
Latin	Ø			Latin	Ø	
Greek	κτείνω	kill, slay		Greek	Ø	
Sanskrit	kṣata	injured		Sanskrit	kṣapaṇa	abstinence

245	क्षम्		!	239	[1P]	kvath
[1U]	√kṣam			240	[1Ā]	kṣaj
W	kṣamati	kṣamate		241	[10P]	kṣaj
English	endure			242	[1Ā]	kṣad
Latin	Ø		!	243	[8P]	kṣan
Greek	Ø			244	[1U]	kṣap
Sanskrit	kṣamā	patience	!	245	[1U]	kṣam

246	क्षम्प्			247	क्षर्	
[1P]	√kṣamp			[1P]	√kṣar	
	kṣampati			W	kṣarati	
English	suffer, bear			English	flow	
Latin	Ø			Latin	Ø	
Greek	Ø			Greek	Ø	
Sanskrit	Ø			Sanskrit	kṣara	melting away

248	क्षल्			249	क्षा	
[10P]	√kṣal			[4P]	√kṣā	
	kṣālayati			W	kṣāyati	
English	wash,	cleanse		English	burn	
Latin	Ø			Latin	Ø	
Greek	Ø			Greek	Ø	
Sanskrit	kṣāla	washing		Sanskrit	Ø	

250	क्षि			251	क्षि	
[2P]	√kṣi			[6P]	√kṣi	
W	kṣeti			W	kṣiyati	
English	possess			English	dwell	
Latin	Ø			Latin	situs	location
Greek	κτάομαι	obtain		Greek	κτίζω	to people
Sanskrit	kṣaya	dominion		Sanskrit	kṣiti	dwelling

252	क्षिप्			246	[1P]	kṣamp
[6U]	√kṣip		!	247	[1P]	kṣar
W	kṣipati	kṣipate		248	[10P]	kṣal
English	throw			249	[4P]	kṣā
Latin	Ø		!	250	[2P]	kṣi
Greek	Ø		!	251	[6P]	kṣi
Sanskrit	kṣipra	swift	!	252	[6U]	kṣip

253	क्षी			254	क्षी	
[5P]	√kṣī			[9P]	√kṣī	
W	kṣiṇoti			W	kṣiṇāti	
English	destroy			English	destroy	
Latin	Ø			Latin	Ø	
Greek	Ø			Greek	Ø	
Sanskrit	kṣīṇā	weak		Sanskrit	kṣīṇā	weak

255	क्षीज्			256	क्षीब्	
[1P]	√ kṣīj			[1P]	√ kṣīb	
	kṣījati				kṣībati	
English	sound	inarticulately		English	be drunk	
Latin	Ø			Latin	Ø	
Greek	Ø			Greek	Ø	
Sanskrit	Ø			Sanskrit	kṣība	intoxicated

257	क्षिव्			258	क्षु	
[1P]	√kṣiv			[2P]	√kṣu	
	kṣevati			W	kṣauti	
English	spit, vomit			English	sneeze	
Latin	Ø			Latin	Ø	
Greek	Ø			Greek	Ø	
Sanskrit	Ø			Sanskrit	kṣáva	sneezing

259	क्षुद्		!	253	[5P]	kṣī
[1U]	√kṣud		!	254	[9P]	kṣī
W	kṣodati	kṣodate		255	[1P]	kṣīj
English	crush			256	[1P]	kṣīb
Latin	Ø			257	[1P]	kṣiv
Greek	Ø		!	258	[2P]	kṣu
Sanskrit	Ø		!	259	[1U]	kṣud

260	क्षुद्			261	क्षुध्	
[7P]	√kṣud			[4P]	√kṣudh	
W	kṣuṇatti			W	kṣudhyati	
English	crush			English	be hungry	
Latin	Ø			Latin	Ø	
Greek	Ø			Greek	Ø	
Sanskrit	kṣuṇṇa	trampled upon		Sanskrit	kṣud	hunger

262	क्षुप्			263	क्षुभ्	
[6P]	√kṣup			[4U]	√kṣubh	
	kṣupati			W	kṣubhyati	kṣubhyate
English	be afraid			English	shake	
Latin	Ø			Latin	Ø	
Greek	Ø			Sanskrit	kṣobha	agitation
Sanskrit	Ø			German	schieben	push, shove

264	क्षुभ्			265	क्षुम्प्	
[9P]	√kṣubh			[1P]	√kṣump	
W	kṣubhnāti				kṣúmpati	
English	shake			English	go	
Latin	Ø			Latin	Ø	
Sanskrit	kṣobha	agitation		Greek	Ø	
German	schieben	push, shove		Sanskrit	Ø	

266	क्षुर्		!	260	[7P]	kṣud
[6P]	√kṣur		!	261	[4P]	kṣudh
	kṣurati			262	[6P]	kṣup
English	cut, dig		!	263	[4U]	kṣubh
Latin	Ø		!	264	[9P]	kṣubh
Greek	ξῠρόν	razor		265	[1P]	kṣump
Sanskrit	kṣurī	knife, dagger		266	[6P]	kṣur

267	क्षै			268	क्ष्णु	
[1P]	√kṣai			[2P]	√kṣṇu	
W	kṣāyati			W	kṣṇauti	
English	burn,	catch fire		English	sharpen	
Latin	Ø			Latin	Ø	
Greek	Ø			Greek	Ø	
Sanskrit	kṣāma	charring		Sanskrit	kṣṇotra	whet-stone

269	क्ष्माय्			270	क्ष्मील्	
[1Ā]	√kṣmāy			[1P]	√kṣmīl	
	kṣmāyate				kṣmīlati	
English	shake,	tremble		English	twinkle	
Latin	Ø			Latin	Ø	
Greek	Ø			Greek	Ø	
Sanskrit	kṣmāyita	shaken		Sanskrit	Ø	

271	क्ष्विड्			272	क्ष्वेल्	
[1P]	√kṣviḍ			[1P]	√kṣvel	
W	kṣveḍati				kṣvelati	
English	buzz, hum			English	leap, play	
Latin	Ø			Latin	Ø	
Greek	Ø			Greek	Ø	
Sanskrit	kṣviṇṇa	humming		Sanskrit	kṣvelana	play, jest

273	खच्			267	[1P]	kṣai
[1P]	√khac			268	[2P]	kṣṇu
	khacati			269	[1Ā]	kṣmāy
English	project			270	[1P]	kṣmīl
Latin	Ø		!	271	[1P]	kṣviḍ
Greek	Ø			272	[1P]	kṣvel
Sanskrit	khacita	prominent (?)	!	273	[1P]	khac

274	खच्			275	खच्	
[9P]	√khac			[10P]	√khac	
	khacñāti				khacayati	
English	be born	again		English	fasten,	bind
Latin	Ø			Latin	Ø	
Greek	Ø			Greek	Ø	
Sanskrit	Ø			Sanskrit	Ø	

276	खज्			277	खञ्ज्	
[1P]	√khaj			[1P]	√khañj	
	khajati			W	khañjati	
English	churn,	agitate		English	limp	
Latin	Ø			Latin	Ø	
Greek	Ø			German	hinken	limp
Sanskrit	khaja	stirring		Sanskrit	khañjā	poetic metre

278	खण्ड्			279	खट्	
[1Ā]	√khaṇḍ			[1P]	√khaṭ	
W	khaṇḍate				khaṭati	
English	break			English	desire	
Latin	Ø			Latin	Ø	
Greek	Ø			Greek	Ø	
Sanskrit	khaṇḍa	broken		Sanskrit	Ø	

280	खट्		!	274	[9P]	khac
[10P]	√khaṭṭ		!	275	[10P]	khac
	khaṭṭayati			276	[1P]	khaj
English	cover,	screen		277	[1P]	khañj
Latin	Ø			278	[1Ā]	khaṇḍ
Greek	Ø			279	[1P]	khaṭ
Sanskrit	Ø			280	[10P]	khaṭṭ

281	खद्			282	खन्	
[6P]	√khad			[1U]	√khan	
	khadati			W	khanati	khanate
English	be steady			English	dig	
Latin	Ø			Latin	canālis	ditch
Greek	Ø			Greek	Ø	
Sanskrit	khadana	firmness		Sanskrit	khanī	a mine

283	खर्ज्			284	खर्द्	
[1P]	√kharj			[1P]	√khard	
	kharjati				khardati	
English	pain			English	bite, sting	
Latin	Ø			Latin	Ø	
Greek	Ø			Greek	Ø	
Sanskrit	Ø			Sanskrit	Ø	

285	खर्ब्			286	खर्व्	
[1P]	√kharb			[1P]	√kharv	
	kharbati				kharvati	
English	go, move			English	be proud	
Latin	Ø			Latin	Ø	
Greek	Ø			Greek	Ø	
Sanskrit	Ø			Sanskrit	Ø	

287	खष्			281	[6P]	khad
[1P]	√khas		!	282	[1U]	khan
	khasati			283	[1P]	kharj
English	hurt, injure			284	[1P]	khard
Latin	Ø			285	[1P]	kharb
Greek	Ø			286	[1P]	kharv
Sanskrit	Ø			287	[1P]	khas

288	खाद्			289	खिट्	
[1P]	√khād			[1P]	√khiṭ	
W	khādati				kheṭati	
English	eat, chew			English	be terrified	
Latin	Ø			Latin	Ø	
Greek	Ø			Greek	Ø	
Sanskrit	khāda	devouring		Sanskrit	Ø	

290	खिद्			291	खु	
[6P]	√khid			[1Ā]	√khu	
W	khidati				khavate	
English	press down			English	sound	
Latin	caedō	cut, strike		Latin	Ø	
Greek	Ø			Greek	Ø	
Sanskrit	khinna	downcast		Sanskrit	Ø	

292	खुज्			293	खुण्ड्	
[1P]	√khuj			[1Ā]	√khuṇḍ	
	khojati				khuṇḍate	
English	steal			English	break in	pieces
Latin	Ø			Latin	Ø	
Greek	Ø			Greek	Ø	
Sanskrit	Ø			Sanskrit	Ø	

294	खेट्					
			!	288	[1P]	khād
[10P]	kheṭ			289	[1P]	khiṭ
	kheṭayati		!	290	[6P]	khid
English	eat			291	[1Ā]	khu
Latin	Ø			292	[1P]	khuj
Greek	Ø			293	[1Ā]	khuṇḍ
Sanskrit	Ø			294	[10P]	kheṭ

295	खेल्		296	ख्या	
[1P]	√khel		[2P]	√khyā	
W	khelati		W	khyāti	
English	swing,	tremble	English	tell, say	
Latin	Ø		Latin	Ø	
Greek	Ø		Greek	Ø	
Sanskrit	khelana	shaking	Sanskrit	khyāti	opinion, view

297	खै		298	गज्	
[1P]	√khai		[1P]	√gaj	
	khāyati		W	gajati	
English	make firm		English	howl, roar	
Latin	Ø		Latin	Ø	
Greek	Ø		Greek	Ø	
Sanskrit	Ø		Sanskrit	Ø	

299	गड्		300	गड्	
[1P]	√gaḍ		[10P]	√gaḍ	
W	gaḍati			gaḍayati	
English	distill		English	cover	
Latin	Ø		Latin	Ø	
Greek	Ø		Greek	Ø	
Sanskrit	Ø		Sanskrit	Ø	

301	गण्			295	[1P]	khel
[10P]	√gaṇ		!	296	[2P]	khyā
W	gaṇayati			297	[1P]	khai
English	count			298	[1P]	gaj
Latin	grex	flock, swarm		299	[1P]	gaḍ
Greek	ἀγών	gathering		300	[10P]	gaḍ
Sanskrit	gaṇa	flock, troop		301	[10P]	gaṇ

302	गण्ड्			303	गद्	
[1P]	√gaṇḍ			[1P]	√gad	
	gaṇḍati			W	gadati	
English	affect the	cheek		English	say	
Latin	Ø			Latin	Ø	
Greek	Ø			English	quethe	quoth
Sanskrit	gaṇḍaka	rhinoceros		Sanskrit	gada	sentence

304	गम्			305	गर्ज्	
[1U]	√gam			[1P]	√garj	
W	gacchati	gacchate		W	garjati	
English	go			English	roar,	trumpet
Latin	veniō	come		Latin	garrio	chatter
Greek	βαινω	go		German	quarren	squeak
Sanskrit	gatá	gone		Sanskrit	garjana	rumbling

306	गर्द्			307	गर्ब्	
[1P]	√gard			[1P]	√garb	
W	gardati				garbati	
English	emit any sound	cry, bray		English	go, move	
Latin	Ø			Latin	Ø	
Greek	Ø			Greek	Ø	
Sanskrit	gardabha	an ass		Sanskrit	Ø	

308	गर्व्			302	[1P]	gaṇḍ
[1P]	√garv		!	303	[1P]	gad
	garvati		!	304	[1U]	gam
English	become	proud	!	305	[1P]	garj
Latin	Ø			306	[1P]	gard
Greek	Ø			307	[1P]	garb
Sanskrit	garva	pride		308	[1P]	garv

309	गर्व्		310	गर्ह्	
[10Ā]	√garv		[1Ā]	√garh	
	garvati	garvayate	W	garhate	
English	become	proud	English	blame	
Latin	Ø		Latin	Ø	
Greek	Ø		Greek	Ø	
Sanskrit	garva	pride	Sanskrit	garhā	censure

311	गर्ह्		312	गल्	
[10P]	√garh		[1P]	√gal	
W	garhayati		W	galati	
English	blame		English	drop	
Latin	Ø		Latin	Ø	
Greek	Ø		Greek	Ø	
Sanskrit	garhā	censure	Sanskrit	gala	oozing, resin

313	गल्भ्		314	गवेष्	
[1Ā]	√galbh		[1Ā]	√gaveṣ	
W	galbhate			gaveṣate	
English	be bold		English	search	
Latin	Ø		Latin	Ø	
Greek	Ø		Greek	Ø	
Sanskrit	galbha	bold	Sanskrit	gaveṣaṇa	desiring

315	गह्			309	[10Ā]	garv
[10P]	√gah		!	310	[1Ā]	garh
W	gahayati		!	311	[10P]	garh
English	enter	deeply into	!	312	[1P]	gal
Latin	Ø			313	[1Ā]	galbh
Greek	Ø			314	[1Ā]	gaveṣ
Sanskrit	gahana	abyss		315	[10P]	gah

316	गा			317	गा	
[3P]	√gā			[1P]	√gā	
W	jigāti			W	gāyati	
English	go			English	sing	
Latin	Ø			Latin	Ø	
German	gehen	go		Greek	Ø	
Sanskrit	Ø			Sanskrit	gāṇa	song

318	गाध्			319	गाह्	
[1Ā]	√gādh			[1Ā]	√gāh	
	gādhate			W	gāhate	
English	stay			English	plunge	
Latin	Ø			Latin	Ø	
Greek	Ø			Greek	Ø	
Sanskrit	gādha	shallow place		Sanskrit	gāḍha	dived into

320	गु			321	गु	
[1Ā]	√gu			[1Ā]	√gu	
	gávate				gavate	
English	go			English	sound	
Latin	Ø			Latin	Ø	
Greek	Ø			Greek	Ø	
Sanskrit	Ø			Sanskrit	Ø	

322	गु		!	316	[3P]	gā
[6P]	√gu		!	317	[1P]	gā
	guvati			318	[1Ā]	gādh
English	void by	stool	!	319	[1Ā]	gāh
Latin	Ø			320	[1Ā]	gu
Greek	Ø			321	[1Ā]	gu
Sanskrit	Ø			322	[6P]	gu

162	kīrt	202	kūrd	242	kṣad	282	khan
163	kīl	203	kai	243	kṣan	283	kharj
164	kuk	204	knath	244	kṣap	284	khard
165	kuc	205	knas	245	kṣam	285	kharb
166	kuj	206	knu	246	kṣamp	286	kharv
167	kuj	207	knūy	247	kṣar	287	khaṣ
168	kuñc	208	kmar	248	kṣal	288	khād
169	kuṭ	209	kṛ	249	kṣā	289	khiṭ
170	kuṭṭ	210	kṛ	250	kṣi	290	khid
171	kuḍ	211	kṛt	251	kṣi	291	khu
172	kuṇ	212	kṛp	252	kṣip	292	khuj
173	kuṇ	213	kṛś	253	kṣī	293	khuṇḍ
174	kuṇṭh	214	kṛṣ	254	kṣī	294	kheṭ
175	kuṇṭh	215	kṝ	255	kṣīj	295	khel
176	kuṇḍ	216	klp	256	kṣīb	296	khyā
177	kuṇḍ	217	krath	257	kṣiv	297	khai
178	kuts	218	krand	258	kṣu	298	gaj
179	kuth	219	krap	259	kṣud	299	gaḍ
180	kud	220	kram	260	kṣud	300	gaḍ
181	kunth	221	krī	261	kṣudh	301	gaṇ
182	kup	222	krīḍ	262	kṣup	302	gaṇḍ
183	kumb	223	kruñc	263	kṣubh	303	gad
184	kumb	224	krudh	264	kṣubh	304	gam
185	kur	225	kruś	265	kṣump	305	garj
186	kul	226	klath	266	kṣur	306	gard
187	kuś	227	kland	267	kṣai	307	garb
188	kuṃś	228	klam	268	kṣṇu	308	garv
189	kuṃś	229	klav	269	kṣmāy	309	garv
190	kuṣ	230	klid	270	kṣmīl	310	garh
191	kuṣ	231	klind	271	kṣviḍ	311	garh
192	kuh	232	kliś	272	kṣvel	312	gal
193	kep	233	kliś	273	khac	313	galbh
194	kel	234	klīb	274	khac	314	gaveṣ
195	kū	235	klīb	275	khac	315	gah
196	kūj	236	klu	276	khaj	316	gā
197	kūḍ	237	kleś	277	khañj	317	gā
198	kūḍ	238	kvaṇ	278	khaṇḍ	318	gādh
199	kūṭ	239	kvath	279	khaṭ	319	gāh
200	kūṭ	240	kṣaj	280	khaṭṭ	320	gu
201	kūrd	241	kṣaj	281	khad	321	gu
						322	gu

Chapter 3

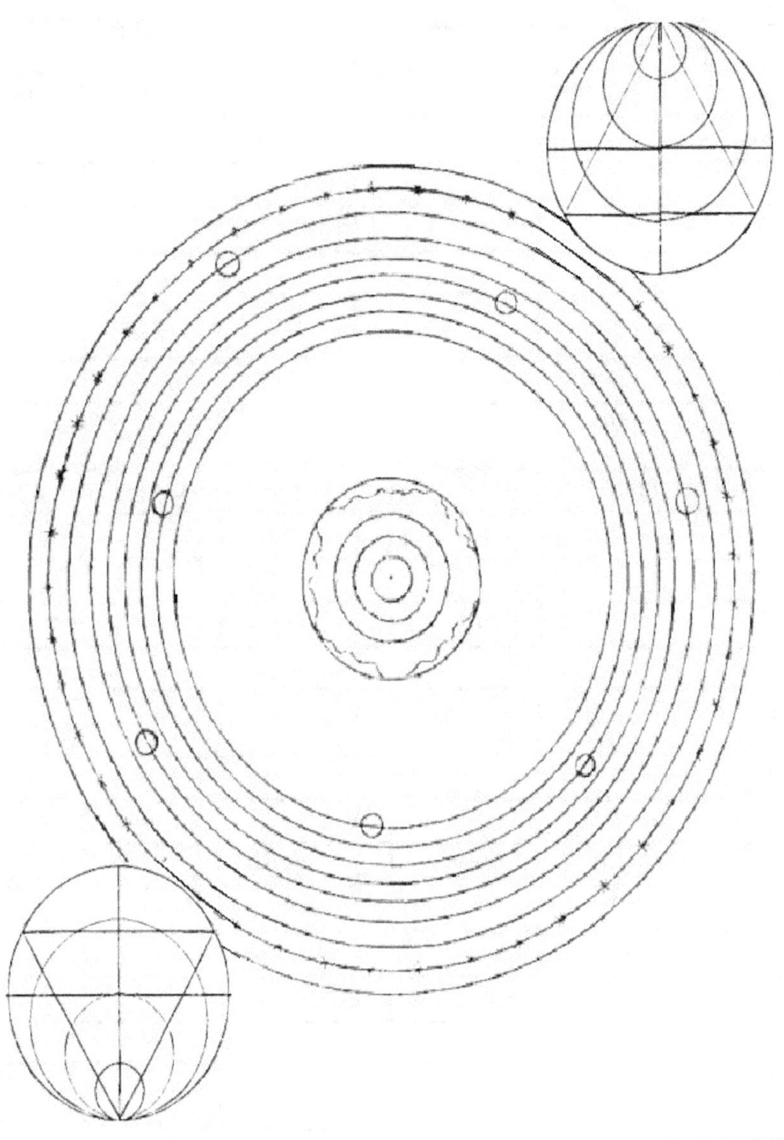

323	गुज्	
[1P]	√guj	
	gojati	
English	buzz, hum	
Latin	Ø	
Greek	Ø	
Sanskrit	Ø	

324	गुज्	
[6P]	√guj	
	gujati	
English	buzz,	hum
Latin	Ø	
Greek	Ø	
Sanskrit	Ø	

325	गुञ्	
[1P]	√guñj	
W	guñjati	
English	buzz, hum	
Latin	Ø	
Greek	Ø	
Sanskrit	guñja	humming

326	गुण्ड्	
[10P]	√guṇḍ	
W	guṇḍayati	
English	cover,	pound
Latin	Ø	
Greek	Ø	
Sanskrit	guṇḍita	pounded

327	गुड्	
[6P]	√guḍ	
	guḍati	
English	guard,	preserve
Latin	Ø	
Greek	Ø	
Sanskrit	guḍa	eleph. armour

328	गुद्	
[1Ā]	√gud	
	godate	
English	play	
Latin	Ø	
Greek	Ø	
Sanskrit	Ø	

329	गुध्		
[4P]	√gudh		
	gudhyati		!
English	cover		
Latin	Ø		
German	Haut	skin, hide	
Sanskrit	gudhita	enclosed	

323	[1P]	guj
324	[6P]	guj
325	[1P]	guñj
326	[10P]	guṇḍ
327	[6P]	guḍ
328	[1Ā]	gud
329	[4P]	gudh

330	गुध्			331	गुध्	
[9P]	√gudh			[1Ā]	√gudh	
	gudhnāti				godhate	
English	be angry			English	play	
Latin	Ø			Latin	Ø	
Greek	Ø			Greek	Ø	
Sanskrit	Ø			Sanskrit	Ø	

332	गुप्			333	गुफ्	
Pft	√gup			[6P]	√guph	
W	jugopa				guphati	
English	protect			English	string	together
Latin	Ø			Latin	Ø	
Greek	Ø			Greek	Ø	
Sanskrit	gupta	protected		Sanskrit	guphita	tied

334	गुर्			335	गुर्	
[6Ā]	√gur			[4Ā]	√gur	
W	gurate				gūryate	
English	lift up			English	hurt, kill	
Latin	Ø			Latin	Ø	
Greek	βάλλω	throw		Greek	Ø	
Sanskrit	Ø			Sanskrit	Ø	

336	गुर्द्			330	[9P]	gudh
336	गुर्द्			331	[1Ā]	gudh
[1Ā]	√gurd		!	332	Pft	gup
	gurdate			333	[6P]	guph
English	play			334	[6Ā]	gur
Latin	Ø			335	[4Ā]	gur
Greek	Ø			336	[1Ā]	gurd

337	गुर्द्			338	गुर्व्	
[10P]	√gurd			[1P]	√gurv	
	gurdayati				gūrvati	
English	dwell			English	lift up	
Latin	∅			Latin	∅	
Greek	∅			Greek	∅	
Sanskrit	∅			Sanskrit	∅	

339	गुह्			340	गृ	
[1P]	√guh			[1P]	√gṛ	
W	gūhati			W	garati	
English	hide			English	sprinkle	
Latin	∅			Latin	∅	
Greek	∅			Greek	∅	
Sanskrit	guhā	hiding-place		Sanskrit	∅	

341	गृज्			342	गृध्	
[1P]	√gṛj			[4P]	√gṛdh	
	garjati			W	gṛdhyati	
English	sound, roar			English	be greedy	
Latin	∅			Latin	∅	
Greek	∅			German	Gier	greed
English	∅			Sanskrit	gṛddhi	greediness

343	गॄ			337	[10P]	gurd
[9U]	√gṝ			338	[1P]	gurv
W	gṛṇāti	gṛṇīte	!	339	[1P]	guh
English	call, sing		!	340	[1P]	gṛ
Latin	garriō	chatter		341	[1P]	gṛj
Greek	γῆρυς	voice	!	342	[4P]	gṛdh
English	garrulous		!	343	[9U]	gṝ

344	गृ			345	गेप्	
[6P]	√gr̄			[1Ā]	√gep	
W	girati				gepate	
English	swallow			English	go, move	
Latin	vorō	devour		Latin	Ø	
Greek	βορά	food		Greek	Ø	
Sanskrit	gará	swallowing		Sanskrit	Ø	

346	गेव्			347	गेष्	
[1Ā]	√gev			[1Ā]	√geṣ	
	gevate				geṣate	
English	serve			English	seek,	search
Latin	Ø			Latin	Ø	
Greek	Ø			Greek	Ø	
Sanskrit	Ø			Sanskrit	Ø	

348	ग्रन्थ्			349	ग्रन्थ्	
[9U]	√granth			[1Ā]	√granth	
W	grathnāti	grathnīte			grathate	
English	tie			English	be crooked	
Latin	glūten (?)	glue		Latin	Ø	
Greek	Ø			Greek	Ø	
Sanskrit	granthí	knot		Sanskrit	granthi	crookedness

350	ग्रह्			343	[6P]	gr̄
[9U]	√grah			345	[1Ā]	gep
W	gṛhṇāti	gṛhṇīte		346	[1Ā]	gev
English	seize, grab			347	[1Ā]	geṣ
Latin	Ø		!	348	[9U]	granth
German	greifen	grasp	!	349	[1Ā]	granth
Sanskrit	graha	seizing	!	350	[9U]	grah

351	ग्रस्			352	गुच्	
[1U]	√gras			[1P]	√gruc	
W	grasati	grasate			grocati	
English	devour			English	steal	
Latin	grā-men	grass		Latin	Ø	
Greek	γράω	eat		Greek	Ø	
Sanskrit	grasta	eaten		Sanskrit	Ø	

353	ग्लह्			354	ग्लुच्	
[1Ā]	√glah			[1P]	√gluc	
W	glahate				glocati	
English	gamble			English	steal,	move
Latin	Ø			Latin	Ø	
Greek	Ø			Greek	Ø	
Sanskrit	glaha	game at dice		Sanskrit	Ø	

355	ग्लुञ्च्			356	ग्लेप्	
[1P]	√gluñc			[1Ā]	√glep	
	gluñcati				glepate	
English	go, move			English	shake,	tremble
Latin	Ø			Latin	Ø	
Greek	Ø			Greek	Ø	
Sanskrit	Ø			Sanskrit	Ø	

357	ग्लेव्		!	351	[1U]	gras
[1Ā]	√glev			352	[1P]	gruc
	glevate			353	[1Ā]	glah
English	serve			354	[1P]	gluc
Latin	Ø			355	[1P]	gluñc
Greek	Ø			356	[1Ā]	glep
Sanskrit	Ø			357	[1Ā]	glev

358	ग्लेष्			359	ग्लै	
[1Ā]	√gleṣ			[1U]	√glai	
	gleṣate				glāyati	glāyate
English	seek			English	feel tired	
Latin	Ø			Latin	Ø	
Greek	Ø			Greek	Ø	
Sanskrit	Ø			Sanskrit	glāni	exhaustion

360	ग्लै			361	ग्ला	
[2P]	√glai			[4U]	√glā	
	glāti			W	glāyati	glāyate
English	feel tired			English	feel tired	
Latin	Ø			Latin	Ø	
Greek	Ø			Greek	Ø	
Sanskrit	glāni	exhaustion		Sanskrit	glāni	exhaustion

362	घघ्			363	घट्	
[1P]	√ghagh			[1Ā]	√ghaṭ	
	ghaghati			W	ghaṭate	
English	laugh			English	strive	
Latin	Ø			Latin	Ø	
Greek	Ø			Greek	Ø	
Sanskrit	Ø			Sanskrit	ghaṭa	busy with

364	घट्ट्			358	[1Ā]	gleṣ
[1Ā]	√ghaṭṭ			359	[1U]	glai
W	ghaṭṭate			360	[2P]	glai
English	rub		!	361	[4U]	glā
Latin	Ø			362	[1P]	ghagh
Greek	Ø		!	363	[1Ā]	ghaṭ
Sanskrit	ghaṭṭana	rubbing		364	[1Ā]	ghaṭṭ

365	घण्ट्			366	घस्	
[1P]	√ghaṇṭ			Pft	√ghas	
	ghaṇṭati			W	jaghāsa	
English	speak, shine			English	eat	
Latin	Ø			Latin	Ø	
Greek	Ø			Greek	Ø	
Sanskrit	Ø			Sanskrit	ghāsa	food, meadow

367	घिण्ण्			368	घु	
[1Ā]	√ghiṇṇ			[1Ā]	√ghu	
	ghiṇṇate				ghavate	
English	take, grasp			English	make a	sound
Latin	Ø			Latin	Ø	
Greek	Ø			Greek	Ø	
Sanskrit	Ø			Sanskrit	Ø	

369	घुट्			370	घुट्	
[1Ā]	√ghuṭ			[6P]	√ghuṭ	
W	ghoṭate			W	ghuṭati	
English	turn			English	resist	
Latin	Ø			Latin	Ø	
Greek	Ø			Greek	Ø	
Sanskrit	Ø			Sanskrit	Ø	

371	घुण्			365	[1P]	ghaṇṭ
[6P]	√ghuṇ			366	Pft	ghas
	ghuṇati			367	[1Ā]	ghiṇṇ
English	go, move			368	[1Ā]	ghu
Latin	Ø			369	[1Ā]	ghuṭ
Greek	Ø			370	[6P]	ghuṭ
Sanskrit	Ø			371	[6P]	ghuṇ

372	घुण्			373	घुण्ण्	
[1Ā]	√ghuṇ			[1Ā]	√ghuṇṇ	
	ghoṇate				ghuṇṇate	
English	go, move			English	take,	grasp
Latin	Ø			Latin	Ø	
Greek	Ø			Greek	Ø	
Sanskrit	Ø			Sanskrit	Ø	

374	घुर्			375	घुष्	
[6P]	√ghur			[1P]	√ghuṣ	
	ghurati			W	ghoṣati	
English	frighten			English	sound	
Latin	Ø			Latin	heus	hey, listen
Greek	Ø			Greek	Ø	
Sanskrit	Ø			Sanskrit	ghoṣa	tumult

376	घूर्ण्			377	घूर्ण्	
[6P]	√ghūrṇ			[1Ā]	√ghūrṇ	
W	ghūrṇati			W	ghūrṇate	
English	be agitated			English	be agitated	
Latin	Ø			Latin	Ø	
Greek	Ø			Greek	Ø	
Sanskrit	ghūrṇa	shaking		Sanskrit	ghūrṇa	shaking

378	घृ			372	[1Ā]	ghuṇ
[3P]	√ghṛ			373	[1Ā]	ghuṇṇ
W	jigharti			374	[6P]	ghur
English	shine, burn			375	[1P]	ghuṣ
Latin	Ø		!	376	[6P]	ghūrṇ
Greek	Ø		!	377	[1Ā]	ghūrṇ
Sanskrit	gharmá	heat, warmth		378	[3P]	ghṛ

379	घृ			380	घृष्	
[1P]	√ghṛ			[1P]	√ghṛṣ	
W	gharati			W	gharṣati	
English	besprinkle			English	rub,	crush
Latin	Ø			Latin	Ø	
Greek	Ø			Greek	χαράσσω	sharpen
Sanskrit	ghṛta	ghee		Sanskrit	gharṣa	rubbing

381	घ्रा			382	चक्	
[1P]	√ghrā			[1U]	√cak	
W	jighrati				cakati	cakate
English	smell			English	be satisfied	
Latin	frōns	brow, front		Latin	Ø	
Greek	ὀσφρησι	smell (?)		Greek	Ø	
Sanskrit	ghrāṇā	nose of a bull		Sanskrit	Ø	

383	चक्क्			384	चकास्	
[10P]	√cakk			[2P]	√cakās	
	cakkayati			W	cakāsti	
English	inflict pain			English	shine	
Latin	Ø			Latin	Ø	
Greek	Ø			Greek	Ø	
Sanskrit	Ø			Sanskrit	cakāsita	illuminated

385	चक्ष्			379	[1P]	ghṛ
[2P]	√cakṣ		!	380	[1P]	ghṛṣ
W	caṣṭe		!	381	[1P]	ghrā
English	see		!	382	[1U]	cak
Latin	Ø			383	[10P]	cakk
Greek	Ø			384	[2P]	cakās
Sanskrit	cákṣas	eye, sight	!	385	[2P]	cakṣ

386	चक्ष्			387	चञ्च्	
[1Ā]	√cakṣ			[1P]	√cañc	
W	cakṣate			W	cañcati	
English	see			English	leap,	jump
Latin	Ø			Latin	Ø	
Greek	Ø			Greek	Ø	
Sanskrit	cákṣus	seeing		Sanskrit	cañcatka	leaping

388	चट्			389	चण्	
[1P]	√caṭ			[1P]	√caṇ	
W	caṭati				caṇati	
English	take place			English	go	
Latin	Ø			Latin	Ø	
Greek	Ø			Greek	Ø	
Sanskrit	Ø			Sanskrit	Ø	

390	चण्ड्			391	चन्	
[1Ā]	√caṇḍ			[1P]	√can	
	caṇḍate				canati	
English	be angry			English	sound	
Latin	Ø			Latin	Ø	
Greek	Ø			Greek	Ø	
Sanskrit	cáṇḍa	fierce		Sanskrit	Ø	

392	चत्			!	386	[1Ā]	cakṣ
[1P]	√cat			!	387	[1P]	cañc
	catati				388	[1P]	caṭ
English	hide one's self				389	[1P]	caṇ
Latin	Ø				390	[1Ā]	caṇḍ
Greek	Ø				391	[1P]	can
Sanskrit	catya	be hidden			392	[1P]	cat

393	चन्द्			394	चप्	
[1P]	√cand			[1P]	√cap	
W	candati				capati	
English	shine			English	caress	
Latin	candidus	shining white		Latin	Ø	
Greek	Ø			Greek	Ø	
Sanskrit	candra	moon		Sanskrit	Ø	

395	चप्			396	चम्	
[10P]	√cap			[1P]	√cam	
	capayati			W	camati	
English	knead			English	sip	
Latin	Ø			Latin	Ø	
Greek	Ø			Greek	Ø	
Sanskrit	Ø			Sanskrit	camasa	cup, flat dish

397	चम्बू			398	चर्	
[1P]	√camb			[1P]	√car	
	cambati			W	carati	
English	go			English	move	
Latin	Ø			Latin	carrus	wagon
Greek	Ø			Greek	πέλομαι	stir
Sanskrit	Ø			Sanskrit	cara	moving

399	चर्च्			393	[1P]	cand
[10P]	√carc			394	[1P]	cap
W	carcayati			395	[10P]	cap
English	repeat			396	[1P]	cam
Latin	Ø			397	[1P]	camb
Greek	Ø		!	398	[1P]	car
Sanskrit	carcā	repetition		399	[10P]	carc

400	चर्ब्			401	चर्व्	
[1P]	√carb			[10P]	√carv	
	carbati			W	carvayati	
English	go			English	chew	
Latin	Ø			Latin	Ø	
Greek	Ø			Greek	Ø	
Sanskrit	Ø			Sanskrit	carvaṇa	chewing

402	चल्			403	चष्	
[1P]	√cal			[1P]	√caṣ	
W	calati				caṣati	
English	stir			English	hurt	
Latin	celer	fast		Latin	Ø	
Greek	Ø			Greek	Ø	
Sanskrit	cala	moving		Sanskrit	Ø	

404	चह्			405	चह्	
[1P]	√cah			[10P]	√cah	
	cahati				cahayati	
English	cheat			English	cheat	
Latin	Ø			Latin	Ø	
Greek	Ø			Greek	Ø	
Sanskrit	Ø			Sanskrit	Ø	

406	चाय्			400	[1P]	carb
[1P]	√cāy		!	401	[10P]	carv
	cāyati		!	402	[1P]	cal
English	observe			403	[1P]	caṣ
Latin	Ø			404	[1P]	cah
Greek	Ø			405	[10P]	cah
Sanskrit	cāyanīya	perceptible		406	[1P]	cāy

407	चि			408	चि	
[5U]	√ci			[1Ā]	√ci	
W	cinoti	cinute		W	cáyate	
English	heap up			English	punish	
Latin	Ø			Latin	Ø	
Greek	ποιέω	make		Greek	τίνομαι	chastise
Sanskrit	caya	collection		Sanskrit	caya	revenging

409	चित्			410	चिन्त्	
[1P]	√cit			[10P]	√cint	
W	cetati			W	cintayati	
English	perceive			English	think	
Latin	Ø			Latin	Ø	
Greek	τίω	honour		Greek	Ø	
Sanskrit	cetanā	consciousness		Sanskrit	cintā	thought, care

411	चिरि			412	चीव्	
[5P]	√ciri			[1U]	√cīv	
	cirṇoti				cīvati	cīvate
English	hurt, kill			English	take	
Latin	Ø			Latin	Ø	
Greek	Ø			Greek	Ø	
Sanskrit	Ø			Sanskrit	Ø	

413	चीव्				407	[5U]	ci
[10P]	√cīv		!	408	[1Ā]	ci
	cīvayati			409	[1P]	cit
English	take			410	[10P]	cint
Latin	Ø			411	[5P]	ciri
Greek	Ø			412	[1U]	cīv
Sanskrit	Ø			413	[10P]	cīv

414	चुक्क्			415	चुट्	
[10P]	√cukk			[6P]	√cuṭ	
	cukkayati			W	cuṭati	
English	suffer pain			English	split	
Latin	Ø			Latin	Ø	
Greek	Ø			Greek	Ø	
Sanskrit	Ø			Sanskrit	Ø	

416	चुट्			417	चुट्	
[10P]	√cuṭ			[1P]	√cuṭ	
W	coṭayati			W	coṭati	
English	split			English	become	small
Latin	Ø			Latin	Ø	
Greek	Ø			Greek	Ø	
Sanskrit	Ø			Sanskrit	Ø	

418	चुड्			419	चुद्	
[6P]	√cuḍ			[1P]	√cud	
	cuḍati			W	codati	
English	conceal			English	impel	
Latin	Ø			Latin	cūdō	strike, beat
Greek	Ø			Greek	σπεύδω	urge on
Sanskrit	Ø			Sanskrit	coda	inspiring

420	चुप्			414	[10P]	cukk
[1P]	√cup			415	[6P]	cuṭ
	copati			416	[10P]	cuṭ
English	move			417	[1P]	cuṭ
Latin	Ø			418	[6P]	cuḍ
Greek	Ø	!		419	[1P]	cud
Sanskrit	copana	moving		420	[1P]	cup

421	चुम्ब्			422	चुर्	
[1P]	√cumb			[10P]	√cur	
W	cumbati			W	corayati	
English	kiss			English	steal	
Latin	Ø			Latin	Ø	
Greek	Ø			French	chouraver	nick (slang)
Sanskrit	cumba	kissing		Sanskrit	cora	thief

423	चुल्			424	चुलुम्प्	
[10P]	√cul			[10P]	√culump	
	colayati				culumpati	
English	raise			English	swing	
Latin	Ø			Latin	Ø	
Greek	Ø			Greek	Ø	
Sanskrit	Ø			Sanskrit	Ø	

425	चूर्			426	चूर्ण्	
[4Ā]	√cūr			[10Ā]	√cūrṇ	
	cūryate				cūrṇyate	
English	burn			English	pulverise	
Latin	Ø			Latin	Ø	
Greek	Ø			Greek	Ø	
Sanskrit	Ø			Sanskrit	cūrṇa	chalk, lime

427	चूष्			421	[1P]	cumb
[1P]	√cūṣ		!	422	[10P]	cur
W	cūṣati			423	[10P]	cul
English	suck			424	[10P]	culump
Latin	Ø			425	[4Ā]	cūr
Greek	Ø			426	[10Ā]	cūrṇ
Sanskrit	cūṣaṇa	sucking leech	!	427	[1P]	cūṣ

428	चृत्			429	चेष्ट्	
[6P]	√cṛt			[1U]	√ceṣṭ	
W	cṛtati			W	ceṣṭati	ceṣṭate
English	bind			English	stir	
Latin	Ø			Latin	Ø	
Greek	Ø			Greek	Ø	
Sanskrit	Ø			Sanskrit	ceṣṭā	action

430	च्यु			431	च्युत्	
[1U]	√cyu			[1P]	√cyut	
W	cyavati	cyavate			cyotati	
English	move			English	flow	
Latin	Ø			Latin	Ø	
Greek	σεύω	drive		Greek	Ø	
Sanskrit	cyuta	moved		Sanskrit	cyut	"distilling"

432	च्युस्			433	छद्	
[10P]	√cyus			[1P]	√chad	
	cyosayati			W	chadati	
English	leave			English	cover	
Latin	Ø			Latin	Ø	
Greek	Ø			Greek	Ø	
Sanskrit	Ø			Sanskrit	chada	cover

434	छन्द्			428	[6P]	cṛt
[1U]	√chand		!	429	[1U]	ceṣṭ
W	chandati	chandate	!	430	[1U]	cyu
English	seem,	please		431	[1P]	cyut
Latin	cēnseō (?)	judge		432	[10P]	cyus
Greek	Ø		!	433	[1P]	chad
Sanskrit	chanda	intention		434	[1U]	chand

435	छम्			436	छष्	
435	छम्			[1U]	√chas	
[1P]	√cham				chaṣati	chaṣate
	chamati			English	hurt	
English	eat			Latin	Ø	
Latin	Ø			Greek	Ø	
Greek	Ø			Sanskrit	Ø	

437	छिद्			438	छुट्	
[7U]	√chid			[6P]	√chuṭ	
W	chinatti	chintte			chuṭati	
English	cut off	schism		English	bind	
Latin	scindo	cut, tear		Latin	Ø	
Greek	σχίζω	split, cleave		Greek	Ø	
Sanskrit	chitti	division		Sanskrit	Ø	

439	छुट्			440	छुप्	
[10P]	√chuṭ			[6P]	√chup	
	choṭayati				chupati	
English	cut			English	touch	
Latin	Ø			Latin	Ø	
Greek	Ø			Greek	Ø	
Sanskrit	choṭana	cutting off		Sanskrit	chupa	touch

441	छुर्			435	[1P]	cham
[6P]	√chur			436	[1U]	chaṣ
	churati		!	437	[7U]	chid
English	cut off			438	[6P]	chuṭ
Latin	Ø			439	[10P]	chuṭ
Greek	Ø			440	[6P]	chup
Sanskrit	chorita	abandoned		441	[6P]	chur

442	छृद्			443	छृद्	
[7P]	√chṛd			[1P]	√chṛd	
W	chṛṇatti			W	chardati	
English	vomit			English	vomit	
Latin	Ø			Latin	Ø	
Greek	Ø			Greek	Ø	
Sanskrit	charda	vomiting		Sanskrit	charda	vomiting

444	जंस्			445	जंस्	
[1P]	√jaṃs			[10P]	√jaṃs	
	jaṃsati				jaṃsayati	
English	protect			English	protect	
Latin	Ø			Latin	Ø	
Greek	Ø			Greek	Ø	
Sanskrit	Ø			Sanskrit	Ø	

446	जक्ष्			447	जक्ष्	
[2P]	√jakṣ			[1P]	√jakṣ	
W	jakṣiti			W	jakṣati	
English	eat			English	eat	
Latin	Ø			Latin	Ø	
Greek	Ø			Greek	Ø	
Sanskrit	jakṣaṇa	consuming		Sanskrit	jakṣaṇa	consuming

448	जज्			442	[7P]	chṛd
[1P]	√jaj			443	[1P]	chṛd
	jajati			444	[1P]	jaṃs
English	fight			445	[10P]	jaṃs
Latin	Ø		!	446	[2P]	jakṣ
Greek	Ø		!	447	[1P]	jakṣ
Sanskrit	jaja	a warrior		448	[1P]	jaj

449	झट्			450	झर्झ्	
[1P]	√jhaṭ			[1P]	√jharjh	
	jhaṭati				jharjhati	
English	become	entangled		English	blame	
Latin	Ø			Latin	Ø	
Greek	Ø			Greek	Ø	
Sanskrit	Ø			Sanskrit	Ø	

451	झष्			452	जन्	
[1P]	√jhaṣ			[1U]	√jan	
	jhaṣati			W	janati	janate
English	hurt			English	give birth	
Latin	Ø			Latin	gignō	give birth to
Greek	Ø			Greek	γίγνομαι	be born
Sanskrit	Ø			Sanskrit	jāti	birth, family

453	जन्			454	जप्	
[4Ā]	√jan			[1P]	√jap	
W	jāyate			W	japati	
English	give birth			English	whisper	
Latin	gignō	give birth to		Latin	Ø	
Greek	γίγνομαι	be born		Greek	Ø	
Sanskrit	jana	creature		Sanskrit	japa	muttering

455	जभ्			449	[1P]	jhaṭ
[1Ā]	√jabh			450	[1P]	jharjh
W	jabhate			451	[1P]	jhaṣ
English	snap at		!	452	[1U]	jan
Latin	Ø		!	453	[4Ā]	jan
Greek	Ø		!	454	[1P]	jap
Sanskrit	jabhya	"snapper"		455	[1Ā]	jabh

456	जम्			457	जल्	
[1P]	√jam			[1P]	√jal	
W	jamati				jalati	
English	eat			English	cover,	to be dull
Latin	Ø			Latin	Ø	
Greek	Ø			Greek	Ø	
Sanskrit	Ø			Sanskrit	jala	stupid

458	जल्प्			459	जष्	
[1U]	√jalp			[1U]	√jaṣ	
W	jalpati	jalpate			jaṣati	jaṣate
English	murmur			English	hurt	
Latin	Ø			Latin	Ø	
Greek	Ø			Greek	Ø	
Sanskrit	jalpa	talk, speech		Sanskrit	Ø	

460	जस्			461	जागृ	
[4P]	√jas			[2P]	√jāgṛ	
W	jasyati			W	jāgarti	
English	be exhausted			English	wake up	
Latin	Ø			Latin	expergiscor	wake up
Greek	Ø			Greek	ἐγείρω	wake up
Sanskrit	jasu	exhaustion		Sanskrit	jāgara	waking

462	जर्च्			456	[1P]	jam
[1P]	√jarc			457	[1P]	jal
	jarcati		!	458	[1U]	jalp
English	speak,	threaten		459	[1U]	jaṣ
Latin	Ø			460	[4P]	jas
Greek	Ø		!	461	[2P]	jāgṛ
Sanskrit	Ø			462	[1P]	jarc

463	जि			464	जिन्व्	
[1U]	√ji			[1P]	√jinv	
W	jayati	jayate		W	jinvati	
English	conquer			English	quicken	
Latin	Ø			Latin	Ø	
Greek	Ø			Greek	Ø	
Sanskrit	jayá	victory		Sanskrit	Ø	

465	जिम्			466	जिष्	
[1P]	√jim			[1P]	√jiṣ	
	jemati				jeṣati	
English	eat			English	sprinkle	
Latin	Ø			Latin	Ø	
Greek	Ø			Greek	Ø	
Sanskrit	Ø			Sanskrit	Ø	

467	जीव्			468	जुड्	
[1U]	√jīv			[6P]	√juḍ	
W	jīvati	jīvate			juḍati	
English	live			English	bind	
Latin	vīvō	live		Latin	Ø	
Greek	βιος	life		Greek	Ø	
Sanskrit	jīva	alive		Sanskrit	Ø	

469	जुड्		!	463	[1U]	ji
[10P]	√juḍ			464	[1P]	jinv
	joḍayati			465	[1P]	jim
English	send out			466	[1P]	jiṣ
Latin	Ø		!	467	[1U]	jīv
Greek	Ø			468	[6P]	juḍ
Sanskrit	Ø			469	[10P]	juḍ

470	जुत्			471	जुष्	
[1Ā]	√jut			[6Ā]	√juṣ	
	jotate			W	juṣate	
English	shine			English	enjoy	
Latin	Ø			Latin	gustō	taste
Greek	Ø			Greek	γεύω	taste
Sanskrit	Ø			Sanskrit	júṣṭi	satisfaction

472	जू			473	जूर्	
[1U]	√jū			[4Ā]	√jūr	
W	javati	javate			jūryate	
English	hurry on			English	hurt	
Latin	Ø			Latin	Ø	
Greek	Ø			Greek	Ø	
Sanskrit	jáva	speed		Sanskrit	Ø	

474	जृ			475	जृम्भ्	
474	जृ			[1P]	√jṛmbh	
[1Ā]	√jṛ			W	jṛmbhate	
	jarate			English	gape	
English	approach			Latin	Ø	
Latin	Ø			Greek	Ø	
Greek	Ø			Sanskrit	jṛmbha	yawning

476	जॄ			470	[1Ā]	jut
[1P]	√jṝ		!	471	[6Ā]	juṣ
W	jarati			472	[1U]	jū
English	grow old			473	[4Ā]	jūr
Latin	Ø		!	474	[1Ā]	jṛ
Greek	γέρων	old man		475	[1P]	jṛmbh
Sanskrit	jaras	old age		476	[1P]	jṝ

477	जॄ			478	जेष्	
[4P]	√jṝ			[1Ā]	√jeṣ	
W	jīryati				jeṣate	
English	grow old			English	move	
Latin	Ø			Latin	Ø	
Greek	γέρων	old man		Greek	Ø	
Sanskrit	jára	old age		Sanskrit	Ø	

479	जेह्			480	जै	
[1Ā]	√jeh			[1P]	√jai	
	jehate				jāyati	
English	open the	mouth		English	wane	
Latin	Ø			Latin	Ø	
Greek	Ø			Greek	Ø	
Sanskrit	Ø			Sanskrit	Ø	

481	ज्ञा			482	ज्या	
[9U]	√jñā			[9P]	√jyā	
W	jānāti	jānīte			jināti	
English	know			English	overpower	
Latin	nōscō	know		Latin	Ø	
Greek	γιγνώσκω	know		Greek	Ø	
Sanskrit	jñāna	knowledge		Sanskrit	jyāna	oppression

483	ज्या			477	[4P]	jṝ
[4Ā]	√jyā			478	[1Ā]	jeṣ
W	jīyate			479	[1Ā]	jeh
English	age			480	[1P]	jai
Latin	Ø		!	481	[9U]	jñā
Greek	Ø			482	[9P]	jyā
Sanskrit	Ø			483	[4Ā]	jyā

323	guj	363	ghaṭ	403	caṣ	443	chṛd
324	guj	364	ghaṭṭ	404	cah	444	jaṃs
325	guñj	365	ghaṇṭ	405	cah	445	jaṃs
326	guṇḍ	366	ghas	406	cāy	446	jakṣ
327	guḍ	367	ghiṇṇ	407	ci	447	jakṣ
328	gud	368	ghu	408	ci	448	jaj
329	gudh	369	ghuṭ	409	cit	449	jhaṭ
330	gudh	370	ghuṭ	410	cint	450	jharjh
331	gudh	371	ghuṇ	411	ciri	451	jhaṣ
332	gup	372	ghuṇ	412	cīv	452	jan
333	guph	373	ghuṇṇ	413	cīv	453	jan
334	gur	374	ghur	414	cukk	454	jap
335	gur	375	ghuṣ	415	cuḍ	455	jabh
336	gurd	376	ghūrṇ	416	cuṭ	456	jam
337	gurd	377	ghūrṇ	417	cuṭ	457	jal
338	gurv	378	ghṛ	418	cuṭ	458	jalp
339	guh	379	ghṛ	419	cud	459	jaṣ
340	gep	380	ghṛṣ	420	cup	460	jas
341	geṣ	381	ghrā	421	cumb	461	jāgṛ
342	gev	382	cak	422	cur	462	jarc
343	gṝ	383	cakk	423	cul	463	ji
344	gṝ	384	cakās	424	culump	464	jinv
345	gr	385	cakṣ	425	cūr	465	jim
346	gṛdh	386	cakṣ	426	cūrṇ	466	jiṣ
347	gṛj	387	cañc	427	cūṣ	467	jīv
348	granth	388	caṭ	428	cṛt	468	juḍ
349	granth	389	caṇ	429	ceṣṭ	469	juḍ
350	grah	390	caṇḍ	430	cyu	470	jut
351	gras	391	can	431	cyut	471	juṣ
352	gruc	392	cat	432	cyus	472	jū
353	glah	393	cand	433	chad	473	jūr
354	gluc	394	cap	434	chand	474	jr
355	gluñc	395	cap	435	cham	475	jṛmbh
356	glep	396	cam	436	chaṣ	476	jṝ
357	glev	397	camb	437	chid	477	jṝ
358	gleṣ	398	car	438	chuṭ	478	jeṣ
359	glai	399	carc	439	chuṭ	479	jeh
360	glai	400	carb	440	chup	480	jai
361	glā	401	carv	441	chur	481	jñā
362	ghagh	402	cal	442	chṛd	482	jyā
						483	jyā

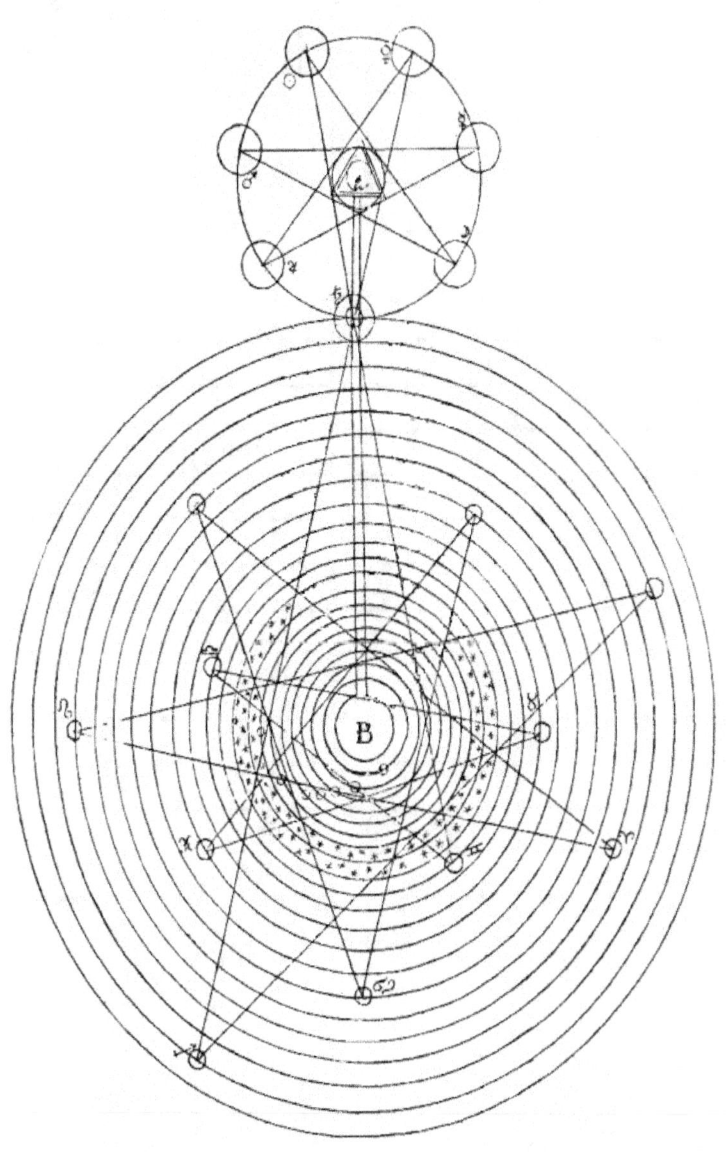

484	ज्युत्			485	ज्रि	
[1U]	√jyut			[1P]	√jri	
W	jyotati	jyotate			jráyati	
English	shine			English	go	
Latin	Ø			Latin	Ø	
Greek	Ø			Greek	Ø	
Sanskrit	jyotis	light		Sanskrit	Ø	

486	ज्रि			487	ज्रि	
[9P]	√jri			[10P]	√jri	
	jriṇāti				jrāyayati	
English	grow old			English	grow old	
Latin	Ø			Latin	Ø	
Greek	Ø			Greek	Ø	
Sanskrit	Ø			Sanskrit	Ø	

488	ज्वर्			489	ज्वल्	
[1P]	√jvar			[1P]	√jval	
W	jvarati			W	jvalati	
English	have fever			English	burn,	blaze
Latin	Ø			Latin	Ø	
Greek	Ø			Greek	Ø	
Sanskrit	jvara	fever		Sanskrit	jvala	flame

490	टङ्क्			484	[1U]	jyut
[10P]	√ṭaṅk			485	[1P]	jri
	ṭaṅkayati			486	[9P]	jri
English	shut			487	[10P]	jri
Latin	Ø		!	488	[1P]	jvar
Greek	Ø		!	489	[1P]	jval
Sanskrit	Ø			490	[10P]	ṭaṅk

491	टल्			492	टिप्	
[1P]	√ṭal			[10P]	√ṭip	
	ṭalati			W	ṭepayati	
English	disturb			English	throw, cast	
Latin	Ø			Latin	Ø	
Greek	Ø			Greek	Ø	
Sanskrit	ṭalana	perturbation		Sanskrit	Ø	

493	टीक्			494	टौक्	
493	टीक्			[1Ā]	√ṭauk	
[1Ā]	√ṭīk				ṭaukate	
	ṭīkate			English	approach	
English	move			Latin	Ø	
Latin	Ø			Greek	Ø	
Greek	Ø			Sanskrit	Ø	

495	ट्वल्			496	डप्	
[1P]	√ṭval			[10Ā]	√ḍap	
	ṭvalati				ḍāpayate	
English	be disturbed			English	accumulate	
Latin	Ø			Latin	Ø	
Greek	Ø			Greek	Ø	
Sanskrit	Ø			Sanskrit	Ø	

497	डम्			491	[1P]	ṭal
[1P]	√ḍam			492	[10P]	ṭip
	ḍamati			493	[1Ā]	ṭīk
English	sound as a	drum		494	[1Ā]	ṭauk
Latin	Ø			495	[1P]	ṭval
Greek	Ø			496	[10Ā]	ḍap
Sanskrit	Ø			497	[1P]	ḍam

498	डम्ब्			499	डिप्	
[10P]	√ḍamb			[10Ā]	√ḍip	
	ḍambayati				ḍepayate	
English	push, throw			English	heap	together
Latin	Ø			Latin	Ø	
Greek	Ø			Greek	Ø	
Sanskrit	Ø			Sanskrit	Ø	

500	डिप्			501	डिप्	
[4P]	√ḍip			[6P]	√ḍip	
	ḍipyati				ḍipati	
English	throw			English	throw	
Latin	Ø			Latin	Ø	
Greek	Ø			Greek	Ø	
Sanskrit	Ø			Sanskrit	Ø	

502	डी			503	डी	
[1Ā]	√ḍī			[4Ā]	√ḍī	
W	ḍayate			W	ḍīyate	
English	fly			English	fly	
Latin	Ø			Latin	Ø	
Greek	Ø			Greek	Ø	
Sanskrit	ḍayana	a bird's flight		Sanskrit	ḍīna	a bird's flight

504	ढौक्					
[1Ā]	√ḍhauk			498	[10P]	ḍamb
	ḍhaukate			499	[10Ā]	ḍip
English	approach			500	[4P]	ḍip
Latin	Ø			501	[6P]	ḍip
Greek	Ø			502	[1Ā]	ḍī
Sanskrit	ḍhaukana	offering		503	[4Ā]	ḍī
				504	[1Ā]	ḍhauk

505	तंस्			506	तक्	
[1P]	√taṃs			[2P]	√tak	
	taṃsati			W	takti	
English	decorate			English	rush	
Latin	Ø			Latin	Ø	
Greek	Ø			Greek	Ø	
Sanskrit	Ø			Sanskrit	takva	quick

507	तक्ष्			508	तङ्कं	
[1P]	√takṣ			[1P]	√taṅk	
W	takṣati				taṅkati	
English	cut, form			English	live in	distress
Latin	texō	weave		Latin	Ø	
Greek	τέχνη	craft, skill		Greek	Ø	
Sanskrit	tákṣa	carpenter		Sanskrit	Ø	

509	तङ्ग			510	तञ्च्	
[1P]	√taṅg			[7P]	√tañc	
	taṅgati			W	tanakti	
English	stumble			English	contract,	coagulate
Latin	Ø			Latin	Ø	
Greek	Ø			Greek	Ø	
Sanskrit	Ø			English	tight	

511	तट्			505	[1P]	taṃs
[1P]	√taṭ			506	[2P]	tak
	taṭati		!	507	[1P]	takṣ
English	rumble			508	[1P]	taṅk
Latin	Ø			509	[1P]	taṅg
Greek	Ø			510	[7P]	tañc
Sanskrit	Ø			511	[1P]	taṭ

512	तड्			513	तण्ड्	
[10P]	√taḍ			[1Ā]	√taṇḍ	
	tāḍayati				taṇḍate	
English	beat			English	beat	
Latin	Ø			Latin	Ø	
Greek	Ø			Greek	Ø	
Sanskrit	taḍit	lightening		Sanskrit	Ø	

514	तन्			515	तन्	
[8U]	√tan			[4P]	√tan	
W	tanoti	tanute		W	tanyati	
English	stretch			English	roar	
Latin	tendō	stretch		Latin	tonō	thunder
Greek	τείνω	stretch		French	tonnerre	thunder
Sanskrit	tántra	loom		Sanskrit	tanyatú	thunder

516	तन्द्र्			517	तप्	
[10Ā]	√tandr			[1U]	√tap	
W	tandrayate			W	tapati	tapate
English	grow	fatigued		English	heat	tepid
Latin	Ø			Latin	tepeō	tepid
Greek	Ø			Greek	Ø	
Sanskrit	tandrā	lassitude		Sanskrit	tápas	heat, penance

518	तम्			512	[10P]	taḍ
[4P]	√tam			513	[1Ā]	taṇḍ
W	tāmyati		!	514	[8U]	tan
English	choke		!	515	[4P]	tan
Latin	Ø			516	[10Ā]	tandr
Greek	Ø		!	517	[1U]	tap
Sanskrit	tāmana	breathless	!	518	[4P]	tam

519	तर्क्			520	तर्ज्	
[10P]	√tark			[1P]	√tarj	
W	tarkayati			W	tarjati	
English	conjecture			English	threathen	
Latin	torqueō	twist		Latin	torvus	dreadful
Greek	τρέπω	turn		Greek	τάρβος	terror
Sanskrit	tarka	conjecture		Sanskrit	tarjana	threathening

521	तर्द्			522	तल्	
[1P]	√tard			[1P]	√tal	
	tardati				talati	
English	injure, kill			English	accomplish	
Latin	Ø			Latin	Ø	
Greek	Ø			Greek	Ø	
Sanskrit	Ø			Sanskrit	Ø	

523	तय्			524	तस्	
[1Ā]	√tay			[4P]	√tas	
	tayate				tasyati	
English	go towards			English	perish,	throw
Latin	Ø			Latin	Ø	
Greek	Ø			Greek	Ø	
Sanskrit	Ø			Sanskrit	Ø	

525	ताय्			519	[10P]	tark
[1Ā]	√tāy			520	[1P]	tarj
	tāyate			521	[1P]	tard
English	proceed			522	[1P]	tal
Latin	Ø			523	[1Ā]	tay
Greek	Ø			524	[4P]	tas
Sanskrit	tāyana	proceeding		525	[1Ā]	tāy

526	तिक्			527	तिक्	
[1Ā]	√tik			[5P]	√tik	
	tekate				tiknoti	
English	go			English	assail,	wound
Latin	Ø			Latin	Ø	
Greek	Ø			Greek	Ø	
Sanskrit	Ø			Sanskrit	Ø	

528	तिघ्			529	तिज्	
[5P]	√tigh			[1Ā]	√tij	
	tighnoti			W	tejate	
English	hurt, kill			English	be sharp	stick
Latin	Ø			Latin	īnstinguō	instigate
Greek	Ø			Greek	στῐ́γμᾰ	mark
Sanskrit	Ø			Sanskrit	tigmá	sharp, pointed

530	तिप्			531	तिम्	
[1P]	√tip			[4P]	√tim	
	tepati				timyati	
English	sprinkle			English	become wet	
Latin	Ø			Latin	Ø	
Greek	Ø			Greek	Ø	
Sanskrit	Ø			Sanskrit	temana	moisture

532	तिल्			526	[1Ā]	tik
[1P]	√til			527	[5P]	tik
	telati			528	[5P]	tigh
English	go			529	[1Ā]	tij
Latin	Ø			530	[1P]	tip
Greek	Ø			531	[4P]	tim
Sanskrit	Ø			532	[1P]	til

533	तिल्ल्			534	तीक्	
[1P]	√till			[1Ā]	√tīk	
	tillati				tīkate	
English	go			English	go	
Latin	Ø			Latin	Ø	
Greek	Ø			Greek	Ø	
Sanskrit	Ø			Sanskrit	Ø	

535	तीव्			536	तु	
[1P]	√tīv			[2P]	√tu	
	tīvati				tauti	
English	be fat			English	strong,	go, injure
Latin	Ø			Latin	tōtus	whole
Greek	Ø			Greek	Ø	
Sanskrit	Ø			Sanskrit	Ø	

537	तुज्			538	तुज्	
[6Ā]	√tuj			[1P]	√tuj	
	tujate				tojati	
English	strike, hit			English	hurt	
Latin	tundō	beat, strike		Latin	Ø	
Greek	τύκος	pick-axe		Greek	Ø	
Sanskrit	tuñjá	assault		Sanskrit	tuja	thunderbolt

539	तुड्			533	[1P]	till
[1P]	√tuṭ			534	[1Ā]	tīk
	tuṭati			535	[1P]	tīv
English	quarrel			536	[2P]	tu
Latin	Ø			537	[6Ā]	tuj
Greek	Ø			538	[1P]	tuj
Sanskrit	Ø			539	[1P]	tuṭ

540	तुइ			541	तुइ	
[1P]	√tuḍ			[6P]	√tuḍ	
	toḍati				tuḍati	
English	strike, split			English	strike, split	
Latin	Ø			Latin	Ø	
Greek	Ø			Greek	Ø	
Sanskrit	Ø			Sanskrit	Ø	

542	तुड्इ			543	तुद्	
[1P]	√tuḍḍ			[6P]	√tud	
W	tuḍḍati			W	tudáti	
English	disregard			English	push,	thrust
Latin	Ø			Latin	tundō	beat, strike
Greek	Ø			Greek	Ø	
Sanskrit	Ø			German	stoßen	push, shove

544	तुण्			545	तुण्ड्	
[6P]	√tuṇ			545	तुण्ड्	
	tuṇati			[1Ā]	√tuṇḍ	
English	curve				tuṇḍate	
Latin	Ø			English	hurt	
French	Ø			Latin	Ø	
Sanskrit	Ø			Greek	Ø	

546	तुभ्			540	[1P]	tuḍ
[1Ā]	√tubh			541	[6P]	tuḍ
	tobhate			542	[1P]	tuḍḍ
English	hurt, kill		!	543	[6P]	tud
Latin	Ø			544	[6P]	tuṇ
Greek	Ø			545	[1Ā]	tuṇḍ
Sanskrit	Ø			546	[1Ā]	tubh

547	तुभ्			548	तुप्	
[4P]	√tubh			[6P]	√tup	
	tubhyati			W	tupati	
English	hurt, kill			English	hurt	
Latin	Ø			Latin	stupeo	numb
Greek	Ø			Greek	τύπτω	hit
Sanskrit	Ø			German	stumpf	dull, blunt

549	तुप्			550	तुफ्	
[1P]	√tup			[1P]	√tuph	
W	topati				topati	
English	hurt			English	hurt	
Latin	stupeo	numb		Latin	stupeo	numb
French	stupeur	amazement		Greek	τύπτω	hit
Sanskrit	Ø			German	stumpf	dull, blunt

551	तुफ्			552	तुम्प्	
[6P]	√tuph			[1P]	√tump	
	tuphati				tumpati	
English	hurt			English	hurt	
Latin	stupeo	numb		Latin	Ø	
Greek	τύπτω	hit		Greek	Ø	
Sanskrit	stumpf	dull, blunt		Sanskrit	Ø	

553	तुम्प्			547	[4P]	tubh
[10P]	√tump			548	[6P]	tup
	tumbayati			549	[1P]	tup
English	be invisible			550	[1P]	tuph
Latin	Ø			551	[6P]	tuph
German	Ø			552	[1P]	tump
Sanskrit	Ø			553	[10P]	tump

554	तुर्			555	तुर्	
[6Ā]	√tur			[4Ā]	√tur	
	turate				turyate	
English	hurry			English	run, hurt	
Latin	Ø			Latin	Ø	
Greek	Ø			Greek	Ø	
Sanskrit	tura	prompt		Sanskrit	tura	prompt

556	तुर्			557	तुर्व्	
[3P]	√tur			[1P]	√turv	
	tutorti				turvati	
English	run			English	overpower	
Latin	Ø			Latin	Ø	
Greek	Ø			Greek	Ø	
Sanskrit	tura	prompt		Sanskrit	turvaṇi	victorious

558	तुल्			559	तुल्	
[10P]	√tul			[10P]	√tul	
W	tolayati			W	tulayati	
English	lift, weigh	tolerate		English	lift,	weigh
Latin	tolerō	bear		Latin	tollō	bear
Greek	τἄλαντον	balance		Greek	τλᾱτός	tolerable
Sanskrit	tulā	balance		Sanskrit	tulya	comparable

560	तुस्			554	[6Ā]	tur
[1P]	√tus			555	[4Ā]	tur
	tosati			556	[3P]	tur
English	sound			557	[1P]	turv
Latin	Ø			558	[10P]	tul
Greek	Ø			559	[10P]	tul
Sanskrit	Ø			560	[1P]	tus

561	तृ			562	तुह्	
[4U]	√tuṣ			[1P]	√tuh	
W	tuṣyati	tuṣyate			tohati	
English	be content			English	pain	
Latin	Ø			Latin	Ø	
Greek	Ø			Greek	Ø	
Sanskrit	tuṣṭi	satisfaction		Sanskrit	Ø	

563	तृ			564	तॄ	
[1P]	√tṝ			[1P]	√tṝ	
W	tarati			W	tirati	
English	pass	cross over		English	pass	cross over
Latin	terminus	boundary		Latin	terminus	boundary
Greek	τέρθρον	end		Greek	τέρθρον	end
Sanskrit	tiras	across		Sanskrit	tāra	carry across

565	तेज्			566	तेप्	
[1P]	√tej			[1Ā]	√tep	
	tejati				tepate	
English	protect			English	ooze,	tremble
Latin	Ø			Latin	Ø	
Greek	Ø			Greek	Ø	
Sanskrit	Ø			Sanskrit	Ø	

567	तेव्		!	561	[4U]	tuṣ
[1Ā]	√tev			562	[1P]	tuh
	tevate			563	[1P]	tṝ
English	sport			564	[1P]	tṝ
Latin	Ø			565	[1P]	tej
Greek	Ø			566	[1Ā]	tep
Sanskrit	tevana	pleasure-gard.		567	[1Ā]	tev

568	त्यज्			569	तृक्ष्	
[1P]	√tyaj			[1P]	√tṛkṣ	
W	tyajati				tṛkṣati	
English	leave	forsake		English	go	
Latin	Ø			Latin	Ø	
Greek	σοβέω	desert		Greek	Ø	
Sanskrit	tyajas	abandonment		Sanskrit	Ø	

570	तृण्			571	तृद्	
[8U]	√tṛṇ			[7U]	√tṛd	
	tṛṇoti	tṛṇute		W	tṛṇatti	tṛntte
English	eat			English	split, bore	
Latin	Ø			Latin	Ø	
Greek	Ø			Greek	Ø	
Sanskrit	tṛṇa	grass, herb		Sanskrit	tṛdila	porous

572	तृप्			573	तृप्	
[4P]	√tṛp			[5P]	√tṛp	
W	tṛpyati			W	tṛpṇoti	
English	be pleased			English	be pleased	
Latin	fruor	enjoy		Latin	fruor	enjoy
Greek	τέρπω	enjoy		Greek	τέρπω	enjoy
Sanskrit	tṛpti	satisfaction		Sanskrit	tṛpat	with pleasure

574	तृष्		!	568	[1P]	tyaj
[4P]	√tṛṣ			569	[1P]	tṛkṣ
W	tṛṣyati			570	[8U]	tṛṇ
English	be thirsty			571	[7U]	tṛd
Latin	torreō	scorch, burn	!	572	[4P]	tṛp
Greek	τερσω	make dry	!	573	[5P]	tṛp
Sanskrit	tṛṣita	thirsty	!	574	[4P]	tṛṣ

575	तृह्			576	त्रंस्	
[7P]	√tṛh			[1P]	√traṃs	
W	tṛṇeḍhi				traṃsati	
English	crush			English	shine, speak	
Latin	Ø			Latin	Ø	
Greek	Ø			Greek	Ø	
Sanskrit	tṛḍha	crushed		Sanskrit	Ø	

577	त्रख्			578	त्रन्द्	
[1P]	√trakh			[1P]	√trand	
	trakhati				trandati	
English	go			English	be busy	
Latin	Ø			Latin	Ø	
Greek	Ø			Greek	Ø	
Sanskrit	Ø			Sanskrit	Ø	

579	त्रप्			580	त्रस्	
[1Ā]	√trap			[1P]	√tras	
W	trapate			W	trásati	
English	be ashamed			English	tremble	quiver
Latin	turpis	ugly, foul		Latin	terreō	terrify
Greek	τρέπω	turn		Greek	τρέω	be afraid
Sanskrit	trapā	shame		Sanskrit	trasta	quivering

581	त्रा			575	[7P]	tṛh
[4Ā]	√trā			576	[1P]	traṃs
W	trāyate			577	[1P]	trakh
English	defend,	protect		578	[1P]	trand
Latin	Ø			579	[1Ā]	trap
Greek	Ø		!	580	[1P]	tras
Sanskrit	trāṇa	protection	!	581	[4Ā]	trā

582	त्रुट्			583	त्रुट्	
[4P]	√truṭ			[6P]	√truṭ	
W	truṭyati			W	truṭati	
English	be torn,	split		English	be torn,	split
Latin	Ø			Latin	Ø	
Greek	Ø			Greek	Ø	
Sanskrit	truṭi	an atom		Sanskrit	truṭi	an atom

584	त्रुप्			585	त्रै	
[1P]	√trup			[1Ā]	√trai	
	tropati			W	trāyate	
English	hurt			English	protect	
Latin	Ø			Latin	Ø	
Greek	Ø			Greek	Ø	
Sanskrit	Ø			Sanskrit	Ø	

586	त्रौक्			587	त्वक्ष्	
586	त्रौक्			[1P]	√tvakṣ	
[1Ā]	√trauk			W	tvakṣati	
W	traukate			English	create	
English	go			Latin	Ø	
Latin	Ø			Greek	Ø	
Greek	Ø			Sanskrit	Ø	

588	त्वङ्ग्					
[1P]	√tvaṅg		!	582	[4P]	truṭ
	tvaṅgati		!	583	[6P]	truṭ
English	wave			584	[1P]	trup
Latin	Ø			585	[1Ā]	trai
Greek	Ø			586	[1Ā]	trauk
Sanskrit	Ø			587	[1P]	tvakṣ
				588	[1P]	tvaṅg

589	त्वच्			590	त्वर्	
[6P]	√tvac			[1Ā]	√tvar	
	tvacati			W	tvarate	
English	cover			English	hasten	
Latin	Ø			Latin	turbō	agitate
Greek	Ø			Greek	ὀτρῡ́νω	stir up
Sanskrit	Ø			Sanskrit	tvari	haste

591	त्विष्			592	त्सर्	
[1U]	√tviṣ			[1P]	√tsar	
W	tveṣati	tveṣate		W	tsárati	
English	excite, shine			English	sneak	
Latin	Ø			Latin	Ø	
Greek	σείω	shake		Greek	Ø	
Sanskrit	tviṣi	energy, light		Sanskrit	tsáru	'snake'

593	दध्			594	दद्	
[1P]	√dadh			[1P]	√dad	
	dadhati				dadati	
English	hold, give			English	give	
Latin	Ø			Latin	Ø	
Greek	Ø			Greek	Ø	
Sanskrit	Ø			Sanskrit	Ø	

595	दंश्			589	[6P]	tvac
[1P]	√daṃś		!	590	[1Ā]	tvar
W	daśati			591	[1U]	tviṣ
English	bite			592	[1P]	tsar
German	Zange	pliers		593	[1P]	dadh
Greek	δάκνω	bite		594	[1P]	dad
Sanskrit	daṃśa	bite, sting	!	595	[1P]	daṃś

596	दक्ष्			597	दघ्	
[1Ā]	√dakṣ			[5P]	√dagh	
W	dakṣate			W	daghnoti	
English	be able			English	reach to	
Latin	dexter	right side		Latin	Ø	
Greek	δεξϊός	right (hand)		Greek	Ø	
Sanskrit	dákṣa	skilled, adroit		Sanskrit	daghna	reaching up to

598	दभ्			599	दम्	
[1P]	√dabh			[4P]	√dam	
W	dabhati			W	dāmyati	
English	hurt,	deceive		English	subdue, tame	domesticate
Latin	Ø			Latin	domō	break in
Greek	ἀτέμβω	afflict		Greek	δάμνημι	tame
Sanskrit	dabha	deceiving		Sanskrit	dáma	taming

600	दम्भ्			601	दम्भ्	
[1P]	√dambh			[5P]	√dambh	
	dambhāti				dabhnóti	
English	deceive,	injure		English	deceive,	injure
Latin	Ø			Latin	Ø	
Greek	ἀτέμβω	maltreat		Greek	ἀτέμβω	maltreat
Sanskrit	dambha	fraud		Sanskrit	dambha	fraud

602	दय्			596	[1Ā]	dakṣ
[1Ā]	√day			597	[5P]	dagh
W	dayate			598	[1P]	dabh
English	divide, allot		!	599	[4P]	dam
Latin	Ø			600	[1P]	dambh
Greek	δαίω	divide, share		601	[5P]	dambh
Sanskrit	dayā	sympathy		602	[1Ā]	day

603	दल्			604	दस्	
[1P]	√dal			[4P]	√das	
W	dalati			W	dasyati	
English	split, burst			English	suffer	want
Latin	dolō	hew, chop		Latin	Ø	
Greek	δαιδαλος	well-wrought		Greek	Ø	
Sanskrit	dála	part, division		Sanskrit	Ø	

605	दस्			606	दह्	
[1P]	√das			[1U]	√dah	
W	dāsati			W	dahati	dahate
English	suffer want			English	burn	
Latin	Ø			Latin	foveō	make warm
Greek	Ø			English	day	
Sanskrit	Ø			Sanskrit	dáha	burning

607	दह्			608	दा	
[4P]	√dah			[3U]	√dā	
W	dahyati			W	dadāti	datte
English	burn			English	give	
Latin	foveō	make warm		Latin	dōnum	gift
German	Tag	day		Greek	δῶρον	gift
Sanskrit	dáha	burning		Sanskrit	dána	gift

609	दा			!	603	[1P]	dal
[1P]	√dā				604	[4P]	das
W	dadati				605	[1P]	das
English	give			!	606	[1U]	dah
Latin	dator	giver		!	607	[4P]	dah
Greek	δώτωρ	giver		!	608	[3U]	dā
Sanskrit	dátṛ	giver		!	609	[1P]	dā

610	दा			611	दा	
[2P]	√dā			[2P]	√dā	
W	dāti			W	dāti	
English	give			English	share, cut	
Latin	datiō	distributing		Latin	daemōn	"dispenser"
Greek	δόσις	the giving		Greek	δαίομαι	divide
Sanskrit	díti	distributing		Sanskrit	dātrá	portion

612	दा			613	दान्	
[4P]	√dā			[1U]	√dān	
W	dyati				dānati	dānate
English	bind			English	cut off	
Latin	Ø			Latin	Ø	
Greek	δέω	bind		Greek	δαίω	divide
Sanskrit	dā́man	rope		Sanskrit	Ø	

614	दाय्			615	दाश्	
[1Ā]	√dāy			[1P]	√dāś	
	dāyate			W	dāśati	
English	give			English	make	offering
Latin	Ø			Latin	decet	proper
Greek	Ø			Greek	δόξᾰ	opinion
Sanskrit	Ø			Sanskrit	dāśu	sacrificing

616	दास्		!	610	[2P]	dā
[1U]	√dās		!	611	[2P]	dā
	dāsati	dāsate	!	612	[4P]	dā
English	give			613	[1U]	dān
Latin	Ø			614	[1Ā]	dāy
Greek	Ø			615	[1P]	dāś
Sanskrit	Ø			616	[1U]	dās

617	दास्			618	दिन्व्	
[5P]	√dās			[1P]	√dinv	
	dāsnoti				dinvati	
English	hurt, injure			English	gladden	
Latin	Ø			Latin	Ø	
Greek	Ø			Greek	Ø	
Sanskrit	Ø			Sanskrit	Ø	

619	दिम्प्			620	दिम्भ्	
[10Ā]	√dimp			[10Ā]	√dimbh	
	dimpayate				dimbhayate	
English	accumulate			English	order	
Latin	Ø			Latin	Ø	
Greek	Ø			Greek	Ø	
Sanskrit	Ø			Sanskrit	Ø	

621	दिव्			622	दिव्	
[1P]	√div			[4U]	√div	
	devati				dívyati	dívyate
English	vex, pain			English	gamble	
Latin	Ø			Latin	Ø	
Greek	Ø			Greek	Ø	
Sanskrit	Ø			Sanskrit	Ø	

623	दिश्			617	[5P]	dās
[3P]	√diś			618	[1P]	dinv
	dideṣṭi			619	[10Ā]	dimp
English	show			620	[10Ā]	dimbh
Latin	digitus	pointer, finger		621	[1P]	div
Greek	δείκνῡμῐ	show		622	[4U]	div
Sanskrit	diśā	direction	!	623	[3P]	diś

624	दिश्			625	दिह्	
[6P]	√diś			[2P]	√dih	
W	diśati			W	degdhi	
English	show			English	smear	anoint
Latin	digitus	pointer, finger		Latin	fingō	shape, form
German	zeigen	show		German	Teig	dough, pastry
Sanskrit	diśā	direction		Sanskrit	deha	body, form

626	दी			627	दी	
[4U]	√dī			[3P]	√dī	
	díyati	díyate			dīdyati	
English	soar, fly			English	shine	
Latin	Ø			Latin	Ø	
Greek	δίω	run away		Greek	δῆλος	visible
Sanskrit	Ø			Sanskrit	dīti	brightness

628	दी			629	दीक्ष्	
[4Ā]	√dī			[1Ā]	√dīkṣ	
	dīyate			W	dīkṣate	
English	decay,	perish		English	be	consecrated
Latin	Ø			Latin	dignus	worthy
Greek	Ø			Greek	δόγμἄ	opinion
Sanskrit	dīda	causing ruin		Sanskrit	dīkṣā	consecr.

630	दीप्		!	624	[6P]	diś
[4Ā]	√dīp		!	625	[2P]	dih
W	dīpyate			626	[4U]	dī
English	shine			627	[3P]	dī
Latin	Ø			628	[4Ā]	dī
Greek	δῆλος	visible	!	629	[1Ā]	dīkṣ
Sanskrit	dīpa	lamp	!	630	[4Ā]	dīp

631	दीव्			632	दु	
[4U]	√dīv			[5P]	√du	
W	dīvyati	dīvyate		W	dunoti	
English	play			English	burn	
Latin	Ø			Latin	bellum(?)	war
Greek	Ø			Greek	δαίω	set on fire
Sanskrit	dyūta	gambling		Sanskrit	dutá	pained

633	दुष्			634	दुर्व्	
[4P]	√duṣ			[1P]	√durv	
W	duṣyati				dūrvati	
English	spoil			English	hurt,	injure
Latin	difficilis			Latin	Ø	
Greek	δυσ	bad, hard		Greek	Ø	
Sanskrit	doṣa	fault, vice		Sanskrit	Ø	

635	दुल्			636	दुह्	
[10P]	√dul			[2P]	√duh	
	dolayati				dogdhi	
English	swing,	shake		English	milk,	extract
Latin	Ø			Latin	Ø	
Greek	Ø			Greek	τύχη	fortune
Sanskrit	dulā	shaking		Sanskrit	dóha	milk

637	दुह्		!	631	[4U]	dīv
[4U]	√duh		!	632	[5P]	du
	duhyati	duhyate	!	633	[4P]	duṣ
English	milk,	extract		634	[1P]	durv
Latin	Ø			635	[10P]	dul
Greek	τύχη	fortune	!	636	[2P]	duh
Sanskrit	dohas	milking	!	637	[4U]	duh

638	दुह्			639	दृ	
[1P]	√duh			[6Ā]	√dr̥	
W	dohati				driyáte	
English	pain			English	respect	
Latin	Ø			Latin	Ø	
Greek	Ø			Greek	Ø	
Sanskrit	Ø			Sanskrit	dr̥ta	honoured

640	दृप्			641	दृप्	
[4P]	√dr̥p			[6P]	√dr̥p	
W	dr̥pyati				dr̥pati	
English	rave			English	pain,	torture
Latin	Ø			Latin	Ø	
Greek	Ø			Greek	Ø	
Sanskrit	dr̥pta	mad, wild		Sanskrit	Ø	

642	दृभ्			643	दृभ्	
[6P]	√dr̥bh			[1P]	√dr̥bh	
W	dr̥bhati				darbhati	
English	bunch			English	fear	
Latin	Ø			Latin	Ø	
Greek	δάρπη	basket		Greek	Ø	
Sanskrit	darbhá	tuft of grass		Sanskrit	Ø	

644	दृश्		!	638	[1P]	duh
[4P]	√dr̥ś		!	639	[6Ā]	dr̥
W	paśyati		!	640	[4P]	dr̥p
English	see		!	641	[6P]	dr̥p
Latin	Ø			642	[6P]	dr̥bh
Greek	δέρκομαι	see		643	[1P]	dr̥bh
Sanskrit	dárśana	doctrine	!	644	[4P]	dr̥ś

484	jyut	524	tas	564	tṝ	604	das
485	jri	525	tāy	565	tej	605	das
486	jri	526	tik	566	tep	606	dah
487	jri	527	tik	567	tev	607	dah
488	jvar	528	tigh	568	tyaj	608	dā
489	jval	529	tij	569	tṛkṣ	609	dā
490	ṭaṅk	530	tip	570	tṛṇ	610	dā
491	ṭal	531	tim	571	tṛd	611	dā
492	ṭip	532	til	572	tṛp	612	dā
493	ṭīk	533	till	573	tṛp	613	dān
494	ṭauk	534	tīk	574	tṛṣ	614	dāy
495	ṭval	535	tīv	575	tṛh	615	dāś
496	ḍap	536	tu	576	traṃs	616	dās
497	ḍam	537	tuj	577	trakh	617	dās
498	ḍamb	538	tuj	578	trand	618	dinv
499	ḍip	539	tuṭ	579	trap	619	dimp
500	ḍip	540	tuḍ	580	tras	620	dimbh
501	ḍip	541	tuḍ	581	trā	621	div
502	ḍī	542	tuḍḍ	582	truṭ	622	div
503	ḍī	543	tud	583	truṭ	623	diś
504	ḍhauk	544	tuṇ	584	trup	624	diś
505	taṃs	545	tuṇḍ	585	trai	625	dih
506	tak	546	tubh	586	trauk	626	dī
507	takṣ	547	tubh	587	tvakṣ	627	dī
508	taṅk	548	tup	588	tvaṅg	628	dī
509	taṅg	549	tup	589	tvac	629	dīkṣ
510	tañc	550	tuph	590	tvar	630	dīp
511	taṭ	551	tuph	591	tviṣ	631	dīv
512	taḍ	552	tump	592	tsar	632	du
513	taṇḍ	553	tump	593	dadh	633	duṣ
514	tan	554	tur	594	dad	634	durv
515	tan	555	tur	595	daṃś	635	dul
516	tandr	556	tur	596	dakṣ	636	duh
517	tap	557	turv	597	dagh	637	duh
518	tam	558	tul	598	dabh	638	duh
519	tark	559	tul	599	dam	639	dṛ
520	tarj	560	tus	600	dambh	640	dṛp
521	tard	561	tuṣ	601	dambh	641	dṛp
522	tal	562	tuh	602	day	642	dṛbh
523	tay	563	tṝ	603	dal	643	dṛbh
						644	dṛś

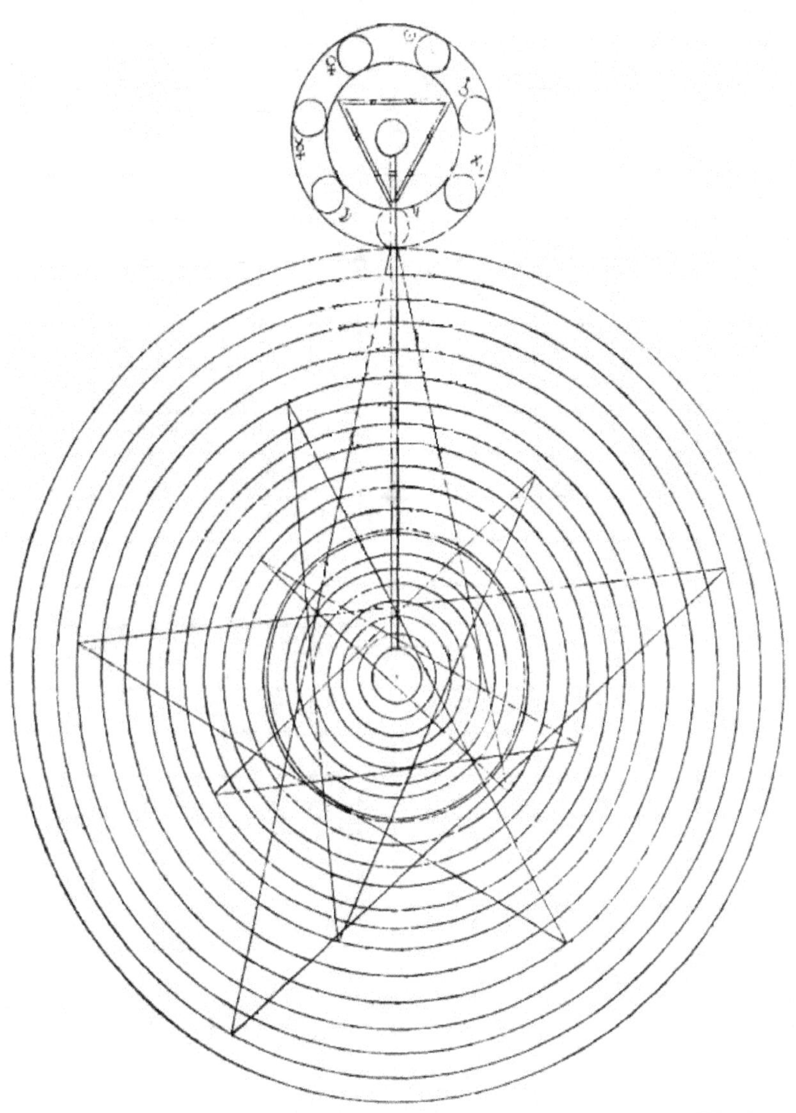

645	ह्ड्			646	दॄ	
[1P]	√dṛh			[9P]	√dṝ	
W	dṛṃhati			W	dṛṇāti	
English	make firm			English	split open	tear
Latin	Ø			German	verzehren	consume
Greek	Ø			Greek	δέρω	flay, skin
Sanskrit	dṛḍha	steadfast, firm		Sanskrit	dāra	cleft

647	दे			648	दै	
[1Ā]	√de			[1P]	√dai	
W	dayate			W	dāyati	
English	protect			English	cleanse	
Latin	Ø			Latin	Ø	
Greek	Ø			Greek	Ø	
Sanskrit	Ø			Sanskrit	Ø	

649	दो			650	दो	
[2P]	√do	[2P]		[4P]	√do	
	dāti				dyáti	
English	cut, divide	English		English	cut,	divide
Latin	Ø	Latin		Latin	Ø	
Greek	Ø	Greek		Greek	Ø	
Sanskrit	Ø	Sanskrit		Sanskrit	Ø	

651	द्रा					
[2P]	√drā			**645**	[1P]	dṛh
W	drāti			**646**	[9P]	dṝ
English	run			**647**	[1Ā]	de
Latin	Ø			**648**	[1P]	dai
Greek	αποδιδράσκω	escape		**649**	[2P]	do
Sanskrit	drāti	run		**650**	[4P]	do
				651	[2P]	drā

652	द्रा		653	द्रा	
[4Ā]	√drā		[2P]	√drā	
W	drāyate		W	drāti	
English	sleep		English	sleep	
Latin	dormiō	sleep	Latin	dormiō	sleep
Greek	δαρθάνω	sleep	Greek	δαρθάνω	sleep
Sanskrit	nidrā	sleep	Sanskrit	nidrā	sleep

654	द्राख्		655	द्राङ्क्ष्	
[1P]	√drākh		[1P]	√drāṅkṣ	
W	drākhati			drāṅkṣati	
English	become dry		English	caw, desire	
Latin	Ø		Latin	Ø	
Greek	Ø		Greek	Ø	
Sanskrit	Ø		Sanskrit	Ø	

656	द्राड्		657	द्राघ्	
[1Ā]	√drāḍ		[1Ā]	√drāgh	
W	drāḍate		W	drāghate	
English	split, divide		English	stretch	
Latin	Ø		Latin	Ø	
Greek	Ø		Greek	Ø	
Sanskrit	Ø		Sanskrit	drāghita	lengthened

658	द्राह्		652	[4Ā]	drā
[1Ā]	√drāh		653	[2P]	drā
	drāhate		654	[1P]	drākh
English	wake,	deposit	655	[1P]	drāṅkṣ
Latin	Ø		656	[1Ā]	drāḍ
Greek	Ø		657	[1Ā]	drāgh
Sanskrit	Ø		658	[1Ā]	drāh

659	दु̣			660	दु̣	
[1P]	√dru			[5P]	√dru	
W	dravati				druṇoti	
English	run, flee			English	hurt	
Latin	Dravus (?)	Drava River		Latin	Ø	
Greek	Ø			Greek	Ø	
Sanskrit	drutā	quick, fast		Sanskrit	Ø	

661	द्रुण्			662	द्रुह्	
[6P]	√druṇ			[4P]	√druh	
	druṇati			W	druhyati	
English	bend, go			English	hurt	deceive
Latin	Ø			Latin	trux	harsh
Greek	Ø			German	trügen	deceive
Sanskrit	Ø			Sanskrit	droha	injury

663	द्रेक्			664	द्रै	
[1Ā]	√drek			[1U]	√drai	
	drekate			W	drāyati	drāyate
English	sound			English	sleep	
Latin	Ø			Latin	dormiō	sleep
Greek	Ø			Greek	δαρθάνω	sleep
Sanskrit	Ø			Sanskrit	Ø	

665	द्रै		!	659	[1P]	dru
[2P]	√drai		!	660	[5P]	dru
W	drāti			661	[6P]	druṇ
English	sleep		!	662	[4P]	druh
Latin	dormiō	sleep		663	[1Ā]	drek
Greek	δαρθάνω	sleep		664	[1U]	drai
Sanskrit	Ø			665	[2P]	drai

666	द्विष्			667	द्विष्	
[6P]	√dviṣ			[2U]	√dviṣ	
W	dviṣati			W	dveṣṭi	dviṣṭe
English	hate	dire		English	hate	dire
Latin	dīrus	fearful		Latin	dīrus	fearful
Greek	δεινός	terrible		German	Zwist	quarrel
Sanskrit	dvéṣa	hatred		Sanskrit	dviṣa	enemy

668	दृ			669	धक्क्	
[1P]	√dvṛ			[10P]	√dhakk	
	dvarati				dhakkayati	
English	obstruct,	cover		English	destroy	
Latin	Ø			Latin	Ø	
Greek	Ø			Greek	Ø	
Sanskrit	Ø			Sanskrit	Ø	

670	धण्			671	धन्	
[1P]	√dhaṇ			[3P]	√dhan	
	dhaṇati				dadhánti	
English	sound			English	run,	bear fruit
Latin	Ø			Latin	Ø	
Greek	Ø			Greek	Ø	
Sanskrit	Ø			Sanskrit	dhana	prize

672	धन्व्			!	666	[6P]	dviṣ
[1U]	√dhanv			!	667	[2U]	dviṣ
	dhanvati	dhanvate			668	[1P]	dvṛ
English	run				669	[10P]	dhakk
Latin	Ø				670	[1P]	dhan
Greek	Ø				671	[3P]	dhan
Sanskrit	dhanutṛ	running			672	[1U]	dhanv

673	धम्			674	धा	
[1P]	√dham			[3U]	√dhā	
W	dhamati			W	dadhāti	dhatte
English	blow			English	put	
Latin	Ø			Latin	faciō	make, do
Greek	θέμερος	dark looking		Greek	θέσις	placement
Sanskrit	dhamani	pipe, tube		Sanskrit	dhātu	layer

675	धा			676	धा	
[1U]	√dhā			[4P]	√dhā	
W	dadhati	dadhate		W	dhayati	
English	put			English	suck, suckle	
Latin	faber	craftsman		Latin	felo	suck
Greek	θέμα	placed		Greek	θῆσθαι	suck
Sanskrit	dhā́man	house		Sanskrit	dhātrī	wet nurse

677	धाव्			678	धाव्	
[1U]	√dhāv			[1U]	√dhāv	
W	dhāvati	dhāvate		W	dhāvati	dhāvate
English	run			English	rinse	
Latin	Ø			Latin	Ø	
Greek	θέω	run, fly		Greek	Ø	
Sanskrit	dhārā	flood		Sanskrit	dhāva	washing

679	धि		!	673	[1P]	dham
[5P]	√dhi		!	674	[3U]	dhā
W	dhinoti		!	675	[1U]	dhā
English	nourish		!	676	[4P]	dhā
Latin	Ø		!	677	[1U]	dhāv
Greek	Ø		!	678	[1U]	dhāv
Sanskrit	dhita	satisfied		679	[5P]	dhi

680	धिक्ष्			681	धिष्	
[1Ā]	√dhikṣ			[3P]	√dhiṣ	
	dhikṣate				didheṣṭi	
English	kindle,	be weary		English	sound	
Latin	Ø			Latin	Ø	
Greek	Ø			Greek	Ø	
Sanskrit	Ø			Sanskrit	dhiṣaṇā	speech, hymn

682	धी			683	द्यु	
[4Ā]	√dhī			[2P]	√dyu	
W	dhīyate			W	dyauti	
English	think			English	attack	
Latin	Ø			Latin	Ø	
Greek	Ø			Greek	Ø	
Sanskrit	dhītí	thought, idea		Sanskrit	Ø	

684	धुक्ष्			685	द्युत्	
[1Ā]	√dhukṣ			[1Ā]	√dyut	
W	dhukṣate			W	dyótate	
English	kindle			English	shine	
Latin	Ø			Latin	Ø	
Greek	Ø			Greek	Ø	
Sanskrit	Ø			Sanskrit	dyuti	glory

686	धू			680	[1Ā]	dhikṣ
[5P]	√dhū			681	[3P]	dhiṣ
W	dhunoti			682	[4Ā]	dhī
English	shake			683	[2P]	dyu
Latin	Ø			684	[1Ā]	dhukṣ
Greek	θύω	storm, rage	!	685	[1Ā]	dyut
Sanskrit	dhūta	shaken, stirred	!	686	[5P]	dhū

687	धूर्व्			688	धूश्	
[1P]	√dhūrv			[10P]	√dhūś	
W	dhūrvati				dhūśayati	
English	injure			English	embellish	
Latin	Ø			Latin	Ø	
Greek	Ø			Greek	Ø	
Sanskrit	dhūrta	rogue		Sanskrit	Ø	

689	धृ			690	धृज्	
[1P]	√dhṛ			[1P]	√dhrj	
W	dharati				dharjati	
English	hold			English	go, move	
Latin	frētus	supported		Latin	Ø	
Greek	Ø			Greek	Ø	
Sanskrit	dhṛta	supported		Sanskrit	Ø	

691	धृञ्			692	धृष्	
[1P]	√dhṛñj			[5P]	√dhṛṣ	
	dhṛñjati			W	dhṛṣṇoti	
English	go, move			English	dare	bold
Latin	Ø			Latin	īnfēstō	harrass
Greek	Ø			Greek	θρᾰσΰς	daring
Sanskrit	Ø			Sanskrit	dhṛṣú	bold

693	धृष्			687	[1P]	dhūrv
[1P]	√dhṛṣ			688	[10P]	dhūś
W	dharṣati		!	689	[1P]	dhṛ
English	dare	bold		690	[1P]	dhrj
Latin	manifestus	caught in act		691	[1P]	dhṛñj
Greek	θρᾰσΰς	daring	!	692	[5P]	dhṛṣ
Sanskrit	dhṛṣṭá	bold	!	693	[1P]	dhṛṣ

694	धे			695	धोर्	
[1P]	√dhe			Pft	√dhor	
	dháyati				dudhora	
English	suck			English	run, trot	
Latin	fēllō	suck, suckle		Latin	Ø	
Greek	Ø			Greek	Ø	
Sanskrit	dhenú	milk cow		Sanskrit	dhoraṇa	vehicle

696	ध्या			697	ध्या	
[4U]	√dhyā			[2P]	√dhyā	
W	dhyāyati	dhyāyate		W	dhyāti	
English	think			English	think	
Latin	Ø			Latin	Ø	
Greek	Ø			Greek	Ø	
Sanskrit	dhyāta	meditated on		Sanskrit	dhyāna	meditation

698	ध्यै			699	ध्यै	
[1U]	√dhyai			[2P]	√dhyai	
	dhyā́yati	dhyā́yate			dhyāti	
English	think,	meditate		English	think,	meditate
Latin	Ø			Latin	Ø	
Greek	σῆμα (?)	sign		Greek	σῆμα (?)	sign
Sanskrit	dhyātṛ	thinker		Sanskrit	dhyātṛ	thinker

700	ध्रज्			694	[1P]	dhe
[1P]	√dhraj			695	Pft	dhor
W	dhrājati		!	696	[4U]	dhyā
English	fly, glide		!	697	[2P]	dhyā
Latin	Ø			698	[1U]	dhyai
Greek	Ø			699	[2P]	dhyai
Sanskrit	dhrajas	gliding course		700	[1P]	dhraj

701	धृण्			702	धृस्	
[1P]	√dhraṇ			[9P]	√dhras	
	dhraṇati				dhrasnāti	
English	sound			English	glean	
Latin	Ø			Latin	Ø	
Greek	Ø			Greek	Ø	
Sanskrit	Ø			Sanskrit	Ø	

703	धृस्			704	ध्राङ्क्षु	
[10P]	√dhras			[1P]	√dhrāṅkṣ	
	dhrāsayati				dhrāṅkṣati	
English	glean			English	caw, croak	
Latin	Ø			Latin	Ø	
Greek	Ø			Greek	Ø	
Sanskrit	Ø			Sanskrit	Ø	

705	ध्राडि			706	ध्रिज्	
[1Ā]	√dhrāḍ			[1P]	dhrij	
	dhrāḍate				dhrejati	
English	divide			English	go, move	
Latin	Ø			Latin	Ø	
Greek	Ø			Greek	Ø	
Sanskrit	Ø			Sanskrit	Ø	

707	ध्रु			701	[1P]	dhraṇ
[6P]	√dhru			702	[9P]	dhras
W	dhruvati			703	[10P]	dhras
English	being solid,	stable		704	[1P]	dhrāṅkṣ
Latin	Ø			705	[1Ā]	dhrāḍ
Greek	Ø			706	[1P]	dhrij
Sanskrit	dhruva	fixed		707	[6P]	dhru

708	ध्रुव्			709	ध्रेक्	
[1P]	√dhruv			[1Ā]	√dhrek	
	dhruvati				dhrekate	
English	being solid,	stable		English	sound	
Latin	Ø			Latin	Ø	
Greek	Ø			Greek	Ø	
Sanskrit	dhruva	fixed		Sanskrit	Ø	

710	ध्रै			711	ध्रै	
[1P]	√dhrai			[2P]	√dhrai	
	dhrāyati				dhrā́ti	
English	be pleased			English	be pleased	
Latin	Ø			Latin	Ø	
Greek	Ø			Greek	Ø	
Sanskrit	Ø			Sanskrit	Ø	

712	ध्वांस्			713	ध्वज्	
[1U]	√dhvaṃs			[1P]	√dhvaj	
W	dhvaṃsati	dhvaṃsate			dhvajati	
English	scatter	perish		English	go, move	
Latin	furō	rave, rage		Latin	Ø	
Greek	θύω	blow, storm		Greek	Ø	
Sanskrit	dhvaṃsa	loss, ruin		Sanskrit	dhvaja	banner

714	ध्वन्			708	[1P]	dhruv
[1P]	√dhvan			709	[1Ā]	dhrek
W	dhvanati			710	[1P]	dhrai
English	sound	din		711	[2P]	dhrai
Latin	Ø		!	712	[1U]	dhvaṃs
Greek	Ø			713	[1P]	dhvaj
Sanskrit	dhvani	sound, noise	!	714	[1P]	dhvan

715	ध्वाङ्क्ष्			716	ध्वृ	
[1P]	√dhvāṅkṣ			[1P]	√dhvṛ	
	dhvāṅkṣati			W	dhvarati	
English	caw, croak,	desire		English	bend, hurt	dull
Latin	Ø			Latin	fraus	deceit
Greek	Ø			German	toll	crazy, mad
Sanskrit	dhvāṅkṣa	crow		Sanskrit	dhvṛt	bending

717	नक्क्			718	नक्ष्	
[10P]	√nakk			[1P]	√nakṣ	
	nakkayati			W	nakṣati	
English	destroy, kill			English	approach	
Latin	Ø			Latin	Ø	
Greek	Ø			Greek	Ø	
Sanskrit	Ø			Sanskrit	nakṣat	approaching

719	नख्			720	नख्	
[1P]	√nakh			[4P]	√nakh	
	nakhati				nakhyati	
English	go, move			English	go, move	
Latin	Ø			Latin	Ø	
Greek	Ø			Greek	Ø	
Sanskrit	Ø			Sanskrit	Ø	

721	नङ्ख्			715	[1P]	dhvāṅkṣ
[1P]	√naṅkh			716	[1P]	dhvṛ
	naṅkhati			717	[10P]	nakk
English	go, move			718	[1P]	nakṣ
Latin	Ø			719	[1P]	nakh
Greek	Ø			720	[4P]	nakh
Sanskrit	Ø			721	[1P]	naṅkh

722	नट्			723	नद्	
[1P]	√naṭ			[1P]	√nad	
W	naṭati			W	nadati	
English	dance			English	sound, roar	
Latin	Ø			Latin	Ø	
Greek	Ø			Greek	Ø	
Sanskrit	naṭa	dancer, mime		Sanskrit	nādá	roaring

724	नन्द्			725	नभ्	
[1U]	√nand			[1Ā]	√nabh	
W	nandati	nandate		W	nabhate	
English	rejoice			English	burst	
Latin	Ø			Latin	Ø	
Greek	Ø			Greek	Ø	
Sanskrit	nanda	joy		Sanskrit	nabha	bursting forth

726	नम्			727	नय्	
[1P]	√nam			[1Ā]	√nay	
W	namati				nayate	
English	bend, bow			English	go,	protect
Latin	nemus	pasture, grove		Latin	Ø	
Greek	νέμος	pasture, grove		Greek	Ø	
Sanskrit	námas	bow		Sanskrit	Ø	

728	नर्द्		!	722	[1P]	naṭ
[1P]	√nard		!	723	[1P]	nad
W	nardati		!	724	[1U]	nand
English	bellow			725	[1Ā]	nabh
Latin	Ø		!	726	[1P]	nam
Greek	Ø			727	[1Ā]	nay
Sanskrit	narda	roaring	!	728	[1P]	nard

729	नल्			730	नल्	
[1P]	√nal			[10P]	√nal	
	nalati				nālayati	
English	smell, bind			English	speak,	shine
Latin	Ø			Latin	Ø	
Greek	Ø			Greek	Ø	
Sanskrit	Ø			Sanskrit	Ø	

731	नश्			732	नह्	
[4P]	√naś			[4P]	√nah	
W	naśyati			W	nahyati	
English	be lost			English	tie	
Latin	noceō	harm		Latin	nectō	bind
Greek	νεκρός	dead		French	nouer	bind
Sanskrit	naśa	destruction		Sanskrit	nahasra	bolt, nail

733	नाथ्			734	नाद्	
[1U]	√nāth			[10P]	√nād	
W	nāthati	nāthate		W	nādayati	
English	seek aid			English	full of	noise
German	Not	need		Latin	Ø	
Greek	ὀνίνημι	benefit		Greek	Ø	
Sanskrit	nātha	protector		Sanskrit	nāda	noise

735	नाय्			729	[1P]	nal
[10P]	√nāy			730	[10P]	nal
W	nāyayati		!	731	[4P]	naś
English	conduct,	lead	!	732	[4P]	nah
Latin	Ø			733	[1U]	nāth
Greek	Ø			734	[10P]	nād
Sanskrit	Ø			735	[10P]	nāy

736	नास्			737	निक्ष्	
[1Ā]	√nās			[1P]	√nikṣ	
	nāsate				nikṣati	
English	sound			English	kiss	
Latin	Ø			Latin	Ø	
Greek	Ø			Greek	Ø	
Sanskrit	Ø			Sanskrit	nikṣa	kissing

738	निज्			739	निज्	
[2Ā]	√nij			[3U]	√nij	
W	niṅkte			W	nenekti	nenikte
English	wash			English	wash	
German	Nixe	water spirit		Latin	noegēum	sweat cloth
Greek	νίζω	wash, cleanse		Greek	ἄνυπτος	unwashed
Sanskrit	niktá	cleansed		Sanskrit	nénekti	wash, cleanse

740	निन्द्			741	निन्व्	
[1P]	√nind			[1P]	√ninv	
W	nindati				ninvati	
English	revile			English	wet,	attend
Latin	Ø			Latin	Ø	
Greek	ὄνειδος	reproach		Greek	Ø	
Sanskrit	nindā	blame		Sanskrit	Ø	

742	निल्			736	[1Ā]	nās
[6P]	√nil			737	[1P]	nikṣ
	nilati			738	[2Ā]	nij
English	understand	with difficulty		739	[3U]	nij
Latin	Ø		!	740	[1P]	nind
Greek	Ø			741	[1P]	ninv
Sanskrit	Ø	Sanskrit		742	[6P]	nil

743	निंस्			744	निष्	
[2Ā]	√niṃs			[1P]	√niṣ	
	niṃsate				neṣati	
English	touch, kiss			English	moisten,	sprinkle
Latin	Ø			Latin	Ø	
Greek	Ø			Greek	Ø	
Sanskrit	Ø			Sanskrit	Ø	

745	निष्क्			746	नी	
[10Ā]	√niṣk			[1P]	√nī	
	niṣkayate			W	nayati	
English	measure	weigh		English	lead	
Latin	Ø			Latin	Ø	
Greek	Ø			Greek	Ø	
Sanskrit	niṣka	golden ornam.		Sanskrit	nīti	guidance

747	नील्			748	नीव्	
[1P]	√nīl			[1P]	√nīv	
	nīlati				nīvati	
English	be dark			English	become fat	
Latin	Ø			Latin	Ø	
Greek	Ø			Greek	Ø	
Sanskrit	nīla	dark colour		Sanskrit	Ø	

749	नु			743	[2Ā]	niṃs
[2P]	√nu			744	[1P]	niṣ
W	nauti			745	[10Ā]	niṣk
English	praise		!	746	[1P]	nī
Latin	nūntius	messenger		747	[1P]	nīl
Greek	Ø			748	[1P]	nīv
Sanskrit	nuti	laudation		749	[2P]	nu

750	नुद्			751	नृत्	
[6P]	√nud			[4P]	√nṛt	
W	nudati			W	nṛtyati	
English	push			English	dance	
Latin	Ø			Latin	Ø	
Greek	Ø			Greek	ναρναξ (?)	crate, box
Sanskrit	nutti	driving away		Sanskrit	nṛtu	dancing

752	नेद्			753	नेष्	
[1P]	√ned			[1Ā]	√neṣ	
W	nedati				neṣate	
English	flow			English	go, move	
Latin	Ø			Latin	Ø	
Greek	Ø			Greek	Ø	
Sanskrit	Ø			Sanskrit	Ø	

754	पक्ष्			755	पक्ष्	
[1P]	√pakṣ			[10P]	√pakṣ	
	pakṣati				pakṣayati	
English	take, seize			English	take, seize	
Latin	Ø			Latin	Ø	
Greek	Ø			Greek	Ø	
Sanskrit	pakṣa	wing		Sanskrit	pakṣa	wing

756	पच्		!	750	[6P]	nud
[1P]	√pac		!	751	[4P]	nṛt
W	pacati			752	[1P]	ned
English	cook			753	[1Ā]	neṣ
Latin	coquo	cook		754	[1P]	pakṣ
Greek	πέσσω	cook		755	[10P]	pakṣ
Sanskrit	pakti	cooking	!	756	[1P]	pac

757	पच्			758	पच्	
[1Ā]	√pac			[4Ā]	√pac	
W	pacate			W	pacyate	
English	cook			English	mature	
Latin	coquo	cook		Latin	coquo	cook
Greek	πέσσω	cook		Greek	πέσσω	cook
Sanskrit	pacaka	a cook		Sanskrit	pacā	maturation

759	पट्			760	पठ्	
[1P]	√paṭ			[1P]	√paṭh	
W	paṭati			W	paṭhati	
English	tear			English	read	
Latin	Ø			Latin	Ø	
German	spalten	split, cleave		Greek	Ø	
Sanskrit	paṭa	cloth		Sanskrit	paṭhana	lecture

761	पण्			762	पण्ड्	
[1Ā]	√paṇ			[1Ā]	√paṇḍ	
W	paṇate				paṇḍate	
English	bargain			English	go, move	
Latin	vēndō	sell		Latin	Ø	
Greek	πωλέω	sell		Greek	Ø	
Sanskrit	paṇa	price		Sanskrit	Ø	

763	पण्ड्					
[1P]	√paṇḍ		!	757	[1Ā]	pac
	paṇḍati		!	758	[4Ā]	pac
English	destroy			759	[1P]	paṭ
Latin	Ø		!	760	[1P]	paṭh
Greek	Ø			761	[1Ā]	paṇ
Sanskrit	Ø			762	[1Ā]	paṇḍ
				763	[1P]	paṇḍ

764	पण्ड्			765	पत्	
[1P]	√paṇḍ			[1P]	√pat	
W	paṇḍati			W	patati	
English	destroy			English	fly, fall	
Latin	Ø			Latin	petō	move towards
Greek	Ø			Greek	πέτομαι	fly
Sanskrit	Ø			Sanskrit	pāta	flying

766	पत्			767	पथ्	
[4Ā]	√pat			[1P]	√path	
W	patyate			W	pathati	
English	govern			English	go	
Latin	potior	be master of		Latin	Ø	
Greek	Ø			Greek	Ø	
Sanskrit	páti	master		Sanskrit	pathá	path

768	पद्			769	पन्	
[4Ā]	√pad			[1Ā]	√pan	
W	padyate			W	panante	
English	go			English	admire	
Latin	Ø			Latin	Ø	
Greek	Ø			Greek	Ø	
Sanskrit	Ø			Sanskrit	panita	admired

770	पन्थ्			764	[1P]	paṇḍ
[10P]	√panth		!	765	[1P]	pat
W	panthayati		!	766	[4Ā]	pat
English	go, move		!	767	[1P]	path
Latin	Ø		!	768	[4Ā]	pad
Greek	Ø			769	[1Ā]	pan
Sanskrit	Ø			770	[10P]	panth

771	पय्			772	पर्द्	
[1Ā]	√pay			[1Ā]	√pard	
	payate				pardate	
English	go, move			English	break wind	
Latin	Ø			German	furzen	fart
Greek	Ø			Greek	πέρδομαι	fart
Sanskrit	Ø			Sanskrit	pardana	farting

773	पर्ण्			774	पर्व्	
[10P]	√parṇ			[1P]	√parv	
	parṇayati				parvati	
English	be green,	verdant		English	fill	
Latin	Ø			Latin	Ø	
Greek	Ø			Greek	Ø	
Sanskrit	Ø			Sanskrit	Ø	

775	पल्			776	पश्	
[1P]	√pal			[4U]	√paś	
	palati			W	paśyati	paśyate
English	go			English	see	
Latin	Ø			Latin	cōn-spiciō	see
Greek	Ø			Greek	Ø	
Sanskrit	Ø			Sanskrit	paśyata	conspicuous

777	पश्			771	[1Ā]	pay
[10P]	√paś			772	[1Ā]	pard
W	pāśayati			773	[10P]	parṇ
English	fasten			774	[1P]	parv
Latin	pac-iscor	contract		775	[1P]	pal
Greek	Ø		!	776	[4U]	paś
Sanskrit	pāśa	noose, bond	!	777	[10P]	paś

778	पष्			779	पष्	
[1U]	√paṣ			[10P]	√paṣ	
	paṣati	paṣate			paṣayati	
English	bind			English	bind	
Latin	Ø			Latin	Ø	
Greek	Ø			Greek	Ø	
Sanskrit	Ø			Sanskrit	Ø	

780	पा			781	पा	
[1P]	√pā			[2P]	√pā	
W	pibati			W	pāti	
English	drink			English	protect	
Latin	pōtō	drink		Latin	pastor	shepherd
Greek	πίνω	drink		Greek	ποιμήν	shepherd
Sanskrit	pītí	draught		Sanskrit	pātṛ́	protector

782	पाल्			783	पाव्	
[10P]	√pāl			[10P]	√pāv	
W	pālayati			W	pāvayati	
English	guard			English	purify	
Latin	Ø			Latin	Ø	
Greek	Ø			Greek	Ø	
Sanskrit	pāla	guard		Sanskrit	pāvanī	pure, sacred

784	पि			778	[1U]	paṣ
[6P]	√pi			779	[10P]	paṣ
	piyati		!	780	[1P]	pā
English	go, move		!	781	[2P]	pā
Latin	Ø			782	[10P]	pāl
Greek	Ø			783	[10P]	pāv
Sanskrit	Ø			784	[6P]	pi

785	पिट्			786	पिण्ड्	
[1P]	√piṭ			[1Ā]	√piṇḍ	
	peṭati				piṇḍate	
English	sound,	assemble		English	roll into a	ball
Latin	Ø			Latin	Ø	
Greek	Ø			Greek	Ø	
Sanskrit	piṭa	basket		Sanskrit	piṇḍa	lump

787	पिण्ड्			788	पिन्व्	
[10P]	√piṇḍ			[1Ā]	√pinv	
W	piṇḍayati				pínvate	
English	roll into a	ball		English	swell	
Latin	Ø			Latin	Ø	
Greek	Ø			Greek	Ø	
Sanskrit	piṇḍa	clod, ball		Sanskrit	pinvita	swollen

789	पिन्व्			790	पिंस्	
[1P]	√pinv			[1P]	√piṃs	
	pínvati				piṃsati	
English	cause to	swell		English	speak,	shine
Latin	Ø			Latin	Ø	
Greek	Ø			Greek	Ø	
Sanskrit	pinvita	swollen		Sanskrit	Ø	

791	पिंस्			785	[1P]	piṭ
[10P]	√piṃs			786	[1Ā]	piṇḍ
	piṃsayati			787	[10P]	piṇḍ
English	speak, shine			788	[1Ā]	pinv
Latin	Ø			789	[1P]	pinv
Greek	Ø			790	[1P]	piṃs
Sanskrit	Ø			791	[10P]	piṃs

792	पिश्			793	पिष्	
[6P]	√piś			[7P]	√piṣ	
W	piṃśati			W	pinaṣṭi	
English	adorn	carve, prepare		English	crush	
Latin	pingō	paint, decorate		Latin	pinsō	beat, pound
Greek	ποικίλος	colourful		Greek	πτίσις	winnowing
Sanskrit	piśita	decorated, cut		Sanskrit	piṣṭá	ground

794	पिस्			795	पिस्	
[4P]	√pis			[1P]	√pis	
	písyati				pesati	
English	stretch,	expand		English	go, move	
Latin	Ø			Latin	Ø	
Greek	Ø			Greek	Ø	
Sanskrit	Ø			Sanskrit	Ø	

796	पिस्			797	पी	
[10P]	√pis			[1Ā]	√pī	
	pesayati			W	payate	
English	hurt,	be strong		English	swell,	fatten
Latin	Ø			Latin	pīnguis	fat, plump
Greek	Ø			Greek	πῖων	fat, rich
Sanskrit	Ø			Sanskrit	pívas	fat

798	पीड्			792	[6P]	piś
[10P]	√pīḍ		!	793	[7P]	piṣ
W	pīḍayati			794	[4P]	pis
English	press			795	[1P]	pis
Latin	Ø			796	[10P]	pis
Greek	πῐέζω	squeeze		797	[1Ā]	pī
Sanskrit	pīḍā	pain		798	[10P]	pīḍ

799	पील्			800	पुट्	
[1P]	√pīl			[6P]	√puṭ	
	pīlati			W	puṭati	
English	stop,	become stupid		English	embrace	
Latin	Ø			Latin	Ø	
Greek	Ø			Greek	Ø	
Sanskrit	Ø			Sanskrit	puṭa	fold, pocket

801	पुट्ट्			802	पुड्	
[10P]	√puṭṭ			[1P]	√puḍ	
	puṭṭayati				poḍati	
English	diminish			English	grind,	pound
Latin	Ø			Latin	Ø	
Greek	Ø			Greek	Ø	
Sanskrit	Ø			Sanskrit	Ø	

803	पुड्			804	पुण्	
[6P]	√puḍ			[6P]	√puṇ	
	puḍati				puṇati	
English	leave, quit			English	act piously	
Latin	Ø			Latin	Ø	
Greek	Ø			Greek	Ø	
Sanskrit	Ø			Sanskrit	Ø	

805	पुण्			799	[1P]	pīl
[10P]	√puṇ		!	800	[6P]	puṭ
	poṇayati			801	[10P]	puṭṭ
English	collect,	accumulate		802	[1P]	puḍ
Latin	Ø			803	[6P]	puḍ
Greek	Ø			804	[6P]	puṇ
Sanskrit	Ø			805	[10P]	puṇ

645	dṛh	685	dyut	725	nabh	765	pat
646	dṝ	686	dhū	726	nam	766	pat
647	de	687	dhūrv	727	nay	767	path
648	dai	688	dhūś	728	nard	768	pad
649	do	689	dhṛ	729	nal	769	pan
650	do	690	dhṛj	730	nal	770	panth
651	drā	691	dhṛñj	731	naś	771	pay
652	drā	692	dhṛṣ	732	nah	772	pard
653	drā	693	dhṛṣ	733	nāth	773	parṇ
654	drākh	694	dhe	734	nād	774	parv
655	drāṅkṣ	695	dhor	735	nāy	775	pal
656	drāḍ	696	dhyā	736	nās	776	paś
657	drāgh	697	dhyā	737	nikṣ	777	paś
658	drāh	698	dhyai	738	nij	778	paṣ
659	dru	699	dhyai	739	nij	779	paṣ
660	dru	700	dhraj	740	nind	780	pā
661	druṇ	701	dhraṇ	741	ninv	781	pā
662	druh	702	dhras	742	nil	782	pāl
663	drek	703	dhras	743	nims	783	pāv
664	drai	704	dhrāṅkṣ	744	niṣ	784	pi
665	drai	705	dhrāḍ	745	niṣk	785	piṭ
666	dviṣ	706	dhrij	746	nī	786	piṇḍ
667	dviṣ	707	dhru	747	nīl	787	piṇḍ
668	dvṛ	708	dhruv	748	nīv	788	pinv
669	dhakk	709	dhrek	749	nu	789	pinv
670	dhaṇ	710	dhrai	750	nud	790	pims
671	dhan	711	dhrai	751	nṛt	791	pims
672	dhanv	712	dhvaṃs	752	ned	792	piś
673	dham	713	dhvaj	753	neṣ	793	piṣ
674	dhā	714	dhvan	754	pakṣ	794	pis
675	dhā	715	dhvāṅkṣ	755	pakṣ	795	pis
676	dhā	716	dhvṛ	756	pac	796	pis
677	dhāv	717	nakk	757	pac	797	pī
678	dhāv	718	nakṣ	758	pac	798	pīḍ
679	dhi	719	nakh	759	paṭ	799	pīl
680	dhikṣ	720	nakh	760	paṭh	800	puṭ
681	dhiṣ	721	naṅkh	761	paṇ	801	puṭṭ
682	dhī	722	naṭ	762	paṇḍ	802	puḍ
683	dyu	723	nad	763	paṇḍ	803	puḍ
684	dhukṣ	724	nand	764	paṇḍ	804	puṇ
						805	puṇ

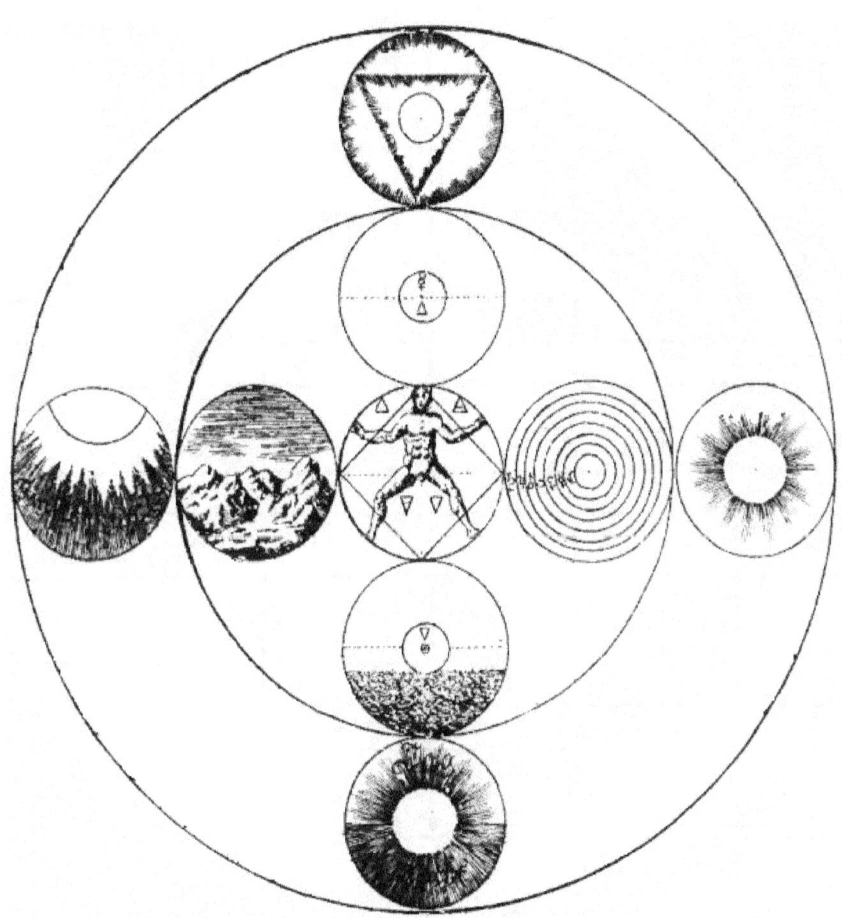

806	पुण्ट्			807	पुण्ड्	
[10P]	√puṇṭ			[1P]	√puṇḍ	
	puṇṭayati				puṇḍati	
English	speak, shine			English	rub,	grind
Latin	Ø			Latin	Ø	
Greek	Ø			Greek	Ø	
Sanskrit	Ø			Sanskrit	Ø	

808	पुथ्			809	पुन्थ्	
[4P]	√puth			[1P]	√punth	
W	puthyati				punthati	
English	crush,	destroy		English	give,	suffer pain
Latin	Ø			Latin	Ø	
Greek	Ø			Greek	Ø	
Sanskrit	pothita	hurt		Sanskrit	Ø	

810	पुर्			811	पुर्व्	
[6P]	√pur			[1P]	√purv	
	purati				pūrvati	
English	precede,	go before		English	fill	
Latin	Ø			Latin	Ø	
Greek	πάρος	before		Greek	Ø	
Sanskrit	purā	before		Sanskrit	Ø	

812	पुर्व्			806	[10P]	puṇṭ
[10P]	√purv			807	[1P]	puṇḍ
	pūrvayati			808	[4P]	puth
English	dwell			809	[1P]	punth
Latin	Ø			810	[6P]	pur
Greek	Ø			811	[1P]	purv
Sanskrit	Ø			812	[10P]	purv

813	पुल्			814	पुल्	
[1P]	√pul			[6P]	√pul	
	polati				pulati	
English	be large			English	be heaped	up
Latin	Ø			Latin	Ø	
Greek	Ø			Greek	Ø	
Sanskrit	pula	extended		Sanskrit	pula	horripilation

815	पुल्			816	पुष्	
[10P]	√pul			[4Ā]	√puṣ	
	polayati			W	puṣyate	
English	be heaped up			English	thrive	
Latin	Ø			Latin	pustula	"bubble"
Greek	Ø			Greek	Ø	
Sanskrit	pulī	a bunch		Sanskrit	póṣa	thriving

817	पुष्			818	पुष्	
[4P]	√puṣ			[9P]	√puṣ	
W	puṣyati			W	puṣṇāti	
English	feed			English	maintain	
Latin	pustula	"bubble"		Latin	pustula	"bubble"
Greek	Ø			Greek	Ø	
Sanskrit	puṣa	nourishing		Sanskrit	poṣaṇa	nourishing

819	पुष्प्			813	[1P]	pul
[4P]	√puṣp			814	[6P]	pul
W	puṣpyati			815	[10P]	pul
English	open,	bloom	!	816	[4Ā]	puṣ
Latin	Ø		!	817	[4P]	puṣ
Greek	Ø		!	818	[9P]	puṣ
Sanskrit	puṣpa	flower		819	[4P]	puṣp

820	पुंस्			821	पुस्त्	
[10P]	√puṃs			[10P]	√pust	
	puṃsayati				pustayati	
English	crush, grind			English	respect	disrespect (?)
Latin	Ø			Latin	Ø	
Greek	Ø			Greek	Ø	
Sanskrit	Ø			Sanskrit	Ø	

822	पू			823	पू	
[9U]	√pū			[1Ā]	√pū	
W	punāti	punīte		W	pavate	
English	cleanse			English	purify	oneself
Latin	pūrus	clear, limpid		Latin	pūrus	clear, limpid
Greek	πῦρ	fire		Greek	πῦρ	fire
Sanskrit	punāna	being purified		Sanskrit	pū́ti	purification

824	पूज्			825	पूय्	
[10U]	√pūj			[1U]	√pūy	
W	pūjayati	pūjayate		W	pūyati	pūyate
English	worship			English	stink	
Latin	Ø			Latin	pūs	"pus"
Greek	Ø			Greek	πῦον	"pus"
Sanskrit	pūjā	reverence		Sanskrit	pū́ya	"pus"

826	पृ			820	[10P]	puṃs
[3P]	√pṛ			821	[10P]	pust
W	piparti		!	822	[9U]	pū
English	bring over	save, rescue	!	823	[1Ā]	pū
Latin	portus	harbour, port		824	[10U]	pūj
Greek	πείρω	pierce		825	[1U]	pūy
Sanskrit	pāra	shore	!	826	[3P]	pṛ

827	पृ			828	पॢ	
[9P]	√pṛ			[9P]	√pṝ	
W	pṛṇāti			W	pṛṇāti	
English	bring over	save, rescue		English	fill	full
Latin	experior	attempt, try		Latin	plenus	full
Greek	πείρω	pierce		Greek	πλήθω	be full
Sanskrit	pāra	shore		Sanskrit	pūra	filling

829	पॄ			830	पृच्	
[6P]	√pṝ			[7U]	√pṛc	
W	priṇāti			W	pṛṇakti	pṛṅkte
English	fill	full		English	mix	
Latin	plūs	more		Latin	plectō	plait, weave
Greek	πληθώρη	fullness		Greek	πλέκω	plait, twine
Sanskrit	pūrtí	filling		German	pflechten	plait, braid

831	पृथ्			832	पृष्	
[10P]	√pṛth			[1P]	√pṛṣ	
W	parthayati			W	parṣati	
English	extend			English	sprinkle,	annoy
Latin	Ø			Latin	Ø	
Greek	Ø			Greek	Ø	
Sanskrit	pṛtha	palm (hand)		Sanskrit	pṛṣat	sprinkling

833	पेल्		!	827	[9P]	pṛ
[1P]	√pel			828	[9P]	pṝ
W	pelati			829	[6P]	pṝ
English	go			830	[7U]	pṛc
Latin	Ø			831	[10P]	pṛth
Greek	Ø			832	[1P]	pṛṣ
Sanskrit	pela	going		833	[1P]	pel

834	पेष्			835	पेस्	
[1Ā]	√peṣ			[1P]	√pes	
	peṣate				pesati	
English	strive	diligently		English	go	
Latin	Ø			Latin	Ø	
Greek	Ø			Greek	Ø	
Sanskrit	Ø			Sanskrit	Ø	

836	पै			837	पैण्	
[1P]	√pai			[1P]	√paiṇ	
	pāyati				paiṇati	
English	dry, wither			English	go, send,	embrace
Latin	Ø			Latin	Ø	
Greek	Ø			Greek	Ø	
Sanskrit	Ø			Sanskrit	Ø	

838	प्या			839	प्याय्	
[1Ā]	√pyā			[1Ā]	√pyāy	
W	pyāyate				pyā́yate	
English	swell,	overflow		English	swell,	overflow
Latin	Ø			Latin	Ø	
Greek	Ø			Greek	Ø	
Sanskrit	Ø			Sanskrit	pyāna	swollen

838	प्या			834	[1Ā]	peṣ
[1Ā]	√pyai			835	[1P]	pes
	pyā́yate			836	[1P]	pai
English	swell,	overflow		837	[1P]	paiṇ
Latin	Ø			838	[1Ā]	pyā
Greek	Ø			839	[1Ā]	pyāy
Sanskrit	pyāyita	grown fat		840	[1Ā]	pyai

841	प्रश्		842	प्रथ्	
[6P]	√praś		[1Ā]	√prath	
W	pṛcchati		W	prathate	
English	ask		English	spread	
Latin	precor	beseech, ask	Latin	planta	sole (foot)
French	prier	ask	Greek	πλᾰτύς	wide, broad
German	fragen	ask	Sanskrit	prathita	spread out

843	प्रा		844	प्री	
[2P]	√prā		[9U]	√prī	
	prāti		W	prīṇāti	prīṇīte
English	fill		English	please	friend
Latin	plenus	full	German	Freund	friend
Greek	Ø		Greek	πραΰς	gentle
Sanskrit	Ø		Sanskrit	priya	beloved

845	प्रु		846	प्रुष्	
[1Ā]	√pru		[5U]	√pruṣ	
W	pravate		W	pruṣṇoti	pruṣṇute
English	emerge		English	sprinkle	freeze
Latin	Ø		Latin	pruīna	hoar frost
Greek	Ø		German	frieren	freeze
Sanskrit	Ø		Sanskrit	pruṣitá	sprinkled

847	प्रुष्			841	[6P]	praś
[1P]	√pruṣ		!	842	[1Ā]	prath
	proṣati			843	[2P]	prā
English	burn		!	844	[9U]	prī
Latin	prūna	burning coal		845	[1Ā]	pru
Greek	Ø			846	[5U]	pruṣ
Sanskrit	pruṣṭa	burnt		847	[1P]	pruṣ

848	प्रेङ्ख्			849	प्रेष्	
[1U]	√preṅkh			[1U]	√preṣ	
	preṅkhati	preṅkhate			preṣyati	preṣyate
English	tremble,	shake		English	drive on,	urge
Latin	Ø			Latin	Ø	
Greek	Ø			Greek	Ø	
Sanskrit	preṅkhaṇa	a swing		Sanskrit	Ø	

850	प्रोथ्			851	प्लक्ष्	
[1U]	√proth			[1U]	√plakṣ	
	prothati	prothate			plakṣati	plakṣate
English	be equal to			English	eat,	consume
Latin	Ø			Latin	Ø	
Greek	Ø			Greek	Ø	
Sanskrit	Ø			Sanskrit	Ø	

852	प्लिह्			853	प्ली	
[1Ā]	√plih			[9P]	√plī	
	plehate				plināti	
English	go, move			English	go, move	
Latin	Ø			Latin	Ø	
Greek	Ø			Greek	Ø	
Sanskrit	Ø			Sanskrit	Ø	

854	प्लु			848	[1U]	preṅkh
[1Ā]	√plu		!	849	[1U]	preṣ
W	plavate			850	[1U]	proth
English	float			851	[1U]	plakṣ
Latin	flūctuō	swell, undulate		852	[1Ā]	plih
Greek	πλέω	float, sail		853	[9P]	plī
Sanskrit	pluta	flood	!	854	[1Ā]	plu

855	प्लुष्			856	प्लुष्	
[1P]	√pluṣ			[4P]	√pluṣ	
W	ploṣati			W	pluṣyati	
English	burn			English	burn	
Latin	Ø			Latin	Ø	
Greek	Ø			Greek	Ø	
Sanskrit	pluṣṭa	burned		Sanskrit	pluṣṭa	burned

857	प्लुष्			858	प्सा	
[9P]	√pluṣ			[2P]	√psā	
W	pluṣṇāti				psāti	
English	sprinkled			English	devour,	eat
Latin	Ø			Latin	Ø	
Greek	Ø			Greek	Ø	
Sanskrit	pluṣṭa	frozen		Sanskrit	psaras	a feast

859	फक्क्			860	फण्	
[1P]	√phakk			[1P]	√phaṇ	
	phakkati				pháṇati	
English	act wrongly			English	go, move	
Latin	Ø			Latin	Ø	
Greek	Ø			Greek	Ø	
Sanskrit	phakkikā	trick, fraud		Sanskrit	phaṇi	serpent

861	फल्		!	855	[1P]	pluṣ
[1P]	√phal		!	856	[4P]	pluṣ
W	phalati		!	857	[9P]	pluṣ
English	burst	split		858	[2P]	psā
Latin	Ø			859	[1P]	phakk
German	spalten	split		860	[1P]	phaṇ
Sanskrit	phala	fruit	!	861	[1P]	phal

862	फेल्			863	बण्	
[1P]	√phel			[1P]	√baṇ	
	phelati				baṇati	
English	go, move			English	sound	
Latin	Ø			Latin	Ø	
Greek	Ø			Greek	Ø	
Sanskrit	Ø			Sanskrit	Ø	

864	बद्			865	बन्ध्	
[1P]	√bad			[9U]	√bandh	
	badati			W	badhnāti	badhnīte
English	be firm,	steady		English	bind	
Latin	Ø			German	binden	bind
Greek	Ø			Greek	πεῖσμα	cord
Sanskrit	Ø			Sanskrit	bandha	bond

866	बर्ह्			867	बर्ह्	
[1Ā]	√barh			[10P]	√barh	
	barhate			W	barhayati	
English	speak			English	speak	
Latin	Ø			Latin	Ø	
Greek	Ø			Greek	Ø	
Sanskrit	Ø			Sanskrit	Ø	

868	बल्			862	[1P]	phel
[1P]	√bal			863	[1P]	baṇ
W	balati			864	[1P]	bad
English	breathe,	live	!	865	[9U]	bandh
Latin	Ø			866	[1Ā]	barh
Greek	Ø			867	[10P]	barh
Sanskrit	Ø			868	[1P]	bal

869	बल्ह्			870	बल्ह्	
[1Ā]	√balh			[10P]	√balh	
	balhate				balhayati	
English	be excellent			English	speak,	shine
Latin	Ø			Latin	Ø	
Greek	Ø			Greek	Ø	
Sanskrit	Ø			Sanskrit	Ø	

871	बंह्			872	बाड्	
[1Ā]	√baṃh			[1Ā]	√bāḍ	
W	baṃhate				bāḍate	
English	grow			English	bathe,	dive
Latin	Ø			Latin	Ø	
Greek	Ø			Greek	Ø	
Sanskrit	Ø			Sanskrit	bāḍita	sunk

873	बाध्			874	बिट्	
[1Ā]	√bādh			[1P]	√biṭ	
W	bādhate				beṭati	
English	oppress			English	swear,	shout
Latin	Ø			Latin	Ø	
Greek	Ø			Greek	Ø	
Sanskrit	bādha	distress		Sanskrit	Ø	

875	बिल्			869	[1Ā]	balh
[6P]	√bil			870	[10P]	balh
	bilati			871	[1Ā]	baṃh
English	split, cleave			872	[1Ā]	bāḍ
Latin	Ø		!	873	[1Ā]	bādh
Greek	Ø			874	[1P]	biṭ
Sanskrit	bila	cave, hole		875	[6P]	bil

876	बिल्			877	बिस्	
[10P]	√bil			[4P]	√bis	
	belayati				bisyati	
English	split, cleave			English	grow,	incite
Latin	Ø			Latin	Ø	
Greek	Ø			Greek	Ø	
Sanskrit	bila	cave, hole		Sanskrit	bisa	shoot

878	बुक्क्			879	बुक्क्	
[1P]	√bukk			[10P]	√bukk	
	bukkati			W	bukkayati	
English	bark, yelp			English	bark,	yelp
Latin	Ø			Latin	Ø	
Greek	Ø			Greek	Ø	
Sanskrit	bukkana	bark		Sanskrit	bukkana	bark

880	बुड्			881	बुध्	
[6P]	√buḍ			[1P]	√budh	
	buḍati			W	bodhati	
English	cover,	conceal		English	know,	wake
Latin	Ø			Latin	Ø	
Greek	Ø			Greek	πεύθομαι	perceive
Sanskrit	Ø			Sanskrit	buddhi	intelligence

882	बुध्			876	[10P]	bil
[4Ā]	√budh			877	[4P]	bis
W	budhyate			878	[1P]	bukk
English	know, wake			879	[10P]	bukk
Latin	Ø			880	[6P]	buḍ
Greek	πεύθομαι	perceive	!	881	[1P]	budh
Sanskrit	bodha	knowing	!	882	[4Ā]	budh

883	बुन्द्			884	बुस्	
[1U]	√bund			[4P]	√bus	
	bundati	bundate			busyati	
English	perceive,	learn		English	divide,	discharge
Latin	Ø			Latin	Ø	
Greek	Ø			Greek	Ø	
Sanskrit	Ø			Sanskrit	Ø	

885	बुस्त्			886	बृह्	
[10P]	√bust			[1U]	√bṛh	
	bustayati			W	bṛṃhati	bṛṃhate
English	honour,	respect		English	grow,	augment
Latin	Ø			Latin	Ø	
Greek	Ø			Greek	Ø	
Sanskrit	Ø			Sanskrit	bṛhát	large

887	बृह्			888	बृह्	
[6P]	√bṛh			[6P]	√bṛh	
W	bṛhati			W	bṛhati	
English	grow,	augment		English	tear	
Latin	Ø			Latin	Ø	
Greek	Ø			Greek	Ø	
Sanskrit	bṛṃhaṇa	nourishing		Sanskrit	bṛḍha	eradicated

889	बेह्			883	[1U]	bund
[1Ā]	√beh			884	[4P]	bus
	behate			885	[10P]	bust
English	endeavour			886	[1U]	bṛh
Latin	Ø			887	[6P]	bṛh
Greek	Ø			888	[6P]	bṛh
Sanskrit	Ø			889	[1Ā]	beh

890	ब्रू			891	ब्रू	
[2U]	√brū			[6P]	√brū	
W	bravīti	brūte		W	bruvati	
English	say			English	say	
Latin	Ø			Latin	Ø	
Greek	Ø			Greek	Ø	
Sanskrit	bruva	pretending		Sanskrit	bruva	pretending

892	भक्ष्			893	भज्	
[1U]	√bhakṣ			[1U]	√bhaj	
W	bhakṣati			W	bhajati	bhajate
English	partake of,	eat		English	share	
Latin	Ø			Latin	Ø	
Greek	Ø			Greek	φἄγεῖν	eat
Sanskrit	bhakṣa	drink, food		Sanskrit	bhaktí	distribution

894	भञ्ज्			895	भट्	
[7P]	√bhañj			[1P]	√bhaṭ	
W	bhanakti				bhaṭati	
English	break			English	hire,	nourish
Latin	frangō	break		Latin	Ø	
Greek	Ø			Greek	Ø	
Sanskrit	bhaṅga	breaking		Sanskrit	Ø	

896	भट्		!	890	[2U]	brū
[10P]	√bhaṭ		!	891	[6P]	brū
	bhaṭayati		!	892	[1U]	bhakṣ
English	speak, hire		!	893	[1U]	bhaj
Latin	Ø		!	894	[7P]	bhañj
Greek	Ø			895	[1P]	bhaṭ
Sanskrit	Ø			896	[10P]	bhaṭ

897	भण्			898	भण्ड्	
[1P]	√bhaṇ			[1Ā]	√bhaṇḍ	
W	bhaṇati			W	bhaṇḍate	
English	talk			English	joke	
Latin	Ø			Latin	Ø	
Greek	Ø			Greek	Ø	
Sanskrit	Ø			Sanskrit	bhaṇḍa	jester

899	भन्द्			900	भर्त्स्	
[1Ā]	√bhand			[1P]	√bharts	
W	bhandate			W	bharsati	
English	be praised			English	revile	
Latin	Ø			Latin	Ø	
Greek	Ø			Greek	Ø	
Sanskrit	bhandanā	acclamation		Sanskrit	bhartsana	threat

901	भर्त्स्			902	भर्व्	
[10P]	√bharts			[1P]	√bharv	
W	bhartsayati				bharvati	
English	revile			English	devour,	eat
Latin	Ø			Latin	Ø	
Greek	Ø			Greek	Ø	
Sanskrit	bhartsita	threatened		Sanskrit	Ø	

903	भष्		!	897	[1P]	bhaṇ
[1P]	√bhaṣ			898	[1Ā]	bhaṇḍ
W	bhaṣati			899	[1Ā]	bhand
English	bark			900	[1P]	bharts
Latin	Ø			901	[10P]	bharts
Greek	Ø			902	[1P]	bharv
Sanskrit	bhaṣa	dog		903	[1P]	bhaṣ

904	भस्			905	भल्	
[3P]	√bhas			[1Ā]	√bhal	
W	babhasti				bhalate	
English	devour			English	perceive	
Latin	Ø			Latin	Ø	
Greek	Ø			Greek	Ø	
Sanskrit	Ø			Sanskrit	bhala	behold

906	भल्			907	भा	
[10Ā]	√bhal			[2P]	√bhā	
W	bhālayate			W	bhāti	
English	describe			English	shine	
Latin	Ø			Latin	Ø	
Greek	Ø			Greek	φαivω	reveal
Sanskrit	Ø			Sanskrit	bhānu	brightness

908	भाम्			909	भास्	
[1Ā]	√bhām			[1U]	√bhās	
W	bhāmate			W	bhāsati	bhāsate
English	be angry			English	shine	
Latin	Ø			Latin	iubar	radiance
Greek	Ø			Greek	φάoς	light
Sanskrit	bhāma	anger		Sanskrit	bhāsa	luster

910	भिक्ष्			904	[3P]	bhas
[1Ā]	√bhikṣ			905	[1Ā]	bhal
W	bhikṣate			906	[10Ā]	bhal
English	ask, beg		!	907	[2P]	bhā
Latin	Ø			908	[1Ā]	bhām
Greek	Ø		!	909	[1U]	bhās
Sanskrit	bhikṣā	alms, begging	!	910	[1Ā]	bhikṣ

911	भिद्			912	भी	
[7U]	√bhid			[3P]	√bhī	
W	bhinatti	bhintte		W	bibheti	
English	split			English	fear	
Latin	findō	cleave		Latin	Ø	
German	beissen	bite		Greek	Ø	
Sanskrit	bhitta	small piece		Sanskrit	bhīti	fear

913	भुज्			914	भुज्	
[6P]	√bhuj			[7Ā]	√bhuj	
W	bhujati			W	bhuṅkte	
English	bend			English	enjoy	
Latin	fugiō	flee, run away		Latin	fungor	enjoy
Greek	φεύγω	flee, run away		Greek	Ø	
Sanskrit	bhuja	arm		Sanskrit	bhoga	enjoyment

915	भू			916	भूष्	
[1P]	√bhū			[1P]	√bhūṣ	
W	bhavati			W	bhūṣati	
English	be			English	strive,	adorn
Latin	fuī (pft sum)	sum, to be		Latin	Ø	
Greek	φύω	bring forth		Greek	Ø	
Sanskrit	bhúvana	living creature		Sanskrit	bhūṣaṇa	ornament

917	भृ		!	911	[7U]	bhid
[1U]	√bhṛ		!	912	[3P]	bhī
W	bharati	bharate	!	913	[6P]	bhuj
English	bear		!	914	[7Ā]	bhuj
Latin	ferō	bear, carry	!	915	[1P]	bhū
Greek	φέρω	bring, bear		916	[1P]	bhūṣ
Sanskrit	bhāra	burden	!	917	[1U]	bhṛ

918	भृज्ज्			919	भृंश्	
[6P]	√bhrjj			[1P]	√bhṛṃś	
W	bhrjjati				bhṛṃśati	
English	roast			English	speak,	shine
Latin	Ø			Latin	Ø	
Greek	Ø			Greek	Ø	
Sanskrit	bhrṣṭa	roasted		Sanskrit	Ø	

920	भृंश्			921	भृश्	
[10P]	√bhṛṃś			[4P]	√bhṛś	
W	bhṛṃśayati				bhṛśyati	
English	speak, shine			English	fall down	
Latin	Ø			Latin	Ø	
Greek	Ø			Greek	Ø	
Sanskrit	Ø			Sanskrit	bhṛśa	falling

922	भृश्			923	भेष्	
[6P]	√bhṛś			[1U]	√bheṣ	
	bhṛśati				bheṣati	bheṣate
English	be strong			English	fear,	dread
Latin	Ø			Latin	Ø	
Greek	Ø			Greek	Ø	
Sanskrit	bhṛśa	vehement		Sanskrit	Ø	

924	भ्यस्		!	918	[6P]	bhrjj
[1Ā]	√bhyas			919	[1P]	bhṛṃś
W	bhyásate			920	[10P]	bhṛṃś
English	fear, dread			921	[4P]	bhṛś
Latin	Ø			922	[6P]	bhṛś
Greek	Ø			923	[1U]	bheṣ
Sanskrit	Ø			924	[1Ā]	bhyas

925	भ्रंश्			926	भ्रश्	
[1Ā]	√bhraṃś			[4U]	√bhraṃś	
	bhramśate				bhraśyati	bhraśyate
English	fall down			English	fall down	
Latin	Ø			Latin	Ø	
Greek	Ø			Greek	Ø	
Sanskrit	bhramśa	decline		Sanskrit	bhramśa	ruin

927	भ्रक्ष्			928	भ्रण्	
[1U]	√bhrakṣ			[1P]	√bhraṇ	
	bhrakṣati	bhrakṣate			bhraṇati	
English	eat			English	sound	
Latin	Ø			Latin	Ø	
Greek	Ø			Greek	Ø	
Sanskrit	Ø			Sanskrit	Ø	

929	भ्रम्			930	भ्रम्	
[1P]	√bhram			[4P]	√bhram	
W	bhramati			W	bhrāmyati	
English	wander			English	wander	
Latin	fremō	mutter, growl		Latin	fremō	mutter, growl
Greek	βρέμω	roar, clash		Greek	βρέμω	roar, clash
Sanskrit	bhrānti	roaming		Sanskrit	bhramara	black bee

931	भ्राज्		!	925	[1Ā]	bhraṃś
[1Ā]	√bhrāj		!	926	[4U]	bhraṃś
W	bhrājate			927	[1U]	bhrakṣ
English	shine			928	[1P]	bhraṇ
Latin	flagrō	burn, blaze	!	929	[1P]	bhram
Greek	φλέγω	burn	!	930	[4P]	bhram
Sanskrit	bhrāja	fire, shining	!	931	[1Ā]	bhrāj

932	भ्राश्			933	भ्राश्	
[1Ā]	√bhrāś			[4Ā]	√bhrāś	
	bhrāśate				bhrāśyate	
English	shine,	glitter		English	shine,	glitter
Latin	Ø			Latin	Ø	
Greek	Ø			Greek	Ø	
Sanskrit	Ø			Sanskrit	Ø	

934	भ्रेज्			935	भ्रेष्	
[1Ā]	√bhrej			[1U]	√bhreṣ	
	bhrejate				bhreṣati	bhreṣate
English	shine,	glitter		English	totter,	slip
Latin	Ø			Latin	Ø	
Greek	Ø			Greek	Ø	
Sanskrit	Ø			Sanskrit	bhreṣa	tottering

936	भ्री			937	भुड्	
[9P]	√bhrī			[6P]	√bhruḍ	
	bhrīṇāti				bhruḍati	
English	fear, bear			English	cover,	collect
Latin	Ø			Latin	Ø	
Greek	Ø			Greek	Ø	
Sanskrit	Ø			Sanskrit	Ø	

938	भ्रूण्			932	[1Ā]	bhrāś
[10Ā]	√bhrūṇ			933	[4Ā]	bhrāś
	bhrūṇayate			934	[1Ā]	bhrej
English	wish, fear			935	[1U]	bhreṣ
Latin	Ø			936	[9P]	bhrī
Greek	Ø			937	[6P]	bhruḍ
Sanskrit	Ø			938	[10Ā]	bhrūṇ

939	भ्लक्ष्		940	भ्लाश्	
[1U]	√bhlakṣ		[1Ā]	√bhlāś	
	bhlakṣati	bhlakṣate		bhlāśate	
English	eat		English	shine,	glitter
Latin	Ø		Latin	Ø	
Greek	Ø		Greek	Ø	
Sanskrit	Ø		Sanskrit	Ø	

941	भ्लाश्		942	मक्ष्	
[4Ā]	√bhlāś		[1P]	√makṣ	
	bhlāśyate			makṣati	
English	shine,	glitter	English	collect,	heap
Latin	Ø		Latin	Ø	
Greek	Ø		Greek	Ø	
Sanskrit	Ø		Sanskrit	Ø	

943	मख्		944	मङ्क्	
[1P]	√makh		[1Ā]	√maṅk	
	makhati			maṅkate	
English	go, move		English	move,	adorn
Latin	Ø		Latin	Ø	
Greek	Ø		Greek	Ø	
Sanskrit	Ø		Sanskrit	Ø	

945	मङ्ख्		939	[1U]	bhlakṣ
[1P]	√maṅkh		940	[1Ā]	bhlāś
	maṅkhati		941	[4Ā]	bhlāś
English	go, move		942	[1P]	makṣ
Latin	Ø		943	[1P]	makh
Greek	Ø		944	[1Ā]	maṅk
Sanskrit	Ø		945	[1P]	maṅkh

946	मङ्घ्			947	मङ्घ्	
[1P]	√maṅgh			[1Ā]	√maṅgh	
	maṅghati				maṅghate	
English	adorn,	decorate		English	go, begin	
Latin	Ø			Latin	Ø	
Greek	Ø			Greek	Ø	
Sanskrit	Ø			Sanskrit	Ø	

948	मच्			949	मज्ज्	
[1Ā]	√mac			[6P]	√majj	
	macate			W	majjati	
English	cheat			English	sink	
Latin	Ø			Latin	mergō	immerse
Greek	Ø			Greek	μίσγω (?)	mix
Sanskrit	Ø			Sanskrit	magna	sunk

950	मठ्			951	मण्	
[1P]	√maṭh			[1P]	√maṇ	
	maṭhati				maṇati	
English	grind,	dwell		English	sound,	murmur
Latin	Ø			Latin	Ø	
Greek	Ø			Greek	Ø	
Sanskrit	maṭha	hut, cottage		Sanskrit	maṇita	sound

952	मण्ड्			946	[1P]	maṅgh
[1P]	√maṇḍ			947	[1Ā]	maṅgh
W	maṇḍati			948	[1Ā]	mac
English	decorate		!	949	[6P]	majj
Latin	Ø			950	[1P]	maṭh
Greek	Ø			951	[1P]	maṇ
Sanskrit	maṇḍa	foam, froth		952	[1P]	maṇḍ

953	मद्			954	मन्	
[4P]	√mad			[4Ā]	√man	
W	mādyati			W	manyate	
English	exhilarate			English	think	
Latin	madeō	to be wet		Latin	meminī	remember
Greek	μαδάω	to be wet		Greek	μέμονἄ	to be minded
Sanskrit	mádana	intoxicating		Sanskrit	mánas	mind

955	मन्			956	मन्त्र्	
[8Ā]	√man			[10Ā]	√mantr	
W	manute			W	mantrayate	
English	think			English	deliberate	
Latin	moneō	remind		Latin	Ø	
Greek	μέμονἄ	to be minded		Greek	Ø	
Sanskrit	matí	thought, idea		Sanskrit	mantra	formula

957	मन्त्र्			958	मन्थ्	
[10P]	√mantr			[1P]	√manth	
W	mantrayati			W	mathati	
English	talk			English	shake	destroy
Latin	Ø			Latin	Ø	
Greek	Ø			Greek	μόθος (?)	battle din
Sanskrit	mantra	formula		Sanskrit	mantha	churning

959	मन्द्		!	953	[4P]	mad
[1Ā]	√mand		!	954	[4Ā]	man
W	mandate		!	955	[8Ā]	man
English	enjoy			956	[10Ā]	mantr
Latin	madeō	to be wet		957	[10P]	mantr
Greek	μαδάω	to be wet		958	[1P]	manth
Sanskrit	mandana	cheerful		959	[1Ā]	mand

960	मभ्र्			940	भ्लाश्	
[1P]	√mabhr			[1Ā]	√may	
	mabhrati				mayate	
English	go, move			English	go, move	
Latin	Ø			Latin	Ø	
Greek	Ø			Greek	Ø	
Sanskrit	Ø			Sanskrit	Ø	

962	मर्च्			963	मर्ब्	
[10P]	√marc			[1P]	√marb	
	marcayati				marbati	
English	sound, take			English	go, move	
Latin	Ø			Latin	Ø	
Greek	Ø			Greek	Ø	
Sanskrit	Ø			Sanskrit	Ø	

964	मर्व्			965	मल्	
[1P]	√marv			[1Ā]	√mal	
	marvati				malate	
English	go, move			English	hold,	possess
Latin	Ø			Latin	Ø	
Greek	Ø			Greek	Ø	
Sanskrit	Ø			Sanskrit	mali	possession

966	मश्			960	[1P]	mabhr
[1P]	√maś			961	[1Ā]	may
	maśati			962	[10P]	marc
English	sound	hum, buzz		963	[1P]	marb
Latin	Ø			964	[1P]	marv
Greek	Ø			965	[1Ā]	mal
Sanskrit	maśa	mosquito		966	[1P]	maś

No.	Root	No.	Root	No.	Root	No.	Root
806	puṇṭ	846	pruṣ	886	bṛh	926	bhraṃś
807	puṇḍ	847	pruṣ	887	bṛh	927	bhrakṣ
808	puth	848	preṅkh	888	bṛh	928	bhraṇ
809	punth	849	preṣ	889	beh	929	bhram
810	pur	850	proth	890	brū	930	bhram
811	purv	851	plakṣ	891	brū	931	bhrāj
812	purv	852	plih	892	bhakṣ	932	bhrāś
813	pul	853	plī	893	bhaj	933	bhrāś
814	pul	854	plu	894	bhañj	934	bhrej
815	pul	855	pluṣ	895	bhaṭ	935	bhreṣ
816	puṣ	856	pluṣ	896	bhaṭ	936	bhrī
817	puṣ	857	pluṣ	897	bhaṇ	937	bhruḍ
818	puṣ	858	psā	898	bhaṇḍ	938	bhrūṇ
819	puṣp	859	phakk	899	bhand	939	bhlakṣ
820	puṃs	860	phaṇ	900	bharts	940	bhlāś
821	pust	861	phal	901	bharts	941	bhlāś
822	pū	862	phel	902	bharv	942	makṣ
823	pū	863	baṇ	903	bhaṣ	943	makh
824	pūj	864	bad	904	bhas	944	maṅk
825	pūy	865	bandh	905	bhal	945	maṅkh
826	pṛ	866	barh	906	bhal	946	maṅgh
827	pṛ	867	barh	907	bhā	947	maṅgh
828	pṝ	868	bal	908	bhām	948	mac
829	pṝ	869	balh	909	bhās	949	majj
830	pṛc	870	balh	910	bhikṣ	950	maṭh
831	pṛth	871	baṃh	911	bhid	951	maṇ
832	pṛṣ	872	bāḍ	912	bhī	952	maṇḍ
833	pel	873	bādh	913	bhuj	953	mad
834	peṣ	874	biṭ	914	bhuj	954	man
835	pes	875	bil	915	bhū	955	man
836	pai	876	bil	916	bhūṣ	956	mantr
837	paiṇ	877	bis	917	bhṛ	957	mantr
838	pyā	878	bukk	918	bhṛjj	958	manth
839	pyāy	879	bukk	919	bhṛṃś	959	mand
840	pyai	880	buḍ	920	bhṛṃś	960	mabhr
841	praś	881	budh	921	bhṛś	961	may
842	prath	882	budh	922	bhṛś	962	marc
843	prā	883	bund	923	bheṣ	963	marb
844	prī	884	bus	924	bhyas	964	marv
845	pru	885	bust	925	bhraṃś	965	mal
						966	maś

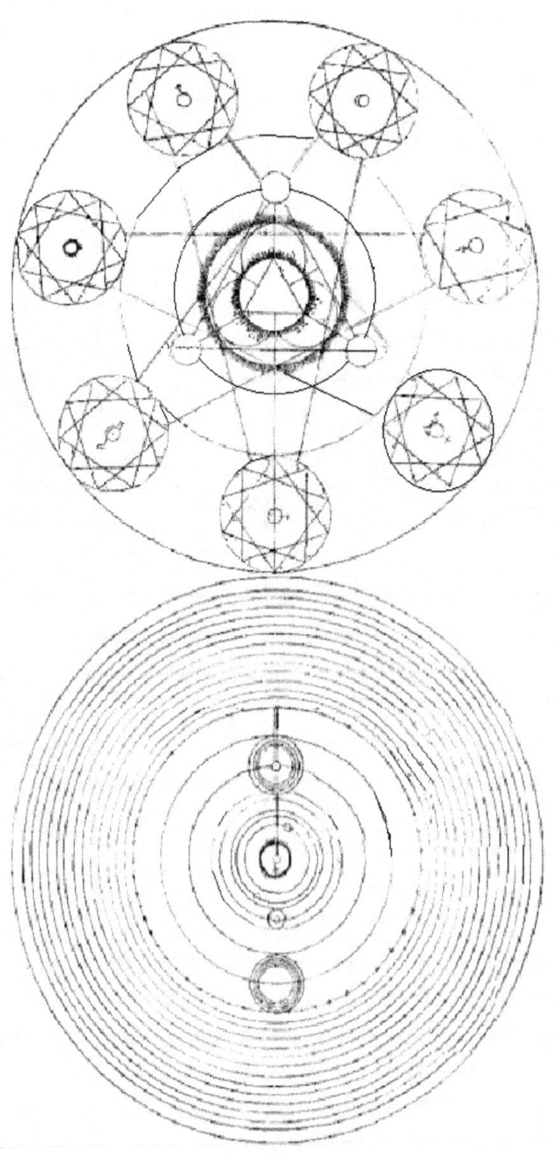

967	मष्			968	मस्	
[1P]	√maṣ			[4P]	√mas	
	maṣati				masyati	
English	hurt, injure			English	measure,	mete
Latin	Ø			Latin	Ø	
Greek	Ø			Greek	Ø	
Sanskrit	Ø			Sanskrit	masa	measure

969	मस्क्			970	मंह्	
[1Ā]	√mask			[1Ā]	√maṃh	
	maskate			W	maṃhate	
English	go, move			English	give	generously
Latin	Ø			Latin	Ø	
Greek	Ø			Greek	Ø	
Sanskrit	Ø			Sanskrit	maṃhana	gift

971	मह्			972	मा	
[1U]	√mah			[3Ā]	√mā	
W	mahati	mahate		W	mimīte	
English	honour, exalt	much		English	measure	
Latin	magnus	great		Latin	mētior	to measure
Greek	μέγας	great		Greek	μέτρον	measure
Sanskrit	mahá	mighty		Sanskrit	māti	measure

973	मा			967	[1P]	maṣ
[2P]	√mā			968	[4P]	mas
W	māti			969	[1Ā]	mask
English	measure			970	[1Ā]	maṃh
Latin	mētior	to measure		971	[1U]	mah
Greek	μέτρον	measure	!	972	[3Ā]	mā
Sanskrit	māti	measure	!	973	[2P]	mā

974	मा			975	माङ्क्षँ	
[3P]	√mā			[1P]	√māṅkṣ	
W	mimāti				māṅkṣati	
English	bellow, roar			English	wish,	desire
Latin	Ø			Latin	Ø	
Greek	μῐνῠρῐζω	hum, warble		Greek	Ø	
Sanskrit	māyu	bleating		Sanskrit	Ø	

976	मान्			977	मार्ग्	
[10P]	√mān			[1U]	√mārg	
W	mānayati			W	mārgati	mārgate
English	respect			English	search	
Latin	Ø			Latin	Ø	
Greek	Ø			Greek	Ø	
Sanskrit	māna	respect		Sanskrit	mārga	path, way

978	मार्ज्			979	माह्	
[10P]	√mārj			[1U]	√māh	
	mārjayati				māhati	māhate
English	cleanse,	purify		English	measure	
Latin	Ø			Latin	Ø	
Greek	Ø			Greek	Ø	
Sanskrit	mārjana	cleaning		Sanskrit	Ø	

980	मि		!	974	[3P]	mā
[5U]	√mi			975	[1P]	māṅkṣ
W	minoti	minute		976	[10P]	mān
English	attach,	measure	!	977	[1U]	mārg
Latin	Ø			978	[10P]	mārj
Greek	Ø			979	[1U]	māh
Sanskrit	mita	fixed		980	[5U]	mi

981	मिथ्			982	मिद्	
[1P]	√mith			[10P]	√mid	
W	methati			W	mindayati	
English	meet, pair			English	be fat	
Latin	mutō	move, alter		Latin	Ø	
Greek	Ø			Greek	Ø	
Sanskrit	mithas	mutually		Sanskrit	minna	obese

983	मिल्			984	मिश्	
[6P]	√mil			[1P]	√miś	
W	milati				meśati	
English	meet	someone		English	sound,	be angry
Latin	Ø			Latin	Ø	
Greek	Ø			Greek	Ø	
Sanskrit	milana	meeting		Sanskrit	Ø	

985	मिश्र्			986	मिष्	
[10P]	√miśr			[6P]	√miṣ	
W	miśrayati			W	miṣati	
English	mix, blend			English	open the	eyes
Latin	misceō	mix		Latin	Ø	
Greek	μίγνυμι	mix		Greek	Ø	
Sanskrit	miśrá	mixed		Sanskrit	Ø	

987	मिष्			981	[1P]	mith
[1P]	√miṣ			982	[10P]	mid
	meṣati		!	983	[6P]	mil
English	sprinkle,	moisten		984	[1P]	miś
Latin	Ø			985	[10P]	miśr
Greek	Ø		!	986	[6P]	miṣ
Sanskrit	Ø		!	987	[1P]	miṣ

988	मिह्			989	मी	
[1P]	√mih			[9P]	√mī	
W	mehati			W	mīnāti	
English	urinate,	rain		English	lessen,	destroy
Latin	meiō	urinate		Latin	minuō	lessen
Greek	όμείχω	urinate		Greek	μινύθω	reduce
Sanskrit	meha	urine		Sanskrit	pra-mīta	dead

990	मी			991	मी	
[5P]	√mī			[4Ā]	√mī	
W	minoti			W	mīyate	
English	lessen,	destroy		English	lessen,	destroy
Latin	minuō	lessen		Latin	minuō	lessen
Greek	μινύθω	reduce		Greek	μινύθω	reduce
Sanskrit	pra-mīta	dead		Sanskrit	pra-mīta	dead

992	मीम्			993	मील्	
[1P]	√mīm			[1P]	√mīl	
	mīmati			W	mīlati	
English	move,	sound		English	close the	eyes
Latin	minurrio	twitter, chirp		Latin	Ø	
Greek	μιμίζω	neigh		Greek	Ø	
Sanskrit	Ø			Sanskrit	mīlita	sleepy

994	मीव्		!	988	[1P]	mih
[1P]	√mīv			989	[9P]	mī
	mīvati			990	[5P]	mī
English	grow fat,	move		991	[4Ā]	mī
Latin	moveō	move		992	[1P]	mīm
Greek	Ø			993	[1P]	mīl
Sanskrit	mūta	moved		994	[1P]	mīv

995	मुच्			996	मुच्	
[1Ā]	√muc			[6P]	√muc	
	mocate			W	muñcati	
English	cheat			English	liberate	
Latin	mūcus	secretion		Latin	mūcus	secretion
Greek	μύσσομαι	blow nose		Greek	μύσσομαι	blow nose
Sanskrit	Ø			Sanskrit	múkti	liberation

997	मुज्			998	मुण्	
[1P]	√muj			[6P]	√muṇ	
W	mojati				muṇati	
English	sound,	cleanse		English	promise	
Latin	Ø			Latin	Ø	
Greek	Ø			Greek	Ø	
Sanskrit	Ø			Sanskrit	Ø	

999	मुण्ट्			1000	मुण्ठ्	
[1P]	√muṇṭ			[1Ā]	√muṇṭh	
	muṇṭati				muṇṭhate	
English	crush, grind			English	protect	run away
Latin	Ø			Latin	Ø	
Greek	Ø			Greek	Ø	
Sanskrit	Ø			Sanskrit	Ø	

1001	मुण्ड्		!	995	[1Ā]	muc
[1Ā]	√muṇḍ		!	996	[6P]	muc
	muṇḍate			997	[1P]	muj
English	cleanse,	shave		998	[6P]	muṇ
Latin	Ø			999	[1P]	muṇṭ
Greek	Ø			1000	[1Ā]	muṇṭh
Sanskrit	muṇḍa	shaved		1001	[1Ā]	muṇḍ

1002	मुण्ड्			1003	मुट्	
[1P]	√muṇḍ			[1P]	√muṭ	
	muṇḍati			W	moṭati	
English	cut			English	crush,	grind
Latin	Ø			Latin	Ø	
Greek	Ø			Greek	Ø	
Sanskrit	muṇḍa	shaved		Sanskrit	Ø	

1004	मुट्			1005	मुद्	
[6P]	√muṭ			[1Ā]	√mud	
W	muṭati			W	modate	
English	crush, grind			English	be happy	
Latin	Ø			Latin	Ø	
Greek	Ø			Greek	Ø	
Sanskrit	Ø			Sanskrit	mudā	pleasure, joy

1006	मुर			1007	मुर्व्	
[6P]	√mur			[1P]	√murv	
	murati				murvati	
English	encompass	entwine		English	bind, tie	
Latin	Ø			Latin	Ø	
Greek	Ø			Greek	Ø	
Sanskrit	mura	encompassing		Sanskrit	Ø	

1008	मुष्			1002	[1P]	muṇḍ
[9P]	√muṣ			1003	[1P]	muṭ
W	muṣṇāti			1004	[6P]	muṭ
English	steal		!	1005	[1Ā]	mud
Latin	mūs	mouse, rat		1006	[6P]	mur
Greek	μῦς	mouse		1007	[1P]	murv
Sanskrit	muṣita	stolen, robbed	!	1008	[9P]	muṣ

1009	मुस्त्			1010	मुह्	
[10P]	√must			[4P]	√muh	
	mustayati			W	muhyati	
English	gather,	collect		English	be confused	
Latin	Ø			Latin	Ø	
Greek	Ø			Greek	Ø	
Sanskrit	Ø			Sanskrit	móha	delusion

1011	मू			1012	मूर्छ्	
[1Ā]	√mū			[1P]	√mūrch	
	mavate			W	mūrchati	
English	bind, tie			English	harden	solidify
Latin	Ø			Latin	Ø	
Greek	Ø			Greek	βρότος	blood (wound)
Sanskrit	mūta	bound, basket		Sanskrit	mūrchā	stupor

1013	मूल्			1014	मूष्	
[1P]	√mūl			[1P]	√mūṣ	
	mūlati			W	mūṣati	
English	be rooted,	firm		English	steal	
Latin	Ø			Latin	mūs	mouse, rat
Greek	μῶλυ (?)	herb		Greek	μῦς	mouse
Sanskrit	mūla	root		Sanskrit	mūṣa	mouse, rat

1015	मे			1009	[10P]	must
[1Ā]	√me		!	1010	[4P]	muh
	mayate			1011	[1Ā]	mū
English	return,	exchange	!	1012	[1P]	mūrch
Latin	Ø			1012	[1P]	mūl
Greek	Ø			1014	[1P]	mūṣ
Sanskrit	Ø			1015	[1Ā]	me

1016	मेप्			1017	मेव्	
1016	मेप्			[1Ā]	√mev	
[1P]	√mep				mevate	
	mepati			English	worship,	serve
English	go			Latin	Ø	
Latin	Ø			Greek	Ø	
Greek	Ø			Sanskrit	Ø	

1018	मृ			1019	मुच्	
[6Ā]	√mṛ			[1P]	√mruc	
W	mriyate				mrocati	
English	die			English	go, move	
Latin	morior	die		Latin	Ø	
Greek	ἔμορτεν	die		Greek	Ø	
Sanskrit	mara	dying, death		Sanskrit	Ø	

1020	मृग्			1021	मृज्	
[4P]	√mṛg			[2P]	√mṛj	
W	mṛgyati			W	mārṣṭi	
English	chase, seek			English	wipe	
Latin	Ø			Latin	mulgeō	milk
Greek	Ø			Greek	ὀμόργνῡμῐ	wipe
Sanskrit	mṛga	forest animal		Sanskrit	mṛjā	cleaning

1022	मृज्			1016	[1P]	mep
[1U]	√mṛj			1017	[1Ā]	mev
W	mārjati	mārjate	!	1018	[6Ā]	mṛ
English	wipe			1019	[1P]	mruc
Latin	amurca	lees, dregs		1020	[4P]	mṛg
Greek	ὀμόργνῡμῐ	wipe	!	1021	[2P]	mrj
Sanskrit	mṛjā	cleaning	!	1022	[1U]	mṛj

1023	मृज्			1024	मृड्	
[6U]	√mṛj			[6P]	√mṛḍ	
	mṛjati	mṛjate		W	mṛḍati	
English	wipe			English	pardon	
Latin	mulgeō	milk		Latin	Ø	
Greek	ὁμόργνῡμῐ	wipe		Greek	Ø	
Sanskrit	mṛjā	cleaning		Sanskrit	mṛḍa	gracious

1025	मृद्			1026	मृद्	
[9P]	√mṛd			[1U]	√mṛd	
W	mṛdnāti			W	mardati	mardate
English	crush			English	crush	
Latin	mordeō	bite		Latin	mordeō	bite
Greek	σμερδνός	terrible		Greek	σμερδνός	terrible
Sanskrit	marda	crushing		Sanskrit	márdana	crushing

1027	मृध्			1028	मृण्	
[1P]	√mṛdh			[6P]	√mṛṇ	
W	mardhati				mṛṇáti	
English	neglect			English	crush, kill	
Latin	Ø			Latin	Ø	
Greek	μαλθακός	weak, gentle		Greek	Ø	
Sanskrit	mṛddha	forsaken		Sanskrit	Ø	

1029	मृश्		!	1023	[6U]	mṛj
[6P]	√mṛś			1024	[6P]	mṛḍ
W	mṛśáti		!	1025	[9P]	mṛd
English	touch		!	1026	[1U]	mṛd
Latin	mulceō	stroke, graze		1027	[1P]	mṛdh
Greek	Ø			1028	[6P]	mṛṇ
Sanskrit	mṛṣṭa	touched	!	1029	[6P]	mṛś

1030	मृष्			1031	मोक्ष्	
[4P]	√mṛṣ			[10P]	√mokṣ	
W	mṛṣyati			W	mokṣayati	
English	forget			English	liberate	
Latin	Ø			Latin	Ø	
Greek	Ø			Greek	Ø	
Sanskrit	mṛṣā	deceit		Sanskrit	mokṣa	liberation

1032	मोक्ष्			1033	म्रक्ष्	
[1Ā]	√mokṣ			[1P]	√mrakṣ	
W	mokṣate			W	mrakṣati	
English	liberate			English	rub,	stroke
Latin	Ø			Latin	Ø	
Greek	Ø			Greek	Ø	
Sanskrit	mokṣita	liberated		Sanskrit	mrakṣa	rubbing

1034	म्ला			1035	म्लुच्	
[1P]	√mlā			[1P]	√mluc	
W	mlāyati			W	mlocati	
English	wilt			English	go, move	
Latin	Ø			Latin	Ø	
Greek	Ø			Greek	Ø	
Sanskrit	mlāni	depression		Sanskrit	Ø	

1036	म्लेच्छ्		!	1030	[4P]	mṛṣ
[1P]	√mlecch			1031	[10P]	mokṣ
W	mlecchati			1032	[1Ā]	mokṣ
English	stammer			1033	[1P]	mrakṣ
Latin	Ø		!	1034	[1P]	mlā
Greek	Ø			1035	[1P]	mluc
Sanskrit	mleccha	barbarian		1036	[1P]	mlecch

1037	म्लेट्			1038	म्लेव्	
[1P]	√mleṭ			[1Ā]	√mlev	
	mleṭati				mlevate	
English	be mad			English	serve,	worship
Latin	Ø			Latin	Ø	
Greek	Ø			Greek	Ø	
Sanskrit	Ø			Sanskrit	Ø	

1039	म्लै			1040	यक्ष्	
[1P]	√mlai			[1U]	√yakṣ	
	mlāyati				yákṣati	yákṣate
English	fade, wither			English	be quick	
Latin	Ø			Latin	Ø	
Greek	Ø			Greek	Ø	
Sanskrit	mlāna	faded		Sanskrit	yakṣa	ghost, spirit

1041	यक्ष्			1042	यज्	
[10Ā]	√yakṣ			[1U]	√yaj	
	yakṣayate			W	yajati	yajate
English	worship,	honour		English	sacrify	
Latin	Ø			Latin	Ø	
Greek	Ø			Greek	ἄζομαι	reverence
Sanskrit	Ø			Sanskrit	yája	sacrifice

1043	यत्			1037	[1P]	mleṭ
[1Ā]	√yat			1038	[1Ā]	mlev
W	yatate			1039	[1P]	mlai
English	join, rival			1040	[1U]	yakṣ
Latin	nītor	brace oneself		1041	[10Ā]	yakṣ
Greek	ὅσιος	pious, hallowed	!	1042	[1U]	yaj
Sanskrit	yatana	exercise	!	1043	[1Ā]	yat

1044	यन्त्र्			1045	यभ्	
[10P]	√yantr			[1P]	√yabh	
	yantrayati			W	yabhati	
English	restrain,	bind		English	copulate	
Latin	Ø			Latin	Ø	
Greek	Ø			Greek	οἴφω	copulate
Sanskrit	yantra	barrier		Sanskrit	yabhana	copulation

1046	यम्			1047	यस्	
[1U]	√yam			[4P]	√yas	
W	yacchati	yacchate		W	yasyati	
English	hold up			English	warm up	
Latin	Ø			Latin	Ø	
Greek	Ø			Greek	ζέω	boil, heat
Sanskrit	yáma	restraint		Sanskrit	yasya	endeavoured

1048	या			1049	याच्	
[2P]	√yā			[1U]	√yāc	
W	yāti			W	yācati	yācate
English	go, proceed			English	ask, beg	
Latin	iānus	arcade		Latin	Ø	
Greek	Ø			Greek	Ø	
Sanskrit	yắna	carriage		Sanskrit	yācana	begging

1050	यौट्			1044	[10P]	yantr
[1P]	√yauṭ			1045	[1P]	yabh
	yauṭati		!	1046	[1U]	yam
English	fasten together	join		1047	[4P]	yas
Latin	Ø		!	1048	[2P]	yā
Greek	Ø		!	1049	[1U]	yāc
Sanskrit	yautra	tie, rope		1050	[1P]	yauṭ

1051	यु	
[2U]	√yu	
W	yauti	yute
English	join	
Latin	Ø	
Greek	Ø	
Sanskrit	yukta	joined

1052	यु	
[6U]	√yu	
W	yuvati	yuvate
English	join	
Latin	Ø	
Greek	Ø	
Sanskrit	yukta	joined

1053	यु	
[9U]	√yu	
W	yunāti	yunīte
English	join	
Latin	Ø	
Greek	Ø	
Sanskrit	yukta	joined

1054	यु	
[3P]	√yu	
W	yuyoti	
English	separate	
Latin	Ø	
Greek	Ø	
Sanskrit	Ø	

1055	यु	
[1P]	√yu	
W	yucchati	
English	separate	
Latin	Ø	
Greek	Ø	
Sanskrit	Ø	

1056	युङ्	
[1P]	√yuṅg	
	yuṅgati	
English	abandon,	desert
Latin	Ø	
Greek	Ø	
Sanskrit	Ø	

1057	युज्	
[7U]	√yuj	
W	yunakti	yuṅkte
English	join	yoke
Latin	iungō	join
Greek	ζεύγνῡμῐ	yoke
Sanskrit	yóga	yoking	!

1051	[2U]	yu
1052	[6U]	yu
1053	[9U]	yu
1054	[3P]	yu
1055	[1P]	yu
1056	[1P]	yuṅg
1057	[7U]	yuj

1058	युज्			1059	युत्	
[4P]	√yuj			[1Ā]	√yut	
W	yujyate				yotate	
English	join	yoke		English	shine	
Latin	iungō	join		Latin	Ø	
Greek	ζεύγνῡμῐ	yoke		Greek	Ø	
Sanskrit	yóga	yoking		Sanskrit	Ø	

1060	युध्			1061	युप्	
[4U]	√yudh			[4P]	√yup	
W	yudhyati	yudhyate			yupyati	
English	fight			English	obstruct,	disturb
Latin	Ø			Latin	Ø	
Greek	Ø			Greek	Ø	
Sanskrit	yuddha	fought		Sanskrit	Ø	

1062	येष्			1063	येष्	
[1P]	√yeṣ			[1Ā]	√yeṣ	
	yéṣati				yéṣate	
English	boil up,	bubble		English	endeavour,	try
Latin	Ø			Latin	Ø	
Greek	Ø			Greek	Ø	
Sanskrit	Ø			Sanskrit	Ø	

1064	रक्		!	1058	[4P]	yuj
[10P]	√rak			1059	[1Ā]	yut
	rākayati		!	1060	[4U]	yudh
English	taste, relish			1061	[4P]	yup
Latin	Ø			1062	[1P]	yeṣ
Greek	Ø			1063	[1Ā]	yeṣ
Sanskrit	Ø			1064	[10P]	rak

1065	रक्ष्			1066	रख्	
[1P]	√rakṣ			[1P]	√rakh	
W	rakṣati				rakhati	
English	protect			English	go, move	
Latin	arceō	ward off		Latin	Ø	
Greek	ἀλέξω	guard		Greek	Ø	
Sanskrit	rakṣa	guarding		Sanskrit	Ø	

1067	रग्			1068	रग्	
[1P]	√rag			[10P]	√rag	
	ragati			W	rāgayati	
English	doubt,	suspect		English	doubt,	suspect
Latin	Ø			Latin	Ø	
Greek	Ø			Greek	Ø	
Sanskrit	Ø			Sanskrit	Ø	

1069	रङ्ख्			1070	रङ्घ्	
[1P]	√raṅkh			[1Ā]	√raṅgh	
	raṅkhati				raṅghate	
English	go, move			English	hasten,	run
Latin	Ø			Latin	Ø	
Greek	Ø			Greek	Ø	
Sanskrit	raṅghas	haste, speed		Sanskrit	Ø	

1071	रच्		!	1065	[1P]	rakṣ
[10P]	√rac			1066	[1P]	rakh
	racayati			1067	[1P]	rag
English	produce	fashion		1068	[10P]	rag
Latin	Ø			1069	[1P]	raṅkh
Greek	Ø			1070	[1Ā]	raṅgh
Sanskrit	racana	arranging		1071	[10P]	rac

1072	रञ्ज्			1073	रञ्ज्	
[4U]	√rañj			[1U]	√rañj	
W	rajyati	rajyate		W	rajati	rajate
English	colour	oneself		English	colour	oneself
Latin	Ø			Latin	Ø	
Greek	ῥέζω	paint		Greek	ῥέζω	paint
Sanskrit	rakta	"blood"		Sanskrit	rañjana	colouring

1074	रट्			1075	रण्	
[1P]	√raṭ			[1P]	√raṇ	
W	raṭati			W	raṇati	
English	cry			English	rejoice	
Latin	Ø			Latin	Ø	
Greek	Ø			Greek	χάρμη	delight
Sanskrit	raṭita	shouting		Sanskrit	raṇa	pleasure

1076	रण्			1077	रद्	
[4P]	√raṇ			[1P]	√rad	
W	raṇyati			W	radati	
English	rejoice			English	scratch	
Latin	Ø			Latin	rōdō	bite, gnaw
Greek	χάρμη	delight		Greek	Ø	
Sanskrit	raṇa	delight		Sanskrit	rada	scratch

1078	रध्		!	1072	[4U]	rañj
[4P]	√radh		!	1073	[1U]	rañj
W	radhyati			1074	[1P]	raṭ
English	be conquered		!	1075	[1P]	raṇ
Latin	Ø		!	1076	[4P]	raṇ
Greek	Ø			1077	[1P]	rad
Sanskrit	raddha	subdued		1078	[4P]	radh

1079	रप्			1080	रफ्	
[1P]	√rap			[1P]	√raph	
	rápati				raphati	
English	talk			English	go, kill	
Latin	Ø			Latin	Ø	
Greek	Ø			Greek	Ø	
Sanskrit	rāpya	to be talked		Sanskrit	Ø	

1081	रभ्			1082	रम्	
[1Ā]	√rabh			[1U]	√ram	
W	rabhate			W	ramati	ramate
English	seize			English	rejoice	
Latin	Ø			Latin	Ø	
Greek	λᾰ́φῡρᾰ	war spoils		Greek	ἠρέμα	gently
Sanskrit	rabhas	violence, force		Sanskrit	ramaṇa	delightful

1083	रम्फ्			1084	रम्ब्	
[1P]	√ramph			[1Ā]	√ramb	
	ramphati				rámbate	
English	go, kill			English	hang	down
Latin	Ø			Latin	Ø	
Greek	Ø			Greek	Ø	
Sanskrit	Ø			Sanskrit	Ø	

1085	रम्ब्			1079	[1P]	rap
[1Ā]	√ramb			1080	[1P]	raph
	rambate			1081	[1Ā]	rabh
English	sound		!	1082	[1U]	ram
Latin	Ø			1083	[1P]	ramph
Greek	Ø			1084	[1Ā]	ramb
Sanskrit	Ø			1085	[1Ā]	ramb

1086	रय्		1087	रस्	
[1Ā]	√ray		[1U]	√ras	
	rayate		W	rasati	rasate
English	go		English	cry	
Latin	Ø		Latin	Ø	
Greek	Ø		Greek	Ø	
Sanskrit	Ø		Sanskrit	rasita	roar, scream

1088	रस्		1089	रह्	
[10P]	√ras		[1P]	√rah	
W	rasáyati		W	rahati	
English	taste, relish		English	abandon	
Latin	rōs	dew, moisture	Latin	Ø	
Greek	ἐξεράω	pour out	Greek	Ø	
Sanskrit	rasa	liquid, taste	Sanskrit	rahas	lonely place

1090	रंह्		1091	रा	
[1P]	√raṃh		[2P]	√rā	
W	raṃhati		W	rāti	
English	hasten		English	give	
Latin	Ø		Latin	rēs	property
Greek	ῥίμφᾰ	fast	Greek	Ø	
Sanskrit	raṃhas	speed	Sanskrit	rayí	property

1092	राख्			1086	[1Ā]	ray
[1P]	√rākh		!	1087	[1U]	ras
	rākhati		!	1088	[10P]	ras
English	be dry,	suffice	!	1089	[1P]	rah
Latin	Ø			1090	[1P]	raṃh
Greek	Ø			1091	[2P]	rā
Sanskrit	Ø			1092	[1P]	rākh

1093	राज्			1094	राध्	
[1U]	√rāj			[5P]	√rādh	
W	rājati	rājate		W	rādhnoti	
English	shine, rule			English	reach	
Latin	rēx	king, ruler		Latin	Ø	
Greek	Ø			Greek	Ø	
Sanskrit	rājan	king		Sanskrit	rāddhi	accomplishmnt

1095	राध्			1096	रि	
[4P]	√rādh			[9P]	√ri	
W	rādhyati			W	riṇāti	
English	reach,	accomplish		English	release	
Latin	Ø			Latin	rīvus	brook, stream
Greek	Ø			Greek	Ø	
Sanskrit	rāddhi	success		Sanskrit	rīṇa	dissolved

1097	रि			1098	रिङ्ख्	
[4Ā]	√ri			[1P]	√riṅkh	
W	rīyate				riṅkhati	
English	release			English	move,	crawl
Latin	rīvus	brook, stream		Latin	Ø	
Greek	Ø			Greek	Ø	
Sanskrit	rīti	motion, course		Sanskrit	riṅkhaṇa	crawling

1099	रिङ्ग्		!	1093	[1U]	rāj
[1P]	√riṅg		!	1094	[5P]	rādh
W	riṅgati		!	1095	[4P]	rādh
English	go, crawl			1096	[9P]	ri
Latin	Ø			1097	[4Ā]	ri
Greek	Ø			1098	[1P]	riṅkh
Sanskrit	riṅgi	going, motion		1099	[1P]	riṅg

1100	रिच्			1101	रिच्	
[4Ā]	√ric			[7U]	√ric	
	ricyate				riṇakti	riṅkte
English	abandon,	release		English	abandon,	release
Latin	linquō	leave		Latin	linquō	leave
Greek	λειπω	leave		Greek	λειπω	leave
Sanskrit	riktá	empty		Sanskrit	riktá	empty

1102	रिण्व्			1103	रिफ्	
[1P]	√riṇv			[6P]	√riph	
	riṇvati				riphati	
English	go			English	speak,	fight
Latin	Ø			Latin	Ø	
Greek	Ø			Greek	Ø	
Sanskrit	Ø			Sanskrit	repha	a word

1104	रिश्			1105	रिष्	
[6P]	√riś			[4U]	√riṣ	
	riśáti			W	riṣyati	riṣyate
English	hurt, tear			English	suffer a loss	
Latin	Ø			Latin	Ø	
Greek	Ø			Greek	Ø	
Sanskrit	riśa	enemy		Sanskrit	riṣṭa	injured

1106	री					
[4P]	√rī		!	1100	[4Ā]	ric
	riṇā́ti		!	1101	[7U]	ric
English	release			1102	[1P]	riṇv
Latin	rīvus	brook, stream		1103	[6P]	riph
Greek	Ø			1104	[6P]	riś
Sanskrit	rīti	going, motion	!	1105	[4U]	riṣ
				1106	[4P]	rī

1107	रु			1108	रुच्	
[2P]	√ru			[1Ā]	√ruc	
W	rauti			W	rocate	
English	make noise			English	shine	
Latin	raucus	hoarse		Latin	lūx	light
Greek	ὠρύομαι	shout, howl		Greek	λευκός	shining
Sanskrit	ráva	roar, howl		Sanskrit	ruci	light

1109	रुज्			1110	रुट्	
[6P]	√ruj			[1Ā]	√ruṭ	
W	rujati				reṭate	
English	break			English	shine	
Latin	lugeō	mourn		Latin	Ø	
Greek	λὔγρός	mournful		Greek	Ø	
Sanskrit	rujā	fracture		Sanskrit	Ø	

1111	रुट्			1112	रुठ्	
[10P]	√ruṭ			[1Ā]	√ruṭh	
	roṭayati				roṭhate	
English	be angry,	speak		English	torment,	pain
Latin	Ø			Latin	Ø	
Greek	Ø			Greek	Ø	
Sanskrit	Ø			Sanskrit	Ø	

1113	रुठ्		!	1107	[2P]	ru
[1P]	√ruṭh		!	1108	[1Ā]	ruc
	roṭhati		!	1109	[6P]	ruj
English	strike down			1110	[1Ā]	ruṭ
Latin	Ø			1111	[10P]	ruṭ
Greek	Ø			1112	[1Ā]	ruṭh
Sanskrit	Ø			1113	[1P]	ruṭh

1114	रुण्ट्			1115	रुण्ठ्	
[1P]	√ruṇṭ			[1P]	√ruṇṭh	
	ruṇṭati			W	ruṇṭhati	
English	steel, rob			English	be idle,	steal
Latin	Ø			Latin	Ø	
Greek	Ø			Greek	Ø	
Sanskrit	Ø			Sanskrit	Ø	

1116	रुद्			1117	रुध्	
[1U]	√rud			[1P]	√rudh	
W	rodati	rodate		W	rodhati	
English	weep			English	grow	
Latin	rŭdō	roar, bray		Latin	līber	free
Greek	Ø			Greek	ἐλεύθερος	free
Sanskrit	rodana	weeping		Sanskrit	rodha	growing

1118	रुध्			1119	रुध्	
[7U]	√rudh			[6P]	√rudh	
W	ruṇaddhi	runddhe		W	rundhati	
English	stop, block			English	stop,	block
Latin	Ø			Latin	Ø	
Greek	Ø			Greek	Ø	
Sanskrit	ruddha	stopped		Sanskrit	ruddha	stopped

1120	रुप्			1114	[1P]	ruṇṭ
[4P]	√rup			1115	[1P]	ruṇṭh
W	rúpyati		!	1116	[1U]	rud
English	violate,	disturb	!	1117	[1P]	rudh
Latin	rumpō	break	!	1118	[7U]	rudh
English	reave	plunder	!	1119	[6P]	rudh
Sanskrit	Ø			1120	[4P]	rup

1121	रुश्			1122	रुष्	
[6P]	√ruś			[4Ā]	√ruṣ	
	ruśáti			W	ruṣyati	ruṣyate
English	hurt, injure			English	be irritated	
Latin	Ø			Latin	Ø	
Greek	Ø			Greek	λὔσσᾰ (?)	rage, fury
Sanskrit	ruśat	injuring		Sanskrit	ruṣṭa	irritated

1123	रुह्			1124	रुह्	
[1P]	√ruh			[6P]	√ruh	
W	rohati			W	ruhati	
English	grow			English	grow	
Latin	Ø			Latin	Ø	
Greek	Ø			Greek	Ø	
Sanskrit	róhaṇa	mounting		Sanskrit	ruha	mounted

1125	रूक्ष्			1126	रूप्	
[10P]	√rūkṣ			[10P]	√rūp	
	rūkṣayati				rūpayati	
English	be rough,	harsh		English	form,	figure
Latin	Ø			Latin	Ø	
Greek	Ø			Greek	Ø	
Sanskrit	rūkṣa	rough, dry		Sanskrit	rūpa	shape

1127	रूष्			1121	[6P]	ruś
[1P]	√rūṣ		!	1122	[4Ā]	ruṣ
	rūṣati		!	1123	[1P]	ruh
English	adorn,	cover	!	1124	[6P]	ruh
Latin	Ø			1125	[10P]	rūkṣ
Greek	Ø			1126	[10P]	rūp
Sanskrit	rūṣaṇa	covering		1127	[1P]	rūṣ

967	maṣ	1007	murv	1047	yas	1087	ras
968	mas	1008	muṣ	1048	yā	1088	ras
969	mask	1009	must	1049	yāc	1089	rah
970	maṃh	1010	muh	1050	yauṭ	1090	raṃh
971	mah	1011	mū	1051	yu	1091	rā
972	mā	1012	mūrch	1052	yu	1092	rākh
973	mā	1013	mūl	1053	yu	1093	rāj
974	mā	1014	mūṣ	1054	yu	1094	rādh
975	māṅkṣ	1015	me	1055	yu	1095	rādh
976	mān	1016	mep	1056	yuṅg	1096	ri
977	mārg	1017	mev	1057	yuj	1097	ri
978	mārj	1018	mṛ	1058	yuj	1098	riṅkh
979	māh	1019	mruc	1059	yut	1099	riṅg
980	mi	1020	mṛg	1060	yudh	1100	ric
981	mith	1021	mṛj	1061	yup	1101	ric
982	mid	1022	mṛj	1062	yeṣ	1102	riṇv
983	mil	1023	mṛj	1063	yeṣ	1103	riph
984	miś	1024	mṛḍ	1064	rak	1104	riś
985	miśr	1025	mṛd	1065	rakṣ	1105	riṣ
986	miṣ	1026	mṛd	1066	rakh	1106	rī
987	miṣ	1027	mṛdh	1067	rag	1107	ru
988	mih	1028	mṛṇ	1068	rag	1108	ruc
989	mī	1029	mṛś	1069	raṅkh	1109	ruj
990	mī	1030	mṛṣ	1070	raṅgh	1110	ruṭ
991	mī	1031	mokṣ	1071	rac	1111	ruṭ
992	mīm	1032	mokṣ	1072	rañj	1112	ruṭh
993	mīl	1033	mrakṣ	1073	rañj	1113	ruṭh
994	mīv	1034	mlā	1074	raṭ	1114	ruṇṭ
995	muc	1035	mluc	1075	raṇ	1115	ruṇṭh
996	muc	1036	mlecch	1076	raṇ	1116	rud
997	muj	1037	mleṭ	1077	rad	1117	rudh
998	muṇ	1038	mlev	1078	radh	1118	rudh
999	muṇṭ	1039	mlai	1079	rap	1119	rudh
1000	muṇṭh	1040	yakṣ	1080	raph	1120	rup
1001	muṇḍ	1041	yakṣ	1081	rabh	1121	ruś
1002	muṇḍ	1042	yaj	1082	ram	1122	ruṣ
1003	muṭ	1043	yat	1083	ramph	1123	ruh
1004	muṭ	1044	yantr	1084	ramb	1124	ruh
1005	mud	1045	yabh	1085	ramb	1125	rūkṣ
1006	mur	1046	yam	1086	ray	1126	rūp
						1127	rūṣ

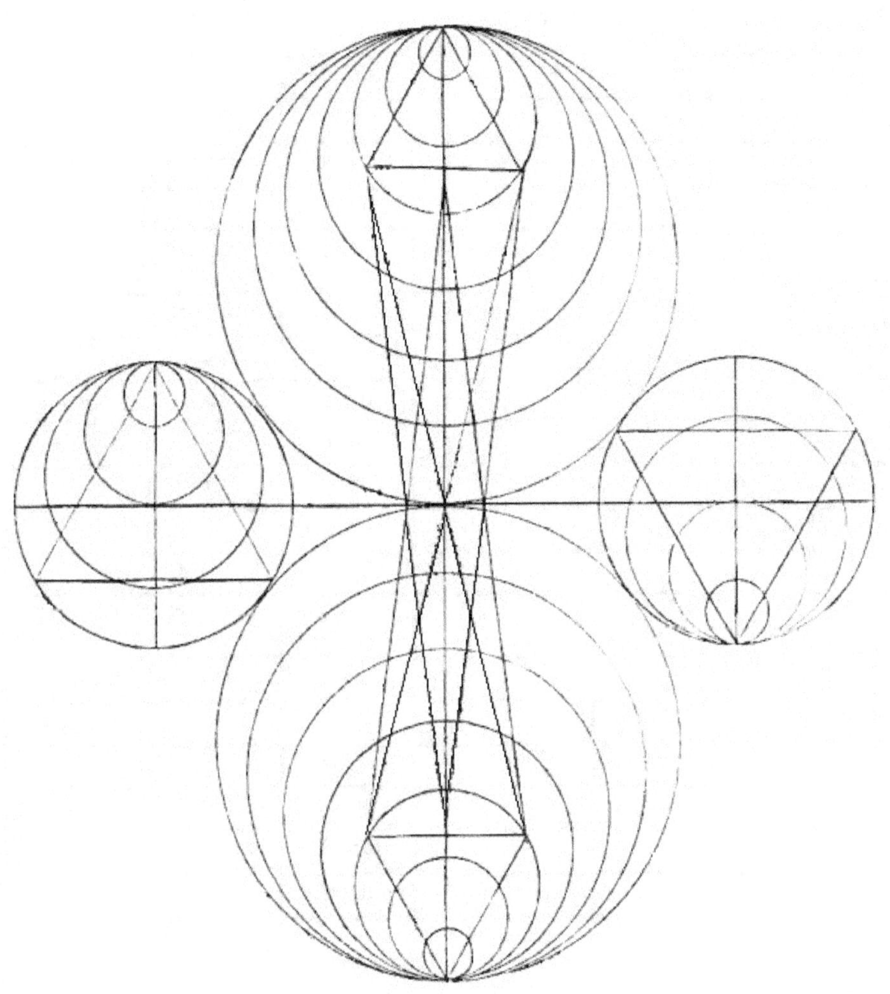

1128	रूष्			1129	रेक्	
[10P]	√rūṣ			[1Ā]	√rek	
	rūṣayati				rekate	
English	tremble,	burst		English	suspect,	doubt
Latin	Ø			Latin	Ø	
Greek	Ø			Greek	Ø	
Sanskrit	Ø			Sanskrit	reka	suspicion

1130	रेट्			1131	रेप्	
[1U]	√reṭ			[1Ā]	√rep	
	reṭati	reṭate			repate	
English	speak			English	go,	sound
Latin	Ø			Latin	Ø	
Greek	Ø			Greek	Ø	
Sanskrit	reṭi	harsh speech		Sanskrit	Ø	

1132	रेभ्			1133	रै	
[1P]	√rebh			[1P]	√rai	
	rébhati				ráyati	
English	crackle,	chatter		English	bark	
Latin	Ø			Latin	lātrō	bark
Greek	Ø			Greek	Ø	
Sanskrit	rebha	crackling		Sanskrit	Ø	

1134	रोड्			1128	[10P]	rūṣ
[1P]	√roḍ			1129	[1Ā]	rek
	roḍati			1130	[1U]	reṭ
English	be mad,	despise		1131	[1Ā]	rep
Latin	Ø			1132	[1P]	rebh
Greek	Ø			1133	[1P]	rai
Sanskrit	Ø			1134	[1P]	roḍ

1135	लक्ष्			1136	लक्ष्	
[1Ā]	√lakṣ			[1P]	√lakṣ	
W	lakṣate			W	lakṣati	
English	perceive			English	recognise	
Latin	Ø			Latin	Ø	
Greek	Ø			Greek	Ø	
Sanskrit	lakṣa	mark, sign		Sanskrit	lakṣmī	mark, sign

1137	लक्ष्			1138	लख्	
[10U]	√lakṣ			[1P]	√lakh	
	lakṣayati	lakṣayate			lakhati	
English	mark, sign			English	go, move	
Latin	Ø			Latin	Ø	
Greek	Ø			Greek	Ø	
Sanskrit	lakṣa	mark, sign		Sanskrit	Ø	

1139	लग्			1140	लङ्	
[1P]	√lag			[1P]	√laṅg	
W	lagati			W	laṅgati	
English	adhere to			English	limp	
Latin	Ø			Latin	langueō	be faint, weak
Greek	λάζομαι (?)	seize, grasp		Greek	λαγώς	hare
Sanskrit	lagna	adhered		Sanskrit	laṅga	limping

1141	लङ्घ्				1135	[1Ā]	lakṣ
[1U]	√laṅgh			!	1136	[1P]	lakṣ
W	laṅghati	laṅghate		!	1137	[10U]	lakṣ
English	jump over				1138	[1P]	lakh
Latin	Ø			!	1139	[1P]	lag
Greek	Ø				1140	[1P]	laṅg
Sanskrit	laṅghana	leaping over		!	1141	[1U]	laṅgh

1142	लज्ज्			1143	लट्	
[6Ā]	√lajj			[1P]	√laṭ	
W	lajjate			W	laṭati	
English	be ashamed			English	be childish	
Latin	Ø			Latin	lascīvus	wanton
Greek	Ø			Greek	λῑλαιομαι	desire
Sanskrit	lajjā	shame		Sanskrit	laṭa	speak foolishly

1144	लड्			1145	लड्	
[1P]	√laḍ			[10P]	√laḍ	
	laḍati				laḍayati	
English	play, sport			English	loll the	tongue
Latin	Ø			Latin	Ø	
Greek	Ø			Greek	Ø	
Sanskrit	laḍaha	beautiful		Sanskrit	laḍaha	beautiful

1146	लण्ड्			1147	लप्	
[10P]	√laṇḍ			[1P]	√lap	
	laṇḍayati			W	lapati	
English	throw,	speak		English	chatter,	prate
Latin	Ø			Latin	lāmentum (?)	wailing
Greek	Ø			Greek	Ø	
Sanskrit	Ø			Sanskrit	lapita	chattered

1148	लभ्		!	1142	[6Ā]	lajj
[1U]	√labh			1143	[1P]	laṭ
W	labhati	labhate		1144	[1P]	laḍ
English	seize			1145	[10P]	laḍ
Latin	Ø			1146	[10P]	laṇḍ
Greek	λᾰφῡρᾰ	war spoils	!	1147	[1P]	lap
Sanskrit	labdha	taken	!	1148	[1U]	labh

1149	लम्ब्			1150	लय्	
[1Ā]	√lamb			[1Ā]	√lay	
W	lambate				layate	
English	hang			English	go	
Latin	limbus	border, hem		Latin	Ø	
Greek	Ø			Greek	Ø	
Sanskrit	lamba	hanging down		Sanskrit	Ø	

1151	लर्ब्			1152	लल्	
[1P]	√larb			[1P]	√lal	
	larbati			W	lalati	
English	go			English	play	
Latin	Ø			Latin	Ø	
Greek	Ø			Greek	Ø	
Sanskrit	Ø			Sanskrit	lala	playful

1153	लश्			1154	लष्	
[10P]	√laś			[1P]	√laṣ	
	lāśayati			W	laṣati	
English	exercise an	art		English	desire	
Latin	Ø			Latin	Ø	
Greek	Ø			Greek	Ø	
Sanskrit	Ø			Sanskrit	laṣaṇa	desiring

1155	लष्		!	1149	[1Ā]	lamb
[4P]	√laṣ			1150	[1Ā]	lay
W	laṣyati			1151	[1P]	larb
English	desire		!	1152	[1P]	lal
Latin	Ø			1153	[10P]	laś
Greek	Ø			1154	[1P]	laṣ
Sanskrit	laṣita	desired		1155	[4P]	laṣ

1156	लस्			1157	ला	
[1P]	√las			[2P]	√lā	
W	lasati			W	lāti	
English	frolic, shine			English	take,	receive
Latin	lascīvus	wanton		Latin	Ø	
Greek	λῑλαίομαι	desire		Greek	Ø	
Sanskrit	lasa	brilliant		Sanskrit	lāta	taken

1158	लाञ्छ्			1159	लाभ्	
[1P]	√lāñch			[10P]	√lābh	
W	lāñchati				lābhayati	
English	indicate,	mark		English	throw,	direct
Latin	Ø			Latin	Ø	
Greek	Ø			Greek	Ø	
Sanskrit	lāñchana	stain, spot		Sanskrit	Ø	

1160	लिख्			1161	लिङ्	
[6P]	√likh			[1P]	√liṅg	
W	likhati				liṅgati	
English	scratch,	scrape		English	go	
Latin	rixa (?)	strife		Latin	Ø	
Greek	ἐρείκω	rend, break		Greek	Ø	
Sanskrit	lekha	line, stroke		Sanskrit	liṅga	mark, sign

1162	लिङ्		!	1156	[1P]	las
[10P]	√liṅg			1157	[2P]	lā
	liṅgayati			1158	[1P]	lāñch
English	paint,	variegate		1159	[10P]	lābh
Latin	Ø		!	1160	[6P]	likh
Greek	Ø			1161	[1P]	liṅg
Sanskrit	liṅga	mark, sign		1162	[10P]	liṅg

1163	लिप्			1164	लिश्	
[6P]	√lip			[6P]	√liś	
W	limpati			W	liśati	
English	smear,	anoint		English	go, move	
Latin	lippus	myopic		Latin	Ø	
Greek	λίπος	fat, lard		Greek	Ø	
Sanskrit	lipi	writing		Sanskrit	Ø	

1165	लिश्			1166	लिह्	
[4Ā]	√liś			[2U]	√lih	
	liśyate			W	leḍhi	līḍhe
English	lessen			English	lick	
Latin	Ø			Latin	lingō	lick
Greek	Ø			Greek	λείχω	lick
Sanskrit	liṣṭa	wasted		Sanskrit	liha	licked

1167	ली			1168	ली	
[4Ā]	√lī			[1Ā]	√lī	
W	līyate			W	layate	
English	adhere to			English	adhere to	
Latin	līmus	mud, slime		Latin	līmus	mud, slime
Greek	Ø			Greek	Ø	
Sanskrit	laya	lying down		Sanskrit	laya	lying down

1169	लुञ्च्		!	1163	[6P]	lip
[1P]	√luñc			1164	[6P]	liś
W	luñcati			1165	[4Ā]	liś
English	pluck		!	1166	[2U]	lih
Latin	runcō	weed, clear	!	1167	[4Ā]	lī
Greek	Ø		!	1168	[1Ā]	lī
Sanskrit	luñcita	plucked	!	1169	[1P]	luñc

1170	लुट्			1171	लुट्	
[1Ā]	√luṭ			[10P]	√luṭ	
	loṭate				loṭayati	
English	resist, suffer	pain		English	speak,	shine
Latin	Ø			Latin	Ø	
Greek	Ø			Greek	Ø	
Sanskrit	Ø			Sanskrit	Ø	

1172	लुठ्			1173	लुड्	
[6U]	√luṭh			[1P]	√luḍ	
W	luṭhati	luṭhate			loḍati	
English	roll			English	agitate,	move
Latin	Ø			Latin	Ø	
Greek	Ø			Greek	Ø	
Sanskrit	luṭhita	rolled down		Sanskrit	loḍita	agitated

1174	लुड्			1175	लुण्ट्	
[6P]	√luḍ			[1P]	√luṇṭ	
	luḍati				luṇṭati	
English	adhere,	cover		English	rob,	plunder
Latin	Ø			Latin	Ø	
Greek	Ø			Greek	Ø	
Sanskrit	Ø			Sanskrit	luṇṭita	robbed

1176	लुण्ट्			1170	[1Ā]	luṭ
[10P]	√luṇṭ			1171	[10P]	luṭ
	luṇṭayati		!	1172	[6U]	luṭh
English	despise			1173	[1P]	luḍ
Latin	Ø			1174	[6P]	luḍ
Greek	Ø			1175	[1P]	luṇṭ
Sanskrit	Ø			1176	[10P]	luṇṭ

1177	लुण्ठ्			1178	लुन्थ्	
[1P]	√luṇṭh			[1P]	√lunth	
W	luṇṭhati				lunthati	
English	rob,	plunder		English	strike,	hurt
Latin	Ø			Latin	Ø	
Greek	Ø			Greek	Ø	
Sanskrit	luṇṭhi	plundering		Sanskrit	Ø	

1179	लुप्			1180	लुभ्	
[6P]	√lup			[4P]	√lubh	
W	lumpati			W	lubhyati	
English	break			English	covet	
Latin	rumpō	break, burst		Latin	libido	desire, fancy
Greek	Ø			Greek	Ø	
Sanskrit	lupta	broken		Sanskrit	lubdha	greedy

1181	लुम्ब्			1182	लुम्ब्	
[1P]	√lumb			[10P]	√lumb	
	lumbati				lumbayati	
English	torment,	harass		English	be invisible	
Latin	Ø			Latin	Ø	
Greek	Ø			Greek	Ø	
Sanskrit	Ø			Sanskrit	Ø	

1183	लुल्			1177	[1P]	luṇṭh
[1P]	√lul			1178	[1P]	lunth
W	lolati		!	1179	[6P]	lup
English	sway		!	1180	[4P]	lubh
Latin	Ø			1181	[1P]	lumb
Greek	Ø			1182	[10P]	lumb
Sanskrit	lulita	moved	!	1183	[1P]	lul

1184	लुष्			1185	लू	
[1P]	√luṣ			[9U]	√lū	
	loṣati			W	lunāti	lunīte
English	rob, steal			English	cut off	
Latin	Ø			Latin	luō	expiate, pay
Greek	Ø			Greek	λύω	loosen, untie
Sanskrit	Ø			Sanskrit	lāva	cutting off

1186	लूष्			1187	लूष्	
[1P]	√lūṣ			[10P]	√lūṣ	
	lūṣati				lūṣayati	
English	adorn			English	hurt,	injure
Latin	Ø			Latin	Ø	
Greek	Ø			Greek	Ø	
Sanskrit	Ø			Sanskrit	Ø	

1188	लेप्			1189	लैण्	
[1Ā]	√lep			[1P]	√laiṇ	
	lepate				laiṇati	
English	go, serve			English	go, send	
Latin	Ø			Latin	Ø	
Greek	Ø			Greek	Ø	
Sanskrit	Ø			Sanskrit	Ø	

1190	लोक्			1184	[1P]	luṣ
[1Ā]	√lok		!	1185	[9U]	lū
W	lokate			1186	[1P]	lūṣ
English	see, look,	behold		1187	[10P]	lūṣ
Latin	lūcus	grove		1188	[1Ā]	lep
Greek	Ø			1189	[1P]	laiṇ
Sanskrit	loka	space		1190	[1Ā]	lok

1191	लोच्			1192	वक्ष्	
[1Ā]	√loc			[pft]	√vakṣ	
W	locate			W	vavakṣa	
English	see			English	grow	wax
Latin	lūceō	be light, clear		Latin	augeō	increase
Greek	Ø			Greek	αὔξω	increase
Sanskrit	locana	eye, sight		Sanskrit	vakṣaṇa	invigorating

1193	वख्			1194	वङ्क्	
[1P]	√vakh			[1Ā]	√vaṅk	
	vakhati				vaṅkate	
English	go, move			English	be crooked	
Latin	Ø			Latin	Ø	
Greek	Ø			Greek	Ø	
Sanskrit	Ø			Sanskrit	vaṅka	crookedness

1195	वङ्ख्			1196	वङ्घ्	
[1P]	√vaṅkh			[1Ā]	√vaṅgh	
	vaṅkhati				vaṅghate	
English	go, move			English	go, begin	
Latin	Ø			Latin	Ø	
Greek	Ø			Greek	Ø	
Sanskrit	Ø			Sanskrit	Ø	

1197	वच्			1191	[1Ā]	loc
[2P]	√vac			1192	[pft]	vakṣ
W	vakti			1193	[1P]	vakh
English	say			1194	[1Ā]	vaṅk
Latin	vōx	voice		1195	[1P]	vaṅkh
Greek	ὄψ	voice		1196	[1Ā]	vaṅgh
Sanskrit	vācana	chanting	!	1197	[2P]	vac

1198	वच्			1199	वज्	
[3P]	√vac			[1P]	√vaj	
W	vivakti				vajati	
English	say			English	go	
Latin	vōx	voice		Latin	Ø	
Greek	ὄψ	voice		Greek	Ø	
Sanskrit	vācana	chanting		Sanskrit	Ø	

1200	वज्			1201	वञ्च्	
[10P]	√vaj			[1P]	√vañc	
	vājayati			W	vañcati	
English	prepare the	way		English	totter,	stagger
Latin	Ø			Latin	con-vexus	arched
Greek	Ø			Greek	Ø	
Sanskrit	Ø			Sanskrit	vañcana	cheating

1202	वट्			1203	वट्	
[1P]	√vaṭ			[10P]	√vaṭ	
	vaṭati				vaṭayati	
English	surround			English	divide	
Latin	Ø			Latin	Ø	
Greek	Ø			Greek	Ø	
Sanskrit	vaṭa	Indian fig-tree		Sanskrit	vaṭa	Indian fig-tree

1204	वठ्		!	1199	[3P]	vac
[1P]	√vaṭh			1199	[1P]	vaj
	vaṭhati			1200	[10P]	vaj
English	be big, fat			1201	[1P]	vañc
Latin	Ø			1202	[1P]	vaṭ
Greek	Ø			1203	[10P]	vaṭ
Sanskrit	vaṭhara	stupid, dull		1204	[1P]	vaṭh

1205	वण्			1206	वण्ट्	
[1P]	√vaṇ			[1P]	√vaṇṭ	
	vaṇati				vaṇṭati	
English	sound			English	partition,	share
Latin	Ø			Latin	Ø	
Greek	Ø			Greek	Ø	
Sanskrit	vaṇa	sound, noise		Sanskrit	vaṇṭa	share

1207	वण्ट्			1208	वद्	
[10P]	√vaṇṭ			[1U]	√vad	
W	vaṇṭayati			W	vadati	vadate
English	partition,	share		English	talk	
Latin	Ø			Latin	Ø	
Greek	Ø			Greek	αὐδάω	speak
Sanskrit	vaṇṭa	share		Sanskrit	vadana	talking

1209	वन्			1210	वन्	
[1P]	√van			[8U]	√van	
W	vanati			W	vanoti	vanute
English	love, gain			English	love, gain	
Latin	venus	charm, love		Latin	venus	charm, love
Greek	Ø			Greek	Ø	
Sanskrit	vanita	loved, desired		Sanskrit	vanita	loved, desired

1211	वन्द्			1205	[1P]	vaṇ
[1Ā]	√vand			1206	[1P]	vaṇṭ
W	vandate			1207	[10P]	vaṇṭ
English	honour,	exalt	!	1208	[1U]	vad
Latin	Ø			1209	[1P]	van
Greek	Ø			1210	[8U]	van
Sanskrit	vandana	worship	!	1211	[1Ā]	vand

1212	वप्			1213	वप्	
[1P]	√vap			[1Ā]	√vap	
W	vapati			W	vapate	
English	shave			English	shave	oneself
Latin	Ø			Latin	Ø	
Greek	Ø			Greek	Ø	
Sanskrit	vapa	shaving		Sanskrit	vapa	shaving

1214	वप्			1215	वम्	
[1P]	√vap			[1P]	√vam	
W	vapati			W	vamati	
English	sow, scatter			English	vomit	
Latin	Ø			Latin	vomō	vomit
Greek	Ø			Greek	ἐμέω	vomit
Sanskrit	vapa	sower		Sanskrit	vama	vomiting

1216	वय्			1217	वर्च्	
[1Ā]	√vay			[1Ā]	√varc	
	vayate				varcate	
English	go			English	shine,	be bright
Latin	Ø			Latin	Ø	
Greek	Ø			Greek	Ø	
Sanskrit	Ø			Sanskrit	Ø	

1218	वर्ण्		!	1212	[1P]	vap
[10P]	√varṇ		!	1213	[1Ā]	vap
W	varṇayati		!	1214	[1P]	vap
English	paint,	describe	!	1215	[1P]	vam
Latin	Ø			1216	[1Ā]	vay
Greek	Ø			1217	[1Ā]	varc
Sanskrit	varṇa	cloak, tint		1218	[10P]	varṇ

1219	वर्ध्			1220	वल्	
[10P]	√vardh			[1Ā]	√val	
	vardhayati			W	valate	
English	cut, divide			English	turn to	
Latin	Ø			Latin	volvō (?)	roll, tumble
Greek	Ø			Greek	εἰλέω (?)	roll, turn
Sanskrit	vardha	cutting		Sanskrit	valita	turned round

1221	वल्			1222	वल्क्	
[1P]	√val			[10P]	√valk	
W	valati				valkayati	
English	turn to			English	speak	
Latin	volvō (?)	roll, tumble		Latin	Ø	
Greek	εἰλέω (?)	roll, turn		Greek	Ø	
Sanskrit	valita	turned round		Sanskrit	Ø	

1223	वल्ग्			1224	वल्भ्	
[1U]	√valg			[1Ā]	√valbh	
W	valgati	valgate			valbhate	
English	bound, leap			English	eat	
Latin	Ø			Latin	Ø	
Greek	Ø			Greek	Ø	
Sanskrit	valgana	jumping		Sanskrit	valbhita	eaten

1225	वल्ल्			1219	[10P]	vardh
[1P]	√vall		!	1220	[1Ā]	val
	vallate		!	1221	[1P]	val
English	be covered,	go		1222	[10P]	valk
Latin	Ø		!	1223	[1U]	valg
Greek	Ø			1224	[1Ā]	valbh
Sanskrit	Ø			1225	[1P]	vall

1226	वल्ह्			1227	वल्ह्	
[1Ā]	√valh			[10P]	√valh	
	valhate				valhayati	
English	speak, kill			English	speak,	shine
Latin	Ø			Latin	Ø	
Greek	Ø			Greek	Ø	
Sanskrit	Ø			Sanskrit	Ø	

1228	वश्			1229	वष्	
[2P]	√vaś			[1P]	√vaṣ	
W	vaṣṭi				vaṣati	
English	desire			English	hurt, kill	
Latin	Ø			Latin	Ø	
Greek	ἑκών	willing		Greek	Ø	
Sanskrit	vaśa	willing		Sanskrit	Ø	

1230	वस्			1231	वस्	
[1P]	√vas			[2Ā]	√vas	
W	vasati			W	vaste	
English	dwell			English	wear	
Latin	Ø			Latin	vestis	garment
Greek	ἄεσα	pass the night		Greek	εἷμα	garment
Sanskrit	vasati	dwelling		Sanskrit	vásana	clothing

1232	वस्			1226	[1Ā]	valh
[6P]	√vas			1227	[10P]	valh
W	ucchati		!	1228	[2P]	vaś
English	shine,	grow bright		1229	[1P]	vaṣ
Latin	Ø		!	1230	[1P]	vas
Greek	Ø		!	1231	[2Ā]	vas
Sanskrit	vasanta	spring	!	1232	[6P]	vas

1233	वस्क्			1234	वस्त्	
[1Ā]	√vask			[10Ā]	√vast	
	vaskate				vastayate	
English	go			English	waste,	hurt
Latin	Ø			Latin	Ø	
Greek	Ø			Greek	Ø	
Sanskrit	vaska	going, motion		Sanskrit	Ø	

1235	वह्			1236	वा	
[1P]	√vah			[2P]	√vā	
W	vahati			W	vāti	
English	carry,	transport		English	blow	
Latin	vehō	carry		Latin	ventus	wind
Greek	ὄχος	cart		Greek	ἄημι	blow
Sanskrit	vaha	bearing		Sanskrit	vāta	wind, air

1237	वा			1238	वाङ्क्ष्	
[4U]	√vā			[1P]	√vāṅkṣ	
W	vayati	vayate			vāṅkṣati	
English	weave			English	desire	
Latin	Ø			Latin	Ø	
Greek	Ø			Greek	Ø	
Sanskrit	Ø			Sanskrit	Ø	

1239	वाञ्छ्			1233	[1Ā]	vask
[1P]	√vāñch			1234	[10Ā]	vast
W	vāñchati		!	1235	[1P]	vah
English	desire		!	1236	[2P]	vā
Latin	Ø		!	1237	[4U]	vā
German	Wunsch	wish		1238	[1P]	vāṅkṣ
Sanskrit	vāñchaka	wishing	!	1239	[1P]	vāñch

1240	वावृत्			1241	वाश्	
[4Ā]	√vāvṛt			[4Ā]	√vāś	
	vāvṛtyate			W	vāśyate	
English	choose			English	low,	bleat
Latin	Ø			Latin	vāgiō (?)	wail
Greek	Ø			Greek	Ø	
Sanskrit	vāvṛtta	chosen		Sanskrit	vāśa	roaring

1242	वास्			1243	वाह्	
[10U]	√vās			[1Ā]	√vāh	
W	vāsayati	vāsayate			vāhate	
English	perfume			English	endeavour,	try
Latin	Ø			Latin	Ø	
Greek	Ø			Greek	Ø	
Sanskrit	vāsana	infusing		Sanskrit	vāhana	exertion

1244	विच्			1245	विज्	
[7U]	√vic			[6Ā]	√vij	
W	vinakti	viṅkte		W	vijate	
English	separate,	sift		English	rush,	recoil
Latin	victima	victim		Latin	Ø	
Greek	Ø			German	weichen	give way
Sanskrit	vikta	separated		Sanskrit	vega	speed

1246	विज्			1240	[4Ā]	vāvṛt
[6P]	√vij		!	1241	[4Ā]	vāś
W	vijati			1242	[10U]	vās
English	rush, recoil			1243	[1Ā]	vāh
Latin	Ø			1244	[7U]	vic
German	weichen	give way		1245	[6Ā]	vij
Sanskrit	vega	speed		1246	[6P]	vij

1247	विडम्ब्			1248	विडम्ब्	
[1Ā]	√viḍamb			[10P]	√viḍamb	
	viḍambate			W	viḍambayati	
English	imitate,	mock		English	imitate,	mock
Latin	Ø			Latin	Ø	
Greek	Ø			Greek	Ø	
Sanskrit	viḍamba	mockery		Sanskrit	viḍamba	mockery

1249	विद्			1250	विद्	
[2P]	√vid			[6P]	√vid	
W	vetti			W	vindati	
English	know			English	find	
Latin	videō	see, perceive		Latin	Ø	
Greek	οῖδα	know		German	weise	wise
Sanskrit	véda	true lore		Sanskrit	vedana	finding

1251	विद्			1252	विद्	
[2Ā]	√vid			[6Ā]	√vid	
W	vitte			W	vindate	
English	find			English	marry	
Latin	Ø			Latin	Ø	
Greek	Ø			Greek	Ø	
Sanskrit	vitta	acquired		Sanskrit	Ø	

1253	विद्			1247	[1Ā]	viḍamb
[7Ā]	√vid			1248	[10P]	viḍamb
W	vintte		!	1249	[2P]	vid
English	discuss		!	1250	[6P]	vid
Latin	Ø		!	1251	[2Ā]	vid
Greek	Ø		!	1252	[6Ā]	vid
Sanskrit	Ø		!	1253	[7Ā]	vid

1254	विध्			1255	विन्ध्	
[6P]	√vidh			[6Ā]	√vidh	
W	vidhati			W	vidhate	
English	worship,	offer		English	lack	
Latin	dīvidō	divide		Latin	vidua	widow
Greek	Ø			Greek	Ø	
Sanskrit	vidhi	worshipper		Sanskrit	vidhavā	widow

1256	विथ्			1257	विप्	
[1Ā]	√vith			[1Ā]	√vip	
	vethate			W	vepate	
English	ask, beg			English	tremble	
Latin	Ø			Latin	vibrō	shake, agitate
Greek	Ø			Greek	Ø	
Sanskrit	Ø			Sanskrit	vipina	stirring

1258	विल्			1259	विल्	
[6P]	√vil			[10P]	√vil	
	vilati				velayati	
English	cover,	conceal		English	throw,	cast
Latin	Ø			Latin	Ø	
Greek	Ø			Greek	Ø	
Sanskrit	Ø			Sanskrit	Ø	

1260	विश्			1254	[6P]	vidh
[6U]	√viś			1255	[6Ā]	vidh
W	viśati	viśate		1256	[1Ā]	vith
English	enter,	settle down	!	1257	[1Ā]	vip
Latin	vīcus	hamlet		1258	[6P]	vil
Greek	οῖκος	house		1259	[10P]	vil
Sanskrit	veśá	settler	!	1260	[6U]	viś

1261	विष्			1262	विष्	
[3P]	√viṣ			[1P]	√viṣ	
W	viveṣṭi			W	veṣati	
English	act			English	be quick	
Latin	vīrus	venom		Latin	vīrus	venom
Greek	ἰός	venom		Greek	ἰός	venom
Sanskrit	viṣa	poison		Sanskrit	viṣa	poison

1263	विष्क्			1264	वी	
[10P]	√viṣk			[2P]	√vī	
	viṣkayati			W	veti	
English	see,	perceive		English	approach	
Latin	Ø			Latin	Ø	
Greek	Ø			Greek	ἵεμαι	aspire
Sanskrit	Ø			Sanskrit	vītí	enjoyment

1265	वीज्			1266	वीड्	
[1P]	√vīj			[10P]	√vīḍ	
W	vījati			W	vīḍayati	
English	fan			English	reinforce	
Latin	Ø			Latin	Ø	
Greek	Ø			Greek	Ø	
Sanskrit	vījita	fanned		Sanskrit	vīḍu	strong, firm

1267	वीड्			1261	[3P]	viṣ
[10Ā]	√vīḍ			1262	[1P]	viṣ
W	vīḍayate			1263	[10P]	viṣk
English	be strong		!	1264	[2P]	vī
Latin	Ø			1265	[1P]	vīj
Greek	Ø			1266	[10P]	vīḍ
Sanskrit	vīḍita	strengthened		1267	[10Ā]	vīḍ

1268	वीर्			1269	वीर्	
[10Ā]	√vīr			[10P]	√vīr	
	vīráyate				vīrayati	
English	be powerful			English	overpower	
Latin	Ø			Latin	Ø	
Greek	Ø			Greek	Ø	
Sanskrit	vīra	hero, man		Sanskrit	vīra	hero, man

1270	वुण्ट्			1271	वृ	
[10P]	√vuṇṭ			[5U]	√vṛ	
	vuṇṭayati			W	vṛṇoti	vṛṇute
English	hurt, kill			English	cover	
Latin	Ø			Latin	operiō	cover, envelop
Greek	Ø			Greek	εἰλύω (?)	wrap, cover
Sanskrit	Ø			Sanskrit	vṛta	concealed

1272	वृ			1273	वृ	
[5P]	√vṛ			[1P]	√vṛ	
W	ūrṇoti			W	varati	
English	cover			English	cover	
Latin	operiō	cover, envelop		Latin	operiō	cover, envelop
Greek	εἰλύω (?)	wrap, cover		Greek	εἰλύω (?)	wrap, cover
Sanskrit	vṛta	concealed		Sanskrit	vṛta	concealed

1274	वृ			1268	[10Ā]	vīr
[9U]	√vṛ			1269	[10P]	vīr
W	vṛṇāti	vṛṇīte		1270	[10P]	vuṇṭ
English	chose		!	1271	[5U]	vṛ
Latin	volō	wish, want	!	1272	[5P]	vṛ
German	wollen	want	!	1273	[1P]	vṛ
Sanskrit	vara	choosing	!	1274	[9U]	vṛ

1275	वृक्			1276	वृक्ष्	
[1Ā]	√vrk			[1Ā]	√vrkṣ	
	varkate				vrkṣate	
English	take, seize			English	select,	accept
Latin	lupus	wolf		Latin	Ø	
Greek	λῠ́κος	wolf		Greek	Ø	
Sanskrit	vrka	wolf		Sanskrit	Ø	

1277	वृज्			1278	वृण्	
[7U]	√vrj			[8U]	√vrṇ	
W	vrṇakti	vrṅkte			vrṇoti	vrṇute
English	twist, bend			English	consume,	eat
Latin	vergō	turn, incline		Latin	Ø	
Greek	Ø			Greek	Ø	
Sanskrit	vrjina	bent, crooked		Sanskrit	Ø	

1279	वृण्			1280	वृत्	
[6P]	√vrṇ			[1Ā]	√vrt	
	vrṇati			W	vartate	
English	please,	gratify		English	turn	
Latin	Ø			Latin	vertō	turn
Greek	Ø			Greek	Ø	
Sanskrit	Ø			Sanskrit	vártana	rotation

1281	वृत्			1275	[1Ā]	vrk
[3P]	√vrt			1276	[1Ā]	vrkṣ
W	vavartti		!	1277	[7U]	vrj
English	turn, be			1278	[8U]	vrṇ
Latin	vertō	turn		1279	[6P]	vrṇ
Greek	Ø		!	1280	[1Ā]	vrt
Sanskrit	vártana	rotation	!	1281	[3P]	vrt

1282	वृध्			1283	वृश्	
[1Ā]	√vṛdh			[4P]	√vṛś	
W	vardhate				vṛśati	
English	grow			English	choose,	select
Latin	Ø			Latin	Ø	
Greek	Ø			Greek	Ø	
Sanskrit	vṛddhi	increase		Sanskrit	Ø	

1284	वृष्			1285	वृह्	
[1P]	√vṛṣ			[6P]	√vṛh	
W	varṣati			W	vṛhati	
English	rain			English	tear off	
Latin	Ø			Latin	Ø	
Greek	ἕρση	raindrops		Greek	Ø	
Sanskrit	varṣá	shower		Sanskrit	Ø	

1286	वे			1287	वेण्	
[1U]	√ve			[1P]	√veṇ	
	váyati	váyate			veṇati	
English	weave, plait			English	go, move	
Latin	Ø			Latin	Ø	
Greek	Ø			Greek	Ø	
Sanskrit	uta	woven		Sanskrit	Ø	

1288	वेन्		!	1282	[1Ā]	vṛdh
[1P]	√ven			1283	[4P]	vṛś
W	venati		!	1284	[1P]	vṛṣ
English	desire			1285	[6P]	vṛh
Latin	Ø			1286	[1U]	ve
Greek	Ø			1287	[1P]	veṇ
Sanskrit	vena	yearning		1288	[1P]	ven

1128	rūṣ	1168	lī	1208	vad	1248	viḍamb
1129	rek	1169	luñc	1209	van	1249	vid
1130	reṭ	1170	luṭ	1210	van	1250	vid
1131	rep	1171	luṭ	1211	vand	1251	vid
1132	rebh	1172	luṭh	1212	vap	1252	vid
1133	rai	1173	luḍ	1213	vap	1253	vid
1134	roḍ	1174	luḍ	1214	vap	1254	vidh
1135	lakṣ	1175	luṇṭ	1215	vam	1255	vidh
1136	lakṣ	1176	luṇṭ	1216	vay	1256	vith
1137	lakṣ	1177	luṇṭh	1217	varc	1257	vip
1138	lakh	1178	lunth	1218	varṇ	1258	vil
1139	lag	1179	lup	1219	vardh	1259	vil
1140	laṅg	1180	lubh	1220	val	1260	viś
1141	laṅgh	1181	lumb	1221	val	1261	viṣ
1142	lajj	1182	lumb	1222	valk	1262	viṣ
1143	laṭ	1183	lul	1223	valg	1263	viṣk
1144	laḍ	1184	luṣ	1224	valbh	1264	vī
1145	laḍ	1185	lū	1225	vall	1265	vīj
1146	laṇḍ	1186	lūṣ	1226	valh	1266	vīḍ
1147	lap	1187	lūṣ	1227	valh	1267	vīḍ
1148	labh	1188	lep	1228	vaś	1268	vīr
1149	lamb	1189	laiṇ	1229	vaṣ	1269	vīr
1150	lay	1190	lok	1230	vas	1270	vuṇṭ
1151	larb	1191	loc	1231	vas	1271	vṛ
1152	lal	1192	vakṣ	1232	vas	1272	vṛ
1153	laś	1193	vakh	1233	vask	1273	vṛ
1154	laṣ	1194	vaṅk	1234	vast	1274	vṛ
1155	laṣ	1195	vaṅkh	1235	vah	1275	vṛk
1156	las	1196	vaṅgh	1236	vā	1276	vṛkṣ
1157	lā	1197	vac	1237	vā	1277	vṛj
1158	lāñch	1198	vac	1238	vāṅkṣ	1278	vṛṇ
1159	lābh	1199	vaj	1239	vāñch	1279	vṛṇ
1160	likh	1200	vaj	1240	vāvṛt	1280	vṛt
1161	liṅg	1201	vañc	1241	vāś	1281	vṛt
1162	liṅg	1202	vaṭ	1242	vās	1282	vṛdh
1163	lip	1203	vaṭ	1243	vāh	1283	vṛś
1164	liś	1204	vaṭh	1244	vic	1284	vṛṣ
1165	liś	1205	vaṇ	1245	vij	1285	vṛh
1166	lih	1206	vaṇṭ	1246	vij	1286	ve
1167	lī	1207	vaṇṭ	1247	viḍamb	1287	veṇ
						1288	ven

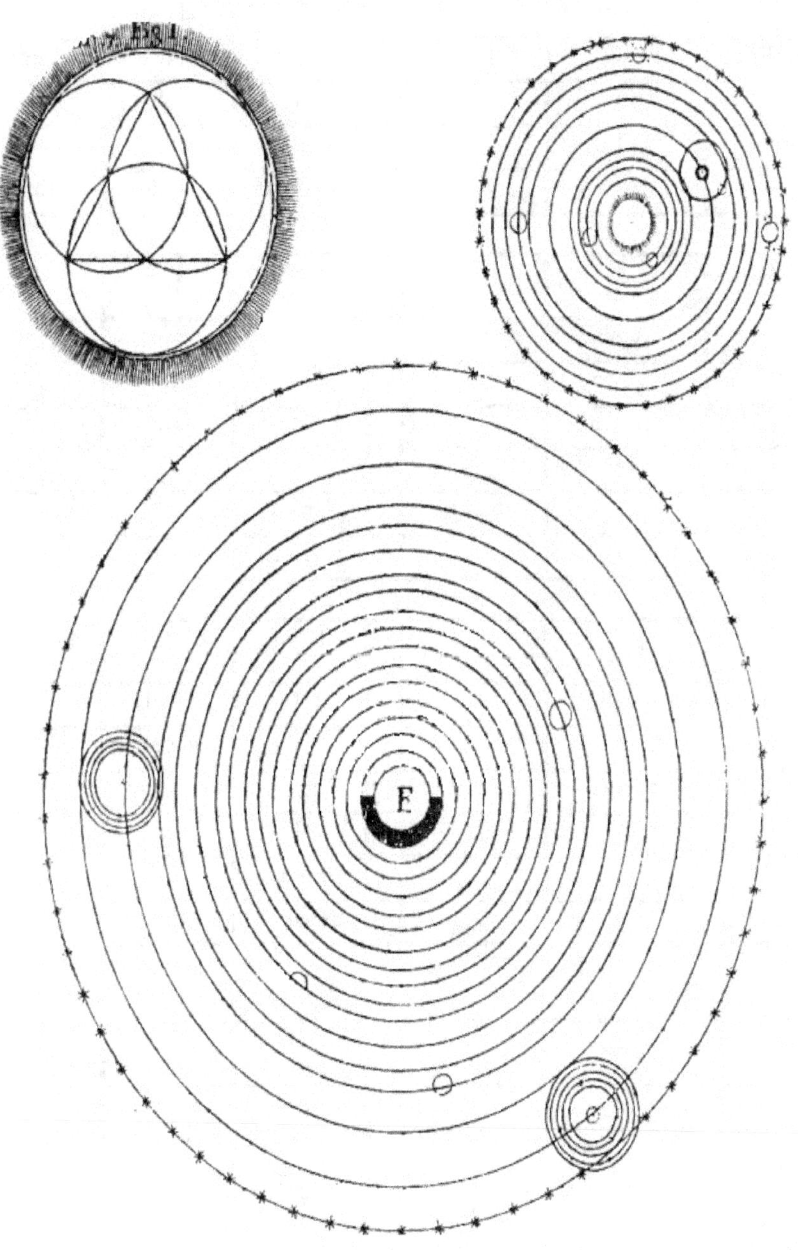

1289	वेल्			1290	वेल्	
[1P]	√vel			[10P]	√vel	
	velati				velayati	
English	move,	shake		English	count the	time
Latin	Ø			Latin	Ø	
Greek	Ø			Greek	Ø	
Sanskrit	Ø			Sanskrit	velā	limit

1291	वेवी			1292	वेष्ट्	
[2Ā]	√vevī			[1P]	√veṣṭ	
	vevīte			W	veṣṭate	
English	go, pervade			English	wind,	wrap
Latin	Ø			Latin	Ø	
Greek	Ø			Greek	Ø	
Sanskrit	Ø			Sanskrit	veṣṭita	enveloped

1293	वेह्			1294	वै	
[1Ā]	√veh			[1P]	√vai	
	vehate			W	vā́yati	
English	strive,	make effort		English	become	weary
Latin	Ø			Latin	Ø	
Greek	Ø			Greek	Ø	
Sanskrit	Ø			Sanskrit	Ø	

1295	व्यच्			1289	[1P]	vel
[3P]	√vyac			1290	[10P]	vel
W	vivyakti			1291	[2Ā]	vevī
English	encompass		!	1292	[1P]	veṣṭ
Latin	Ø			1293	[1Ā]	veh
Greek	Ø			1294	[1P]	vai
Sanskrit	vyacas	wide space		1295	[3P]	vyac

1296	व्यथ्			1297	व्यध्	
[1U]	√vyath			[4P]	√vyadh	
W	vyathati	vyathate		W	vidhyati	
English	tremble			English	pierce	
Latin	Ø			Latin	Ø	
Greek	Ø			Greek	Ø	
Sanskrit	vyathā	agitation		Sanskrit	vyadhā	bleeding

1298	व्यय्			1299	व्यय्	
[1U]	√vyay			[10P]	√vyay	
	vyayati	vyayate			vyayayati	
English	expend			English	go, move	
Latin	Ø			Latin	Ø	
Greek	Ø			Greek	Ø	
Sanskrit	vyaya	spending		Sanskrit	Ø	

1300	व्यय्			1301	व्या	
[10P]	√vyay			[1U]	√vyā	
	vyāyayati			W	vyayati	vyayate
English	throw, cast			English	cover	
Latin	Ø			Latin	Ø	
Greek	Ø			Greek	Ø	
Sanskrit	Ø			Sanskrit	Ø	

1302	व्युष्			!	1296	[1U]	vyath
[4P]	√vyuṣ			!	1297	[4P]	vyadh
	vyuṣati				1298	[1U]	vyay
English	burn,	divide			1299	[10P]	vyay
Latin	Ø				1300	[10P]	vyay
Greek	Ø				1301	[1U]	vyā
Sanskrit	vyuṣṭa	burnt			1302	[4P]	vyuṣ

1303	व्युष्			1304	व्ये	
[10P]	√vyuṣ			[1U]	√vye	
	vyoṣayati				vyáyati	vyáyate
English	reject,	discharge		English	cover	
Latin	Ø			Latin	vieō	bend, twist
Greek	Ø			Greek	Ø	
Sanskrit	Ø			Sanskrit	vyo-man	heaven, sky

1305	व्रज्			1306	व्रण्	
[1P]	√vraj			[1P]	√vraṇ	
W	vrajati				vraṇati	
English	graze, walk			English	sound	
Latin	Ø			Latin	Ø	
Greek	Ø			Greek	Ø	
Sanskrit	vraja	wandering		Sanskrit	Ø	

1307	व्रण्			1308	व्रण्	
[1P]	√vraṇ			[10P]	√vraṇ	
	vraṇati			W	vraṇayati	
English	wound			English	wound	
Latin	Ø			Latin	Ø	
Greek	Ø			Greek	Ø	
Sanskrit	vraṇa	wound		Sanskrit	vraṇa	wound

1309	व्रश्च्			1303	[10P]	vyuṣ
[6P]	√vraśc			1304	[1U]	vye
W	vṛścati		!	1305	[1P]	vraj
English	cut off,	down		1306	[1P]	vraṇ
Latin	Ø			1307	[1P]	vraṇ
Greek	ῥάκος (?)	wrinkles (pl)		1308	[10P]	vraṇ
Sanskrit	vraścana	cutting	!	1309	[6P]	vraśc

1310	निष्			1311	निष्	
[9P]	√vrī			[4Ā]	√vrī	
W	vrīṇāti			W	vrīyate	
English	choose			English	choose	
Latin	Ø			Latin	Ø	
Greek	Ø			Greek	Ø	
Sanskrit	vrīṇa	chosen		Sanskrit	vrīṇa	chosen

1312	व्रीड्			1313	व्रुड्	
[1Ā]	√vrīḍ			[6P]	√vruḍ	
W	vrīḍate			W	vruḍati	
English	be ashamed			English	cover,	sink
Latin	Ø			Latin	Ø	
Greek	Ø			Greek	Ø	
Sanskrit	vrīḍā	shame		Sanskrit	vruḍita	immersed

1314	व्ली			1315	शक्	
[9P]	√vlī			[5P]	√śak	
W	vlīnāti			W	śaknoti	
English	crush			English	be able to	
Latin	Ø			Latin	Ø	
Greek	Ø			German	behagen	delight, please
Sanskrit	vlīna	crushed		Sanskrit	śakti	power

1316	शक्			1310	[9P]	vrī
[4P]	√śak			1311	[4Ā]	vrī
W	śakyati		!	1312	[1Ā]	vrīḍ
English	be able to			1313	[6P]	vruḍ
Latin	Ø			1314	[9P]	vlī
German	behagen	delight, please	!	1315	[5P]	śak
Sanskrit	śakti	power	!	1316	[4P]	śak

1317	शङ्कू			1318	शच्	
[1Ā]	√śaṅk			[1Ā]	√śac	
W	śaṅkate				śacate	
English	suspect,	doubt		English	be strong,	say
Latin	cūnctor	delay		Latin	Ø	
Greek	Ø			Greek	Ø	
Sanskrit	śaṅka	doubt		Sanskrit	śacī	speech

1319	शट्			1320	शट्	
[1P]	√śaṭ			[10Ā]	√śaṭ	
	śaṭati				śāṭayate	
English	be sick,	weary		English	be sick,	weary
Latin	Ø			Latin	Ø	
Greek	Ø			Greek	Ø	
Sanskrit	Ø			Sanskrit	Ø	

1321	शठ्			1322	शठ्	
[10Ā]	√śaṭh			[10P]	√śaṭh	
	śāṭhayate				śaṭhayati	
English	praise,	flatter		English	speak ill	
Latin	Ø			Latin	scelus (?)	wicked
Greek	Ø			Greek	σκολἴός	curved, bent
Sanskrit	Ø			Sanskrit	śaṭha	deceitful

1323	शठ्		!	1317	[1Ā]	śaṅk
[10P]	√śaṭh			1318	[1Ā]	śac
	śaṭhayati			1319	[1P]	śaṭ
English	accomplish,	adorn		1320	[10Ā]	śaṭ
Latin	Ø			1321	[10Ā]	śaṭh
Greek	Ø			1322	[10P]	śaṭh
Sanskrit	Ø			1323	[10P]	śaṭh

1324	शठ्			1325	शठ्	
[1P]	√śaṭh			[10P]	√śaṭh	
	śaṭhati				śāṭhayati	
English	deceive,	hurt		English	be idle,	lazy
Latin	Ø			Latin	Ø	
Greek	Ø			Greek	Ø	
Sanskrit	śaṭha	deceitful		Sanskrit	Ø	

1326	शण्			1327	शण्	
[1P]	√śaṇ			[10P]	√śaṇ	
	śaṇati			W	śaṇayati	
English	give, go			English	give, go	
Latin	Ø			Latin	Ø	
Greek	Ø			Greek	Ø	
Sanskrit	Ø			Sanskrit	Ø	

1328	शद्			1329	शप्	
[1Ā]	√śad			[1U]	√śap	
W	śīyate			W	śapati	śapate
English	fall			English	curse,	swear
Latin	cadō (?)	fall		Latin	Ø	
Greek	Ø			Greek	Ø	
Sanskrit	śada	falling		Sanskrit	śāpa	spell, curse

1330	शब्द्			1324	[1P]	śaṭh
[10P]	√śabd			1325	[10P]	śaṭh
	śabdayati			1326	[1P]	śaṇ
English	make noise			1327	[10P]	śaṇ
Latin	Ø			1328	[1Ā]	śad
Greek	Ø		!	1329	[1U]	śap
Sanskrit	śabda	sound, noise		1330	[10P]	śabd

1331	शम्			1332	शम्ब्	
[4P]	√śam			[1P]	√śamb	
W	śāmyati				śambati	
English	work,	be calm		English	go	
Latin	Ø			Latin	Ø	
Greek	κάμνω	labour		Greek	Ø	
Sanskrit	śānti	peace		Sanskrit	Ø	

1333	शम्ब्			1334	शर्ब्	
[10P]	√śamb			[1P]	√śarb	
	śambayati				śarbati	
English	collect			English	go, kill	
Latin	Ø			Latin	Ø	
Greek	Ø			Greek	Ø	
Sanskrit	Ø			Sanskrit	Ø	

1335	शर्व्			1336	शल्	
[1P]	√śarv			[1P]	√śal	
	śarvati			W	śalati	
English	hurt, kill			English	jump	over
Latin	Ø			Latin	Ø	
Greek	Ø			Greek	Ø	
Sanskrit	Ø			Sanskrit	Ø	

1337	शव्		!	1331	[4P]	śam
[1P]	√śav			1332	[1P]	śamb
	śavati			1333	[10P]	śamb
English	go, change			1334	[1P]	śarb
Latin	Ø			1335	[1P]	śarv
Greek	Ø			1336	[1P]	śal
Sanskrit	Ø			1337	[1P]	śav

1338	शश्			1339	शष्	
[1P]	√śaś			[1P]	√śaṣ	
	śaśati				śaṣati	
English	jump			English	hurt, kill	
Latin	cānus	white, hoary		Latin	Ø	
Greek	Ø			Greek	Ø	
Sanskrit	śaśa	hare, rabbit		Sanskrit	Ø	

1340	शस्			1341	शा	
[1P]	√śas			[3U]	√śā	
W	śasati			W	śiśāti	śiśīte
English	cut, kill			English	sharpen	
Latin	castrō	amputate		Latin	catus	clever, sharp
Greek	Ø			Greek	κῶνος	pine cone
Sanskrit	śastra	sword		Sanskrit	śāṇa	whetstone

1342	शा			1343	शाख्	
[4P]	√śā			[1P]	√śākh	
W	śyati				śākhati	
English	sharpen			English	embrace,	pervade
Latin	catus	clever, sharp		Latin	Ø	
Greek	κῶνος	pine cone		Greek	Ø	
Sanskrit	śāṇa	whetstone		Sanskrit	Ø	

1344	शाड्			1338	[1P]	śaś
[1Ā]	√śāḍ			1339	[1P]	śaṣ
	śāḍate			1340	[1P]	śas
English	praise		!	1341	[3U]	śā
Latin	Ø		!	1342	[4P]	śā
Greek	Ø			1343	[1P]	śākh
Sanskrit	Ø			1344	[1Ā]	śāḍ

1345	शाल्			1346	शाल्	
[1Ā]	√śāl			[10Ā]	√śāl	
	śālate			W	śālayate	
English	shine			English	praise	
Latin	Ø			Latin	Ø	
Greek	Ø			Greek	Ø	
Sanskrit	śālita	distinguished		Sanskrit	Ø	

1347	शल्भ्			1348	शास्	
[1Ā]	√śalbh			[2P]	√śās	
	śalbhate			W	śāsti	
English	praise,	boast		English	punish,	govern
Latin	Ø			Latin	Ø	
Greek	Ø			Greek	Ø	
Sanskrit	Ø			Sanskrit	śāsana	punishing

1349	शास्			1350	शि	
[1P]	√śās			[3P]	√śi	
W	śāsati				śiśāti	
English	punish,	teach		English	grant,	bestow
Latin	Ø			Latin	Ø	
Greek	Ø			Greek	Ø	
Sanskrit	śiṣya	student		Sanskrit	śita	satisfied

1351	शि			1345	[1Ā]	śāl
[5U]	√śi			1346	[10Ā]	śāl
	śinoti	śinote		1347	[1Ā]	śalbh
English	sharpen		!	1348	[2P]	śās
Latin	Ø		!	1349	[1P]	śās
Greek	Ø			1350	[3P]	śi
Sanskrit	Ø			1351	[5U]	śi

1352	शिञ्ज्			1353	शिट्	
[2Ā]	√śiñj			[1P]	√śiṭ	
W	śiṅkte				śeṭati	
English	ring, tinkle			English	despise	
Latin	Ø			Latin	Ø	
Greek	Ø			Greek	Ø	
Sanskrit	śiñjā	tinkling		Sanskrit	Ø	

1354	शिष्			1355	शिल्	
[7P]	√śiṣ			[6P]	√śil	
W	śinaṣṭi				śilati	
English	leave			English	glean	
Latin	Ø			Latin	Ø	
Greek	Ø			Greek	Ø	
Sanskrit	śiṣṭa	left		Sanskrit	śila	gleaning

1356	शी			1357	शी	
[2Ā]	√śī			[1Ā]	√śī	
W	śete			W	śayate	
English	rest			English	rest	
Latin	Ø			Latin	Ø	
Greek	Ø			Greek	Ø	
Sanskrit	śayana	bed, couch		Sanskrit	śaya	resting

1358	शीक्			1352	[2Ā]	śiñj
[1Ā]	√śīk			1353	[1P]	śiṭ
W	śīkate		!	1354	[7P]	śiṣ
English	drizzle			1355	[6P]	śil
Latin	Ø		!	1356	[2Ā]	śī
Greek	Ø		!	1357	[1Ā]	śī
Sanskrit	śīkara	drizzle		1358	[1Ā]	śīk

1359	शिक्ष्			1360	शीभ्	
[1U]	√śikṣ			[1Ā]	√śībh	
	śíkṣati	śíkṣate			śībhate	
English	learn,	acquire		English	boast	
Latin	Ø			Latin	Ø	
Greek	Ø			Greek	Ø	
Sanskrit	śikṣaṇa	teaching		Sanskrit	Ø	

1361	शील्			1362	शुच्	
[1P]	√śīl			[1P]	√śuc	
W	śīlati			W	śocati	
English	practise			English	burn,	suffer
Latin	Ø			Latin	Ø	
Greek	Ø			Greek	Ø	
Sanskrit	śīla	conduct		Sanskrit	śúci	bright, pure

1363	शुच्			1364	शुच्य्	
[4U]	√śuc			[1P]	√śucy	
	śucyati	śucyate			śucyati	
English	be bright,	pure		English	distil	
Latin	Ø			Latin	Ø	
Greek	Ø			Greek	Ø	
Sanskrit	śúci	pure		Sanskrit	Ø	

1365	शुठ्		!	1359	[1U]	śikṣ
[1P]	√śuṭh			1360	[1Ā]	śībh
	śoṭhati			1361	[1P]	śīl
English	limp		!	1362	[1P]	śuc
Latin	Ø		!	1363	[4U]	śuc
Greek	Ø			1364	[1P]	śucy
Sanskrit	Ø			1365	[1P]	śuṭh

1366	शुठ्			1367	शुण्ठ्	
[10P]	√śuṭh			[1P]	√śuṇṭh	
W	śoṭhayati				śuṇṭhati	
English	be dull,	slow		English	limp,	be lame
Latin	Ø			Latin	Ø	
Greek	Ø			Greek	Ø	
Sanskrit	śoṭha	foolish		Sanskrit	Ø	

1368	शुण्ठ्			1369	शुध्	
[10P]	√śuṇṭh			[4U]	√śudh	
	śuṇṭhayati			W	śudhyati	śudhyate
English	become dry			English	purify	
Latin	Ø			Latin	Ø	
Greek	Ø			Greek	Ø	
Sanskrit	śuṇṭhī	dry ginger		Sanskrit	śodha	cleansing

1370	शुभ्			1371	शुभ्	
[1Ā]	√śubh			[1P]	√śubh	
W	śobhate			W	śobhati	
English	shine			English	shine	
Latin	Ø			Latin	Ø	
Greek	Ø			Greek	Ø	
Sanskrit	śubha	bright		Sanskrit	śubha	bright

1372	शुन्			1366	[10P]	śuṭh
[6P]	√śun			1367	[1P]	śuṇṭh
	śunati			1368	[10P]	śuṇṭh
English	go		!	1369	[4U]	śudh
Latin	Ø		!	1370	[1Ā]	śubh
Greek	Ø		!	1371	[1P]	śubh
Sanskrit	Ø			1372	[6P]	śun

1373	शुन्ध्			1374	शुन्ध्	
[1U]	√śundh			[4U]	√śundh	
	śundhati	śundhate			śudhyati	śudhyate
English	purify			English	be cleansed	
Latin	Ø			Latin	Ø	
Greek	Ø			Greek	Ø	
Sanskrit	śuddha	cleansed, pure		Sanskrit	śuddha	pure

1375	शुम्भ्			1376	शुष्	
[1P]	√śumbh			[1U]	√śuṣ	
W	śumbhati			W	śuṣyati	śuṣyate
English	wound, kill			English	dry out	
Latin	Ø			Latin	sūdus	dry
Greek	Ø			Greek	αὔω	dry, kindle
Sanskrit	Ø			Sanskrit	śuṣa	drying up

1377	शुल्क्			1378	शू	
[10P]	√śulk			[1P]	√śū	
	śulkayati			W	śvayati	
English	pay, give			English	swell	
Latin	ōs-cillum (?)	swing		Latin	inciēns	be pregnant
Greek	Ø			Greek	κυέω	be pregnant
Sanskrit	śulka	price, value		Sanskrit	śūna	swollen

1379	शूर्			1373	[1U]	śundh
[4Ā]	√śūr			1374	[4U]	śundh
	śūryate			1375	[1P]	śumbh
English	hurt, kill		!	1376	[1U]	śuṣ
Latin	Ø			1377	[10P]	śulk
Greek	Ø			1378	[1P]	śū
Sanskrit	Ø			1379	[4Ā]	śūr

1380	शूर्			1381	शूल्	
[10Ā]	√śūr			[1P]	√śūl	
	śūrayate				śūlati	
English	be powerful			English	cause	pain
Latin	Ø			Latin	Ø	
Greek	κύριος	master		Greek	Ø	
Sanskrit	Ø			Sanskrit	śūla	pike, spear

1382	शूल्			1383	श्रृध्	
[4U]	√śūl			[1U]	√śrdh	
	śūlyati	śūlyate		W	śardhati	śardhate
English	sound,	collect		English	defy,	mock
Latin	Ø			Latin	Ø	
Greek	Ø			Greek	Ø	
Sanskrit	Ø			Sanskrit	śardhamāna	mocking

1384	श्रृध्			1385	जुष्	
[1U]	√śrdh			[9U]	√śṝ	
	śárdhati	śárdhate		W	śṛṇāti	śṛṇīte
English	break wind			English	break	
Latin	Ø			Latin	Ø	
Greek	Ø			Greek	κεραΐζω	tear, destroy
Sanskrit	śṛddha	moistened		Sanskrit	śarāru	injurious

1386	शेल्			1380	[10Ā]	śūr
[1P]	√śel			1381	[1P]	śūl
	śelati			1382	[4U]	śūl
English	go			1383	[1U]	śrdh
Latin	Ø			1384	[1U]	śrdh
Greek	Ø			1385	[9U]	śṝ
Sanskrit	Ø			1386	[1P]	śel

1387	शेव्			1388	शौट्	
[1Ā]	√śev			[1P]	√śauṭ	
	śevate				śauṭati	
English	worship,	serve		English	be proud	
Latin	Ø			Latin	Ø	
Greek	Ø			Greek	Ø	
Sanskrit	Ø			Sanskrit	śauṭīra	arrogant

1389	शंस्			1390	श्चुत्	
[1P]	√śaṃs			[1P]	√ścut	
W	śaṃsati			W	ścotati	
English	show, tell			English	seep,	sprinkle
Latin	cēnseō	advise		Latin	Ø	
Greek	κῶμος	song		Greek	Ø	
Sanskrit	śaṃsa	recitation		Sanskrit	ścutita	sprinkled

1391	श्च्युत्			1392	श्मील्	
[1P]	√ścyut			[1P]	√śmīl	
W	ścyotati				śmīlati	
English	seep,	sprinkle		English	wink,	twinkle
Latin	Ø			Latin	Ø	
Greek	Ø			Greek	Ø	
Sanskrit	śścyutita	sprinkled		Sanskrit	śmīla	winking

1393	श्या			1387	[1Ā]	śev
[1P]	√śyā			1388	[1P]	śauṭ
W	śyāyati	śyāyate	!	1389	[1P]	śaṃs
English	freeze			1390	[1P]	ścut
Latin	Ø			1391	[1P]	ścyut
Greek	Ø			1392	[1P]	śmīl
Sanskrit	śyāna	coagulated		1393	[1P]	śyā

1394	श्यै			1395	श्रङ्कृ	
[1P]	√śyai			[1Ā]	√śraṅk	
	śyāyati				śraṅkate	
English	freeze			English	go, move	
Latin	Ø			Latin	Ø	
Greek	κιἐλλη (?)	mist, haze		Greek	Ø	
Sanskrit	śiśira	cool, chilly		Sanskrit	Ø	

1396	श्रण्			1397	श्रण्	
[1P]	√śraṇ			[10P]	√śraṇ	
	śraṇati			W	śrāṇayati	
English	give			English	give	
Latin	Ø			Latin	Ø	
Greek	Ø			Greek	Ø	
Sanskrit	Ø			Sanskrit	Ø	

1398	श्रथ्			1399	श्रन्थ्	
[9U]	√śrath			[9P]	√śranth	
W	śrathnāti	śrathnīte			śranthnāti	
English	become	loose		English	become	loose
Latin	Ø			Latin	Ø	
Greek	Ø			Greek	Ø	
Sanskrit	śrathana	untying		Sanskrit	śranthana	untying

1400	श्रम्			1394	[1P]	śyai
[4P]	√śram			1395	[1Ā]	śraṅk
W	śrāmyati			1396	[1P]	śraṇ
English	be tired			1397	[10P]	śraṇ
Latin	Ø			1398	[9U]	śrath
Greek	κρέμαμαι	hang		1399	[9P]	śranth
Sanskrit	śrama	weariness	!	1400	[4P]	śram

1401	श्रम्			1402	श्रम्भ्	
[1U]	√śram			[1P]	√śrambh	
W	śramati	śramate		W	śrambhate	
English	be tired			English	be careless	
Latin	Ø			Latin	Ø	
Greek	κρέμαμαι	hang		Greek	Ø	
Sanskrit	śramaṇa	toiling		Sanskrit	Ø	

1403	श्रा			1404	श्रा	
[4P]	√śrā			[9P]	√śrā	
W	śrāyati			W	śrīṇāti	
English	boil			English	boil	
Latin	Ø			Latin	Ø	
Greek	Ø			Greek	Ø	
Sanskrit	śrapaṇa	boiling		Sanskrit	śrapaṇa	cooking

1405	श्रि			1406	श्री	
[1U]	√śri			[9U]	√śrī	
W	śrayati	śrayate		W	śrīṇáti	śrīṇīté
English	rely on			English	mix, cook	
Latin	clīnō	bend, incline		Latin	Ø	
Greek	κλῑ́νω	bend, lean		Greek	κεράννυμι	mix, blend
Sanskrit	śrita	attached to		Sanskrit	śrīta	mixed

1407	श्रु		!	1401	[1U]	śram
[5U]	√śru			1402	[1P]	śrambh
W	śṛṇoti	śṛṇute		1403	[4P]	śrā
English	hear, learn			1404	[9P]	śrā
Latin	clueō	be called	!	1405	[1U]	śri
Greek	κλΰω	hear, listen	!	1406	[9U]	śrī
Sanskrit	ślóka	verse	!	1407	[5U]	śru

1408	श्रोण्			1409	श्लङ्कृ	
[1P]	√śroṇ			[1Ā]	√ślank	
	śroṇati				ślaṅkate	
English	collect,	accumulate		English	go, move	
Latin	Ø			Latin	Ø	
Greek	Ø			Greek	Ø	
Sanskrit	Ø			Sanskrit	Ø	

1410	श्लथ्			1411	श्लाख्	
[1U]	√ślath			[1P]	√ślākh	
W	ślathati	ślathate			ślākhati	
English	be free			English	pervade,	penetrate
Latin	Ø			Latin	Ø	
Greek	Ø			Greek	Ø	
Sanskrit	ślatha	loose, relaxed		Sanskrit	Ø	

1412	श्लाघ्			1413	श्लिष्	
[1Ā]	√ślāgh			[4U]	√śliṣ	
W	ślāghate			W	śliṣyati	śliṣyate
English	praise			English	adhere to	
Latin	Ø			Latin	Ø	
Greek	Ø			Greek	Ø	
Sanskrit	ślāghā	vaunt		Sanskrit	śliṣā	clinging

1414	जुष्			1408	[1P]	śroṇ
[1Ā]	√ślok			1409	[1Ā]	ślank
	ślokate			1410	[1U]	ślath
English	compose			1411	[1P]	ślākh
Latin	Ø		!	1412	[1Ā]	ślāgh
Greek	Ø		!	1413	[4U]	śliṣ
Sanskrit	Ø			1414	[1Ā]	ślok

1415	श्लोण्			1416	श्वङ्क्	
[1P]	√śloṇ			[1Ā]	√śvaṅk	
	śloṇati				śvaṅkate	
English	heap,	collect		English	go, move	
Latin	Ø			Latin	Ø	
Greek	Ø			Greek	Ø	
Sanskrit	Ø			Sanskrit	Ø	

1417	श्वस्			1418	श्वस्	
[2P]	√śvas			[1U]	√śvas	
W	śvasiti			W	śvasati	śvasate
English	blow, breathe	(wheeze)		English	blow, breathe	(wheeze)
Latin	querī	complain		Latin	querī	complain
Greek	Ø			Greek	Ø	
Sanskrit	śvasana	air, wind		Sanskrit	śvasana	air, wind

1419	श्वल्			1420	श्वल्क्	
[1P]	√śval			[10P]	√śvalk	
	śvalati				śvalkayati	
English	go quickly,	run		English	tell, narrate	
Latin	Ø			Latin	Ø	
Greek	Ø			Greek	Ø	
Sanskrit	Ø			Sanskrit	Ø	

1421	श्वि			1415	[1P]	śloṇ
[1P]	√śvi			1416	[1Ā]	śvaṅk
	śvayati		!	1417	[2P]	śvas
English	swell		!	1418	[1U]	śvas
Latin	inciēns	be pregnant		1419	[1P]	śval
Greek	κυέω	be pregnant		1420	[10P]	śvalk
Sanskrit	śvaya	swelling	!	1421	[1P]	śvi

1422	श्वित्			1423	श्विन्द्	
[1Ā]	√śvit			[1Ā]	√śvind	
W	śvetate				śvindate	
English	be white			English	be white	
Latin	Ø			Latin	Ø	
German	weiss	white		Greek	Ø	
Sanskrit	śvita	white		Sanskrit	Ø	

1424	ष्ठीव्			1425	ष्ठीव्	
[1P]	√ṣṭhīv			[4P]	√ṣṭhīv	
W	ṣṭhīvati			W	ṣṭhīvyati	
English	spit, spew			English	spit, spew	
Latin	spuo	spit, spew		Latin	spuo	spit, spew
Greek	πτύω	spit out		Greek	πτύω	spit out
Sanskrit	ṣṭhīvana	saliva		Sanskrit	ṣṭhyūta	expectorated

1426	ष्वष्क्			1427	सग्	
[1U]	√ṣvaṣk			[1P]	√sag	
	ṣvaṣkati	ṣvaṣkate			sagati	
English	go, move			English	cover	
Latin	Ø			Latin	Ø	
Greek	Ø			Greek	Ø	
Sanskrit	Ø			Sanskrit	Ø	

1428	सघ्			1422	[1Ā]	śvit
[5P]	√sagh			1423	[1Ā]	śvind
	saghnoti		!	1424	[1P]	ṣṭhīv
English	hurt, kill		!	1425	[4P]	ṣṭhīv
Latin	Ø			1426	[1U]	ṣvaṣk
Greek	Ø			1427	[1P]	sag
Sanskrit	Ø			1428	[5P]	sagh

1429	सच्			1430	सञ्ज्	
[1Ā]	√sac			[1P]	√sañj	
W	sacate			W	sajati	
English	familiar with			English	adhere	
Latin	sequor	follow		Latin	sēgnis (?)	slow, tardy
Greek	ἕπομαι	follow		Greek	Ø	
Sanskrit	saciva	companion		Sanskrit	sakta	adhering to

1431	सञ्ज्			1432	सद्	
[1Ā]	√sañj			[1P]	√sad	
W	sajjate			W	sīdati	
English	be attached to			English	be seated	
Latin	sēgnis (?)	slow, tardy		Latin	sedeō	sit, be seated
Greek	Ø			Greek	ἕζομαι	sit, be seated
Sanskrit	sakta	adhering to		Sanskrit	satta	seated

1433	सट्			1434	सट्ट्	
[1P]	√saṭ			[10P]	√saṭṭ	
	saṭati				saṭṭayati	
English	be a part of			English	hurt	
Latin	Ø			Latin	Ø	
Greek	Ø			Greek	Ø	
Sanskrit	Ø			Sanskrit	Ø	

1435	सत्र्			1429	[1Ā]	sac
[10Ā]	√satr		!	1430	[1P]	sañj
	satrayate		!	1431	[1Ā]	sañj
English	extend		!	1432	[1P]	sad
Latin	Ø			1433	[1P]	saṭ
Greek	Ø			1434	[10P]	saṭṭ
Sanskrit	Ø			1435	[10Ā]	satr

1436	सन्			1437	सप्	
[8P]	√san			[1P]	√sap	
W	sanoti			W	sapati	
English	obtain			English	follow	
Latin	Ø			Latin	sepeliō	bury, inter
Greek	ἀνύω	cause, effect		Greek	ἕπω	busy oneself
Sanskrit	sana	acquisition		Sanskrit	kéta-sáp	obedient

1438	सभाज्			1439	सम्	
[10P]	√sabhāj			[1P]	√sam	
	sabhājayati				samati	
English	serve,	honour		English	be disturbed	
Latin	Ø			Latin	Ø	
Greek	Ø			Greek	Ø	
Sanskrit	sabhājana	courtesy		Sanskrit	Ø	

1440	सम्			1441	सर्ब्	
[10P]	√sam			[1P]	√sarb	
W	samayati				sarbati	
English	be disturbed			English	go, move	
Latin	Ø			Latin	Ø	
Greek	Ø			Greek	Ø	
Sanskrit	Ø			Sanskrit	Ø	

1442	सल्			1436	[8P]	san
[1P]	√sal			1437	[1P]	sap
	salati			1438	[10P]	sabhāj
English	go, move			1439	[1P]	sam
Latin	Ø			1440	[10P]	sam
Greek	Ø			1441	[1P]	sarb
Sanskrit	Ø			1442	[1P]	sal

1443	सस्			1444	सह्	
[2P]	√sas			[1Ā]	√sah	
	sásti			W	sahate	
English	sleep			English	overcome	
Latin	Ø			Latin	harsh, strict	harsh, strict
Greek	Ø			Greek	ἔχω	possess
Sanskrit	sasa	sleeping		Sanskrit	sahana	powerful

1445	सह्			1446	सा	
[1P]	√sah			[4P]	√sā	
W	sahati			W	syati	
English	overcome			English	stop	
Latin	sevērus	harsh, strict		Latin	Ø	
Greek	ἔχω	possess		Greek	Ø	
Sanskrit	sahana	powerful		Sanskrit	Ø	

1447	साध्			1448	साध्	
[1U]	√sādh			[4P]	√sādh	
	sádati	sádate		W	sādhyati	
English	attain,	succeed		English	attain,	succeed
Latin	Ø			Latin	Ø	
Greek	ἰθύς (?)	straight		Greek	ἰθύς (?)	straight
Sanskrit	sādhaka	effective		Sanskrit	sādha	fulfilment

1449	साध्			1443	[2P]	sas
[5P]	√sādh		!	1444	[1Ā]	sah
	sādhnoti		!	1445	[1P]	sah
English	attain,	succeed	!	1446	[4P]	sā
Latin	Ø		!	1447	[1U]	sādh
Greek	ἰθύς (?)	straight	!	1448	[4P]	sādh
Sanskrit	sādhú	holy man	!	1449	[5P]	sādh

1289	vel	1329	śap	1369	śudh	1409	ślaṅk
1290	vel	1330	śabd	1370	śubh	1410	ślath
1291	vevī	1331	śam	1371	śubh	1411	ślākh
1292	veṣṭ	1332	śamb	1372	śun	1412	ślāgh
1293	veh	1333	śamb	1373	śundh	1413	śliṣ
1294	vai	1334	śarb	1374	śundh	1414	ślok
1295	vyac	1335	śarv	1375	śumbh	1415	śloṇ
1296	vyath	1336	śal	1376	śuṣ	1416	śvaṅk
1297	vyadh	1337	śav	1377	śulk	1417	śvas
1298	vyay	1338	śaś	1378	śū	1418	śvas
1299	vyay	1339	śaṣ	1379	śūr	1419	śval
1300	vyay	1340	śas	1380	śūr	1420	śvalk
1301	vyā	1341	śā	1381	śūl	1421	śvi
1302	vyuṣ	1342	śā	1382	śūl	1422	śvit
1303	vyuṣ	1343	śākh	1383	śr̥dh	1423	śvind
1304	vye	1344	śāḍ	1384	śr̥dh	1424	ṣṭhīv
1305	vraj	1345	śāl	1385	śr̥̄	1425	ṣṭhīv
1306	vraṇ	1346	śāl	1386	śel	1426	ṣvaṣk
1307	vraṇ	1347	śalbh	1387	śev	1427	sag
1308	vraṇ	1348	śās	1388	śauṭ	1428	sagh
1309	vraśc	1349	śās	1389	śaṃs	1429	sac
1310	vrī	1350	śi	1390	ścut	1430	sañj
1311	vrī	1351	śi	1391	ścyut	1431	sañj
1312	vrīḍ	1352	śiñj	1392	śmīl	1432	sad
1313	vruḍ	1353	śiṭ	1393	śyā	1433	saṭ
1314	vlı	1354	śiṣ	1394	śyai	1434	saṭṭ
1315	śak	1355	śil	1395	śraṅk	1435	satr
1316	śak	1356	śī	1396	śraṇ	1436	san
1317	śaṅk	1357	śī	1397	śraṇ	1437	sap
1318	śac	1358	śīk	1398	śrath	1438	sabhāj
1319	śaṭ	1359	śikṣ	1399	śranth	1439	sam
1320	śaṭ	1360	śībh	1400	śram	1440	sam
1321	śaṭh	1361	śīl	1401	śram	1441	sarb
1322	śaṭh	1362	śuc	1402	śrambh	1442	sal
1323	śaṭh	1363	śuc	1403	śrā	1443	sas
1324	śaṭh	1364	śucy	1404	śrā	1444	sah
1325	śaṭh	1365	śuṭh	1405	śri	1445	sah
1326	śaṇ	1366	śuṭh	1406	śrī	1446	sā
1327	śaṇ	1367	śuṇṭh	1407	śru	1447	sādh
1328	śad	1368	śuṇṭh	1408	śroṇ	1448	sādh
						1449	sādh

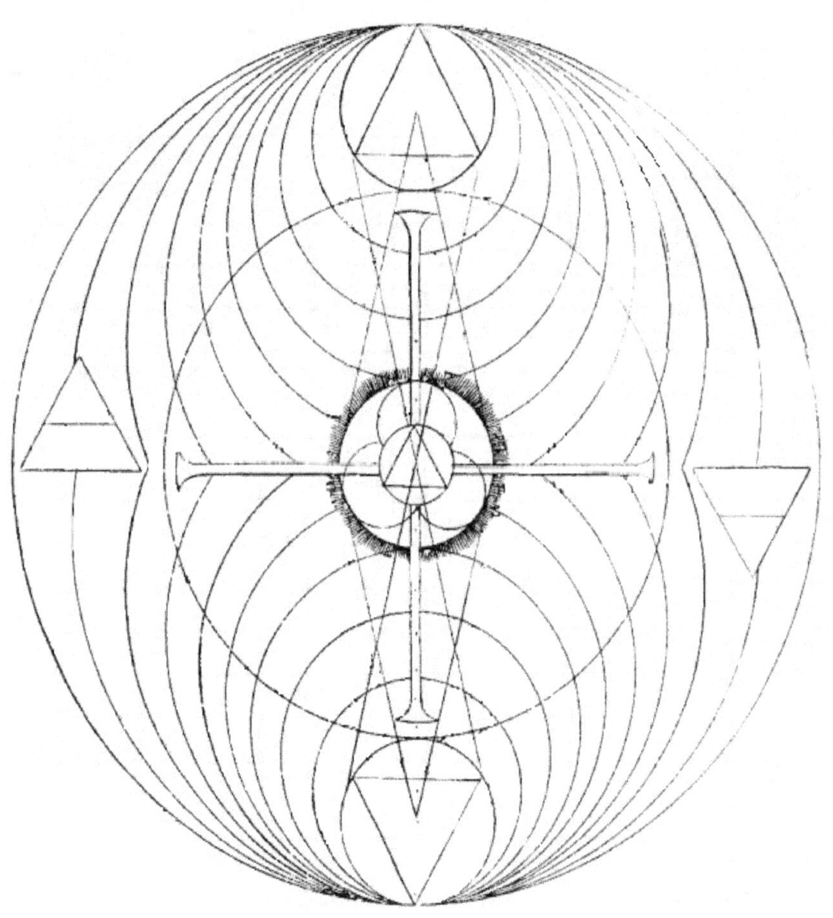

1450	सान्त्व्			1451	सामय	
[10U]	√sāntv			[10P]	√sāmaya	
	sāntvayati	sāntvayate			sāmayati	
English	console			English	conciliate	appease
Latin	Ø			Latin	Ø	
Greek	Ø			Greek	Ø	
Sanskrit	sāntva	consolation		Sanskrit	Ø	

1452	सि			1453	सि	
[9P]	√si			[5P]	√si	
W	sināti			W	sinoti	
English	bind, attach			English	bind,	attach
Latin	Ø			Latin	Ø	
German	Seil	rope		Greek	Seil	rope
Sanskrit	sétu	binding		Sanskrit	sétu	binding

1454	सिच्			1455	सिट्	
[6P]	√sic			[1P]	√siṭ	
W	siñcati				seṭati	
English	pour			English	despise	
Latin	Ø			Latin	Ø	
Greek	ἰκμάς	moisture		Greek	Ø	
Sanskrit	séka	sprinkling		Sanskrit	Ø	

1456	सिध्			1450	[10U]	sāntv
[4P]	√sidh			1451	[10P]	sāmaya
W	sidhyati			1452	[9P]	si
English	succeed			1453	[5P]	si
Latin	Ø		!	1454	[6P]	sic
Greek	Ø			1455	[1P]	siṭ
Sanskrit	siddha	accomplished	!	1456	[4P]	sidh

1457	सिध्			1458	सिल्	
[1P]	√sidh			[6P]	√sil	
W	sedhati				silati	
English	drive off,	repel		English	glean	
Latin	cēdō	go, move		Latin	Ø	
Greek	Ø			Greek	Ø	
Sanskrit	siddha	driven off		Sanskrit	Ø	

1459	सीव्			1460	सु	
[4P]	√sīv			[5U]	√su	
W	sīvyati			W	sunoti	sunute
English	sew			English	press	
Latin	suō	sew, stitch		Latin	Ø	
Greek	Ø			Greek	Ø	
Sanskrit	sūtra	thread		Sanskrit	suta	pressed out

1461	सुख्			1462	सुख्	
[10P]	√sukh			[4P]	√sukh	
	sukhayati				sukhyati	
English	please,	delight		English	please,	delight
Latin	Ø			Latin	Ø	
Greek	Ø			Greek	Ø	
Sanskrit	sukha (?)	happy		Sanskrit	sukha (?)	happy

1463	सुट्ट्		!	1457	[1P]	sidh
[10P]	√suṭṭ			1458	[6P]	sil
	suṭṭayati		!	1459	[4P]	sīv
English	disregard,	despise	!	1460	[5U]	su
Latin	Ø			1461	[10P]	sukh
Greek	Ø			1462	[4P]	sukh
Sanskrit	Ø			1463	[10P]	suṭṭ

1464	सुभ्			1465	सुभ्	
[9P]	√subh			[6P]	√subh	
	subhnāti				sumbhati	
English	smother			English	smother	
Latin	Ø			Latin	Ø	
Greek	Ø			Greek	Ø	
Sanskrit	subdha	smothered		Sanskrit	subdha	smothered

1466	सुर्			1467	सुह्	
[6P]	√sur			[4P]	√suh	
W	surati				suhyati	
English	have super	powers		English	satisfy,	gladden
Latin	Ø			Latin	Ø	
Greek	Ø			Greek	Ø	
Sanskrit	sura	god		Sanskrit	Ø	

1468	सू			1469	सू	
[1P]	√sū			[6P]	√sū	
	savati				suvati	
English	conceive			English	conceive	
Latin	Ø			Latin	Ø	
Greek	υἰός	son		Greek	υἰός	son
Sanskrit	sūta	born		Sanskrit	sūta	born

1470	सू			1464	[9P]	subh
[2P]	√sū			1465	[6P]	subh
	sauti			1466	[6P]	sur
English	conceive			1467	[4P]	suh
Latin	Ø		!	1468	[1P]	sū
Greek	υἰός	son	!	1469	[6P]	sū
Sanskrit	sūta	born	!	1470	[2P]	sū

1471	सू			1472	सूच्	
[2Ā]	√sū			[10P]	√sūc	
W	sūte			W	sūcayati	
English	conceive			English	indicate	
Latin	Ø			Latin	Ø	
Greek	υἱός	son		Greek	στίζω (?)	mark
Sanskrit	sūta	born		Sanskrit	sūcana	indicating

1473	सूद्			1474	सूर्क्ष्	
[1Ā]	√sūd			[1P]	√sūrkṣ	
W	sūdate				sūrkṣati	
English	arrange, kill			English	trouble	about
Latin	Ø			Latin	Ø	
Greek	Ø			German	Sorge (?)	concern
Sanskrit	sūdana	destruction		Sanskrit	sūrkṣya	heeded

1475	सृ			1476	सृ	
[1P]	√sṛ			[3P]	√sṛ	
W	sarati			W	sisarti	
English	spring, run			English	spring,	run
Latin	saliō	leap, jump		Latin	saliō	leap, jump
Greek	ἅλλομαι	leap, jump		Greek	ἅλλομαι	leap, jump
Sanskrit	sṛta	running		Sanskrit	sṛta	running

1477	सृज्		!	1471	[2Ā]	sū
[6P]	√sṛj			1472	[10P]	sūc
W	sṛjati			1473	[1Ā]	sūd
English	let go,	throw		1474	[1P]	sūrkṣ
Latin	Ø		!	1475	[1P]	sṛ
English	sulky	(morose)	!	1476	[3P]	sṛ
Sanskrit	sárga	discharging	!	1477	[6P]	sṛj

1478	सृप्			1479	सृभ्	
[1P]	√sṛp			[1P]	√sṛbh	
W	sarpati				sarbhati	
English	crawl			English	injure,	kill
Latin	serpō	creep, crawl		Latin	Ø	
Greek	ἕρπω	creep, crawl		Greek	Ø	
Sanskrit	sarpá	snake, serpent		Sanskrit	Ø	

1480	सेक्			1481	सेव्	
[1Ā]	√sek			[1Ā]	√sev	
	sekate			W	sevate	
English	go, move			English	stay,	serve
Latin	Ø			Latin	Ø	
Greek	Ø			Greek	Ø	
Sanskrit	Ø			Sanskrit	sevā	service

1482	सै			1483	सो	
[1P]	√sai			[4P]	√so	
	sāyati				syati	
English	waste away,	decline		English	destroy,	kill
Latin	Ø			Latin	Ø	
Greek	Ø			Greek	Ø	
Sanskrit	Ø			Sanskrit	Ø	

1484	स्कन्द्		!	1478	[1P]	sṛp
[1P]	√skand			1479	[1P]	sṛbh
W	skandati			1480	[1Ā]	sek
English	leap, jump		!	1481	[1Ā]	sev
Latin	scandō	climb, mount		1482	[1P]	sai
Greek	σκἄνδἄλον	trap, snare		1483	[4P]	so
Sanskrit	skanda	hopping	!	1484	[1P]	skand

1485	स्कम्भ्			1486	स्कु	
[9P]	√skambh			[5U]	√sku	
W	skabhnāti				skunoti	skunute
English	prop,	support		English	tear,	pluck
Latin	scamnum	stool, step		Latin	cutis	skin
Greek	σκαμνίον	bench		Greek	δέρω	flay
Sanskrit	skambha	pillar		Sanskrit	Ø	

1487	स्कु			1488	स्कुन्द्	
[9U]	√sku			[1Ā]	√skund	
	skunāti	skunīte			skundate	
English	tear, pluck			English	jump	
Latin	cutis	skin		Latin	Ø	
Greek	δέρω	flay		Greek	Ø	
Sanskrit	Ø			Sanskrit	Ø	

1489	स्कुम्भ्			1490	स्कुम्भ्	
[5P]	√skumbh			[9P]	√skumbh	
	skubhnoti				skumbhnāti	
English	stop, hinder			English	stop,	hinder
Latin	Ø			Latin	Ø	
Greek	Ø			Greek	Ø	
Sanskrit	Ø			Sanskrit	Ø	

1491	स्खद्			1485	[9U]	skambh
[1Ā]	√skhad			1486	[5U]	sku
	skhadate			1487	[9U]	sku
English	destroy, cut			1488	[1Ā]	skund
Latin	Ø			1489	[5P]	skumbh
Greek	Ø			1490	[9P]	skumbh
Sanskrit	skhadana	hurting		1491	[1Ā]	skhad

1492	स्खल्			1493	स्तक्	
[1P]	√skhal			[1P]	√stak	
W	skhalati				stakati	
English	stumble			English	strike	against
Latin	Ø			Latin	Ø	
Greek	σφάλλομαι	tottering		Greek	Ø	
Sanskrit	skhalana	stumbling		Sanskrit	Ø	

1494	स्तन्			1495	स्तम्भ्	
[1P]	√stan			[9P]	√stambh	
W	stanati			W	stabhnāti	
English	resound,	thunder		English	fasten,	stamp
Latin	tonō	thunder		Latin	Ø	
Greek	στένω	moan		Greek	Ø	
Sanskrit	stanita	thunder		Sanskrit	stambha	pillar

1496	स्तम्भ्			1497	स्तम्भ्	
[5P]	√stambh			[1Ā]	√stambh	
W	stabhnoti			W	stambhate	
English	fasten,	stamp		English	fasten,	stamp
Latin	Ø			Latin	Ø	
Greek	Ø			Greek	Ø	
Sanskrit	stambha	pillar		Sanskrit	stambha	pillar

1498	स्तिम्		!	1492	[1P]	skhal
[4P]	√stim			1493	[1P]	stak
W	stimyati			1494	[1P]	stan
English	become	moist	!	1495	[9P]	stambh
Latin	Ø		!	1496	[5P]	stambh
Greek	Ø		!	1497	[1Ā]	stambh
Sanskrit	stimita	wet, moist		1498	[4P]	stim

1499	स्तिप्			1500	स्तु	
[1Ā]	√stip			[2P]	√stu	
	stepate			W	stauti	
English	ooze, drip			English	praise	
Latin	Ø			Latin	Ø	
Greek	Ø			Greek	στεῦται	announce
Sanskrit	Ø			Sanskrit	stava	eulogy

1501	स्तु			1502	स्तुच्	
[5P]	√stu			[1Ā]	√stuc	
W	stunoti				stocate	
English	praise			English	be bright,	propitious
Latin	Ø			Latin	Ø	
Greek	στεῦται	announce		Greek	Ø	
Sanskrit	stutá	praised		Sanskrit	Ø	

1503	स्तुभ्			1504	स्तूप्	
[1P]	√stubh			[4P]	√stūp	
W	stobhati				stūpyati	
English	celebrate			English	heap up,	pile
Latin	Ø			Latin	Ø	
Greek	Ø			Greek	στῦφω (?)	contract
Sanskrit	stubdha	praised		Sanskrit	stūpa	monument

1505	स्तूप्			1499	[1Ā]	stip
[10P]	√stūp		!	1500	[2P]	stu
W	stūpayati		!	1501	[5P]	stu
English	heap up,	pile		1502	[1Ā]	stuc
Latin	Ø			1503	[1P]	stubh
Greek	στῦφω (?)	contract		1504	[4P]	stūp
Sanskrit	stūpa	monument		1505	[10P]	stūp

1506	स्तृ			1507	स्तृ	
[9U]	√stṝ			[5U]	√stṝ	
W	stṛṇāti	stṛṇīte		W	stṛṇoti	stṛṇute
English	extend	(strew)		English	extend	(strew)
Latin	sternō	spread		Latin	sternō	spread
Greek	στόρνῡμι	spread		Greek	στόρνῡμι	spread
Sanskrit	stara	stratum		Sanskrit	stara	stratum

1508	स्तृह्			1509	स्तेन्	
[6P]	√stṝh			[10P]	√sten	
	strihati				stenayati	
English	injure,	harm		English	steal, rob	
Latin	Ø			Latin	Ø	
Greek	Ø			Greek	Ø	
Sanskrit	Ø			Sanskrit	stena	robber

1510	स्तेप्			1511	स्तेप्	
[1Ā]	√step			[10P]	√step	
	stepate				stepayati	
English	flow			English	send,	throw
Latin	Ø			Latin	Ø	
Greek	Ø			Greek	Ø	
Sanskrit	Ø			Sanskrit	Ø	

1512	स्तै			1506	[9U]	stṝ
[1P]	√stai			1507	[5U]	stṝ
	stāyati			1508	[6P]	stṝh
English	steal			1509	[10P]	sten
Latin	Ø			1510	[1Ā]	step
Greek	Ø			1511	[10P]	step
Sanskrit	stāyu	thief, robber		1512	[1P]	stai

1513	स्त्या			1514	स्त्यै	
[4Ā]	√styā			[1P]	√styai	
W	styāyate				styāyati	
English	harden			English	collected into	a heap
Latin	Ø			Latin	Ø	
Greek	σῶμα (?)	dead body		Greek	σῶμα (?)	body
Sanskrit	stiyā	stagnt. water		Sanskrit	styāna	stiff

1515	जुष्			1516	स्थग्	
[1Ā]	√styai			[1P]	√sthag	
	styāyate			W	sthagati	
English	stiffen			English	cover,	hide
Latin	Ø			Latin	toga	garment
Greek	σῶμα (?)	dead body		Greek	στέγω	cover
Sanskrit	styāna	stiffened		Sanskrit	sthagita	concealed

1517	स्थल्			1518	स्था	
[1P]	√sthal			[6Ā]	√sthā	
	sthalati			W	tiṣṭhati	tiṣṭhate
English	stand firm			English	stand,	exist
Latin	locus	place, spot		Latin	stō	stand
Greek	στήλη	support block		Greek	ἵστημι	stand
Sanskrit	sthala	ground, soil		Sanskrit	sthāna	standing

1519	स्थुड्			1513	[4Ā]	styā
[6P]	√sthuḍ			1514	[1P]	styai
	sthuḍati			1515	[1Ā]	styai
English	cover			1516	[1P]	sthag
Latin	Ø			1517	[1P]	sthal
Greek	Ø		!	1518	[6Ā]	sthā
Sanskrit	Ø			1519	[6P]	sthuḍ

1520	स्थूल्			1521	जुष्	
[10Ā]	√sthūl			[2P]	√snā	
	sthūlayate			W	snāti	
English	grow fat			English	bathe	
Latin	Ø			Latin	natō	swim, float
Greek	Ø			Greek	νέω	swim
Sanskrit	sthūla	thick, stout		Sanskrit	snāna	bathing

1522	स्निह्			1523	स्निह्	
[4P]	√snih			[1P]	√snih	
W	snihyati			W	snehati	
English	stick, love			English	glue, love	
Latin	ningit	snow		Latin	ningit	snow
Greek	νειφει	snow		Greek	νειφει	snow
Sanskrit	sneha	oiliness		Sanskrit	sneha	oiliness

1524	स्नु			1525	स्नुस्	
[2U]	√snu			[4P]	√snus	
W	snauti	snute			snusyati	
English	distill, flow			English	eat,	disappear
Latin	Ø			Latin	Ø	
Greek	Ø			Greek	Ø	
Sanskrit	snava	oozing		Sanskrit	Ø	

1526	स्नुह्			1520	[10Ā]	sthūl
[4P]	√snuh		!	1521	[2P]	snā
W	snuhyati		!	1522	[4P]	snih
English	vomit		!	1523	[1P]	snih
Latin	Ø			1524	[2U]	snu
Greek	Ø			1525	[4P]	snus
Sanskrit	Ø			1526	[4P]	snuh

1527	स्नै			1528	स्पन्द्	
[1P]	√snai			[1Ā]	√spand	
	snāyati			W	spandate	
English	clothe,	wrap round		English	tremble	
Latin	Ø			Latin	Ø	
Greek	Ø			Greek	σφᾰδᾁζω	struggle
Sanskrit	Ø			Sanskrit	spanda	throbbing

1529	स्फल्			1530	स्फर्	
[1P]	√sphal			[6P]	√sphar	
W	sphalati				spharati	
English	tremble			English	expand,	open
Latin	Ø			Latin	Ø	
Greek	Ø			Greek	Ø	
Sanskrit	sphālana	quivering		Sanskrit	sphāra	wide, large

1531	स्पर्ध्			1532	स्पश्	
[1Ā]	√spardh			[pft]	√spaś	
W	spardhate			W	paspaśe	
English	rival			English	observe	
Latin	Ø			Latin	haru-spex	diviner
Greek	Ø			Greek	σκώψ (?)	small owl
Sanskrit	spardhā	rivalry		Sanskrit	spaś	spy

1533	स्पृ			1527	[1P]	snai
[5P]	√spṛ		!	1528	[1Ā]	spand
W	spṛṇoti			1529	[1P]	sphal
English	save			1530	[6P]	sphar
Latin	Ø			1531	[1Ā]	spardh
Greek	Ø			1532	[pft]	spaś
Sanskrit	spṛtā	saved		1533	[5P]	spṛ

1534	स्पृश्			1535	स्पृह्	
[6U]	√spṛś			[10P]	√spṛh	
W	spṛśati	spṛśate		W	spṛhayati	
English	touch			English	desire, envy	(spring)
Latin	Ø			Latin	Ø	
Greek	Ø			Greek	σπέρχω	haste, hurry
Sanskrit	sparśa	touch		Sanskrit	spṛhā	desire

1536	स्फा			1537	स्फाय्	
[1Ā]	√sphā			[1Ā]	√sphāy	
W	sphāyate			W	sphāyate	
English	swell,	get fat		English	swell,	increase
Latin	spēs	hope		Latin	spēs	hope
Greek	Ø			Greek	Ø	
Sanskrit	sphīta	rich		Sanskrit	sphāyat	expanding

1538	स्फिट्			1539	स्फिट्ट्	
[10P]	√sphiṭ			[10P]	√sphiṭṭ	
	spheṭayati			W	sphiṭṭayati	
English	hurt, injure			English	hurt,	injure
Latin	Ø			Latin	Ø	
Greek	Ø			Greek	Ø	
Sanskrit	Ø			Sanskrit	Ø	

1540	स्फुट्		!	1534	[6U]	spṛś
[6P]	√sphuṭ		!	1535	[10P]	spṛh
W	sphuṭati			1536	[1Ā]	sphā
English	split			1537	[1Ā]	sphāy
Latin	Ø			1538	[10P]	sphiṭ
Greek	Ø			1539	[10P]	sphiṭṭ
Sanskrit	sphuṭa	wide, broad	!	1540	[6P]	sphuṭ

1541	स्फुट्			1542	स्फुड्	
[1P]	√sphuṭ			[6P]	√sphuḍ	
W	sphoṭati				sphuḍati	
English	split			English	cover	
Latin	Ø			Latin	Ø	
Greek	Ø			Greek	Ø	
Sanskrit	sphuṭa	wide, broad		Sanskrit	Ø	

1543	स्फुण्ट्			1544	स्फुण्ट्	
[1P]	√sphuṇṭ			[10P]	√sphuṇṭ	
	sphuṇṭati				sphuṇṭayati	
English	open,	expand		English	jest, joke	
Latin	Ø			Latin	Ø	
Greek	Ø			Greek	Ø	
Sanskrit	Ø			Sanskrit	Ø	

1545	स्फुर्			1546	स्फुल्	
[6U]	√sphur			[6P]	√sphul	
W	sphurati	sphurate			sphulati	
English	tremble,	spurn		English	tremble,	throb
Latin	spernō	push away		Latin	spernō	push away
Greek	σπαίρω	twitch		Greek	σπαίρω	twitch
Sanskrit	sphura	quiver		Sanskrit	sphulana	throbbing

1547	स्फूर्ज्			1541	[1P]	sphuṭ
[1P]	√sphūrj			1542	[6P]	sphuḍ
	sphūrjati			1543	[1P]	sphuṇṭ
English	rumble,	roar		1544	[10P]	sphuṇṭ
Latin	Ø		!	1545	[6U]	sphur
Greek	σφαραγέομαι	crackle		1546	[6P]	sphul
Sanskrit	sphūrja	thunderclap		1547	[1P]	sphūrj

1548	सि			1549	स्मिट्	
[1U]	√smi			[10P]	√smiṭ	
W	smayati	smayate			smeṭayati	
English	smile			English	despise	
Latin	mīror	marvel at		Latin	Ø	
Greek	μειδάω	smile		Greek	Ø	
Sanskrit	smita	smile		Sanskrit	Ø	

1550	स्मृ			1551	स्यन्द्	
[1P]	√smṛ			[1Ā]	√syand	
W	smarati			W	syandate	
English	remember			English	flow, run	
Latin	memor	remembering		Latin	Ø	
Greek	μέριμνα	care, thought		Greek	Ø	
Sanskrit	smara	recollecting		Sanskrit	syanna	flowing

1552	स्यम्			1553	स्यम्	
[1P]	√syam			[10P]	√syam	
W	syamati			W	syamayati	
English	accord			English	sound,	shout
Latin	Ø			Latin	Ø	
Greek	Ø			Greek	Ø	
Sanskrit	Ø			Sanskrit	Ø	

1554	स्यम्		!	1548	[1U]	smi
[10Ā]	√syam			1549	[10P]	smiṭ
W	syāmayate		!	1550	[1P]	smṛ
English	consider,	reflect	!	1551	[1Ā]	syand
Latin	Ø			1552	[1P]	syam
Greek	Ø			1553	[10P]	syam
Sanskrit	Ø			1554	[10Ā]	syam

1555	स्रंस्			1556	सु	
[1Ā]	√srams			[1P]	√sru	
W	sraṃsate			W	sravati	
English	fall			English	stream	
Latin	Ø			German	Strom	stream, flow
Greek	Ø			Greek	ῥέω	flow, stream
Sanskrit	sraṃsana	loosening		Sanskrit	srutí	stream, flow

1557	स्रेक्			1558	स्वज्	
[1Ā]	√srek			[1Ā]	√svaj	
W	srekate				svájate	
English	go, move			English	embrace	
Latin	Ø			Latin	Ø	
Greek	Ø			Greek	Ø	
Sanskrit	Ø			Sanskrit	pari-ṣvakta	embraced

1559	स्वज़्			1560	स्वद्	
[1Ā]	√svañj			[1U]	√svad	
W	svajate			W	svadati	svadate
English	embrace			English	taste,	be sweet
Latin	Ø			Latin	suavis	sweet
Greek	Ø			Greek	ἡδύς	sweet
Sanskrit	pari-ṣvaṅga	embrace		Sanskrit	svādú	sweet

1561	स्वन्					
			!	1555	[1Ā]	srams
[1P]	√svan		!	1556	[1P]	sru
W	svanati			1557	[1Ā]	srek
English	sound		!	1558	[1Ā]	svaj
Latin	sonō	sound		1559	[1Ā]	svañj
Greek	Ø		!	1560	[1U]	svad
Sanskrit	svaná	sound, noise	!	1561	[1P]	svan

1562	स्वप्			1563	स्वप्	
[2P]	√svap			[1P]	√svap	
W	svapiti			W	svapati	
English	sleep			English	sleep	
Latin	somnus	sleep		Latin	somnus	sleep
Greek	ὕπνος	sleep		Greek	ὕπνος	sleep
Sanskrit	svápna	sleeping		Sanskrit	svapanā	sleepy

1564	स्वर्			1565	स्वर्	
[1P]	√svar			[1P]	√svar	
W	svarati			W	svarati	
English	sound			English	shine	
Latin	susurrus (?)	whisper		Latin	sōl	sun
Greek	ὐράξ	shrewmouse		Greek	ἥλιος	sun
Sanskrit	svara	sound, noise		Sanskrit	svar	heaven

1566	स्वर्द्			1567	स्वाद्	
[1Ā]	√svard			[1Ā]	√svād	
	svardate				svádate	
English	taste, please			English	relish	
Latin	Ø			Latin	suādeō	recommend
Greek	Ø			Greek	ἡδύς	sweet
Sanskrit	Ø			Sanskrit	svāda	taste, flavour

1568	स्विद्		!	1562	[2P]	svap
[1Ā]	√svid		!	1563	[1P]	svap
	svedate			1564	[1P]	svar
English	sweat			1565	[1P]	svar
Latin	sūdō	sweat		1566	[1Ā]	svard
Greek	ἰδρώς	sweat		1567	[1Ā]	svād
Sanskrit	svéda	sweat	!	1568	[1Ā]	svid

1569	स्विद्			1570	स्वृ	
[4P]	√svid			[1P]	√svṛ	
W	svidyati				svárati	
English	being	sweaty		English	sound	
Latin	sūdō	sweat		Latin	susurrus (?)	whisper
Greek	ἴδρώς	sweat		Greek	ὑράξ	shrewmouse
Sanskrit	svinna	sweating		Sanskrit	svara	sound, noise

1571	हट्			1572	हठ्	
[1P]	√haṭ			[1P]	√haṭh	
	haṭati			W	haṭhati	
English	shine,	be bright		English	commit	evil
Latin	Ø			Latin	Ø	
Greek	Ø			Greek	Ø	
Sanskrit	Ø			Sanskrit	haṭha	violence

1573	हद्			1574	हन्	
[1U]	√had			[2P]	√han	
W	hadati	hadate		W	hanti	
English	defecate			English	kill	
Latin	Ø			Latin	offendō	hit, strike
Greek	Ø			Greek	θείνω	strike
Sanskrit	hanna	evacuated		Sanskrit	hatyā	slaying

1575	हम्म्			1569	[4P]	svid
[1P]	√hamm			1570	[1P]	svṛ
	hammati			1571	[1P]	haṭ
English	go			1572	[1P]	haṭh
Latin	Ø			1573	[1U]	had
Greek	Ø		!	1574	[2P]	han
Sanskrit	Ø			1575	[1P]	hamm

1576	हल्			1577	हस्	
[1P]	√hal			[1U]	√has	
	halati			W	hasati	hasate
English	plough			English	laugh	
Latin	Ø			Latin	Ø	
Greek	Ø			Greek	Ø	
Sanskrit	hāla	plough		Sanskrit	hasa	mirth

1578	हा			1579	हा	
[3P]	√hā			[3Ā]	√hā	
W	jahāti			W	jihīte	
English	abandon			English	spring	forward
Latin	Ø			Latin	Ø	
Greek	κίχημι	overtake		Greek	κίχημι	overtake
Sanskrit	hāni	abandonment		Sanskrit	Ø	

1580	हि			1581	हिंस्	
[5P]	√hi			[7P]	√hiṃs	
W	hinoti			W	hinasti	
English	send forth			English	do wrong	
Latin	Ø			Latin	Ø	
Greek	Ø			Greek	Ø	
Sanskrit	hetí	missile		Sanskrit	hiṃsitā	injured

1582	हिंस्			1576	[1P]	hal
[1P]	√hiṃs		!	1577	[1U]	has
W	hiṃsati		!	1578	[3P]	hā
English	do wrong		!	1579	[3Ā]	hā
Latin	Ø			1580	[5P]	hi
Greek	Ø		!	1581	[7P]	hiṃs
Sanskrit	hiṃsā	injury	!	1582	[1P]	hiṃs

1583	हिक्क्			1584	हु	
[1P]	√hikk			[3U]	√hu	
W	hikkati			W	juhoti	juhute
English	hiccup			English	sacrifice,	pour
Latin	Ø			Latin	fūtilis	leaky
Greek	Ø			Greek	χέω	pour
Sanskrit	hikkā	hiccup		Sanskrit	havyá	oblation

1585	हुड्			1586	हुड्	
[6P]	√huḍ			[1P]	√huḍ	
	huḍati				hoḍati	
English	collect			English	go	
Latin	Ø			Latin	Ø	
Greek	Ø			Greek	Ø	
Sanskrit	Ø			Sanskrit	Ø	

1587	हुण्ड्			1588	हुर्छ्	
[1Ā]	√huṇḍ			[1P]	√hurch	
W	huṇḍate				hūrchati	
English	collect			English	creep	
Latin	Ø			Latin	Ø	
Greek	Ø			Greek	Ø	
Sanskrit	Ø			Sanskrit	huras	stealthily

1589	हुल्			1583	[1P]	hikk
[1P]	√hul		!	1584	[3U]	hu
	holati			1585	[6P]	huḍ
English	go, conceal			1586	[1P]	huḍ
Latin	Ø			1587	[1Ā]	huṇḍ
Greek	Ø			1588	[1P]	hurch
Sanskrit	Ø			1589	[1P]	hul

1590	हू			1591	हृ	
[1U]	√hū			[1U]	√hṛ	
W	hvayati	hvayate		W	harati	harate
English	call, invite			English	transport	
Latin	Ø			Latin	cohors	farmyard
Greek	Ø			Greek	χορός	dance ring
Sanskrit	hūtā	called		Sanskrit	hṛtá	taken away

1592	हृ			1593	हृ	
[3P]	√hṛ			[9Ā]	√hṛ	
W	jiharti			W	hṛṇīte	
English	transport			English	be angry	
Latin	cohors	farmyard		Latin	Ø	
Greek	χορός	dance ring		Greek	Ø	
Sanskrit	hṛtá	taken away		Sanskrit	hṛṇāna	angry

1594	हृष्			1595	हृष्	
[4P]	√hṛṣ			[1P]	√hṛṣ	
W	hṛṣyati			W	harṣati	
English	be excited			English	be excited	
Latin	horreō	shiver		Latin	horreō	shiver
Greek	χέρσος	dry land		Greek	χέρσος	dry land
Sanskrit	hṛṣita	cheerful		Sanskrit	hṛṣita	cheerful

1596	हेठ्			1590	[1U]	hū
[1U]	√heṭh		!	1591	[1U]	hṛ
	heṭhati	heṭhate	!	1592	[3P]	hṛ
English	vex, harrass		!	1593	[9Ā]	hṛ
Latin	Ø		!	1594	[4P]	hṛṣ
Greek	Ø		!	1595	[1P]	hṛṣ
Sanskrit	heṭha	vexation		1596	[1U]	heṭh

1597	हेड्			1598	हेड्	
[1P]	√heḍ			[1Ā]	√heḍ	
	heḍati				heḍate	
English	surround			English	be angry	
Latin	Ø			Latin	Ø	
Greek	Geist	spirit		German	Geist	spirit
Sanskrit	Ø			Sanskrit	heḍa	anger

1599	हेष्			1600	ह्नु	
[1Ā]	√heṣ			[2Ā]	√hnu	
	héṣate			W	hnute	
English	neigh			English	hide from	
Latin	Ø			Latin	Ø	
Greek	Ø			Greek	Ø	
Sanskrit	heṣā	neighing		Sanskrit	hnavana	concealing

1601	हस्			1602	ह्राद्	
[1P]	√hras				√	
W	hrasati			W	hrādate	
English	diminish			English	make noise	
Latin	Ø			Latin	Ø	
Greek	Ø			Greek	Ø	
Sanskrit	hrasita	shortened		Sanskrit	hrāda	sound, noise

1603	ह्री			1597	[1P]	heḍ
[3P]	√hrī			1598	[1Ā]	heḍ
W	jihreti		!	1599	[1Ā]	heṣ
English	be ashamed			1600	[2Ā]	hnu
Latin	Ø		!	1601	[1P]	hras
Greek	Ø			1602	[1Ā]	hrād
Sanskrit	hrīti	shame	!	1603	[3P]	hrī

1604	हेष्			1605	ह्लग्	
[1Ā]	√hreṣ			[1Ā]	√hlag	
	hreṣate				hlagate	
English	neigh			English	cover	
Latin	Ø			Latin	Ø	
Greek	Ø			Greek	Ø	
Sanskrit	hreṣā	neighing		Sanskrit	Ø	

1606	ह्लस्			1607	ह्लाद्	
[1P]	√hlas			[1Ā]	√hlād	
	hlasati			W	hlādate	
English	sound			English	rejoice,	be glad
Latin	Ø			Latin	Ø	
Greek	Ø			Greek	κέχλᾱδα	ring out
Sanskrit	Ø			Sanskrit	hlāda	delight

1608	ह्वल्			1609	ह्वृ	
[1U]	√hval			[1P]	√hvṛ	
W	hvalati	hvalate		W	hvarati	
English	go astray			English	deviate	
Latin	Ø			Latin	Ø	
Greek	φῆλος	deceitful		Greek	φῆλος	deceitful
Sanskrit	hvāla	failure		Sanskrit	hvaras	crookedness

1610	हे			1604	[1Ā]	hreṣ
[1U]	√hve			1605	[1Ā]	hlag
	hváyati	hváyate		1606	[1P]	hlas
English	call,	summon		1607	[1Ā]	hlād
Latin	Ø			1608	[1U]	hval
Greek	καυχάομαι	boast		1609	[1P]	hvṛ
Sanskrit	hūta	summoned		1610	[1U]	hve

1450	sāntv	1490	skumbh	1530	sphar	1570	svṛ
1451	sāmaya	1491	skhad	1531	spardh	1571	haṭ
1452	si	1492	skhal	1532	spaś	1572	haṭh
1453	si	1493	stak	1533	spṛ	1573	had
1454	sic	1494	stan	1534	spṛś	1574	han
1455	siṭ	1495	stambh	1535	spṛh	1575	hamm
1456	sidh	1496	stambh	1536	sphā	1576	hal
1457	sidh	1497	stambh	1537	sphāy	1577	has
1458	sil	1498	stim	1538	sphiṭ	1578	hā
1459	sīv	1499	stip	1539	sphiṭṭ	1579	hā
1460	su	1500	stu	1540	sphuṭ	1580	hi
1461	sukh	1501	stu	1541	sphuṭ	1581	hiṃs
1462	sukh	1502	stuc	1542	sphuḍ	1582	hiṃs
1463	suṭṭ	1503	stubh	1543	sphuṇṭ	1583	hikk
1464	subh	1504	stūp	1544	sphuṇṭ	1584	hu
1465	subh	1505	stūp	1545	sphur	1585	huḍ
1466	sur	1506	stṝ	1546	sphul	1586	huḍ
1467	suh	1507	stṝ	1547	sphūrj	1587	huṇḍ
1468	sū	1508	stṝh	1548	smi	1588	hurch
1469	sū	1509	sten	1549	smiṭ	1589	hul
1470	sū	1510	step	1550	smṛ	1590	hū
1471	sū	1511	step	1551	syand	1591	hṛ
1472	sūc	1512	stai	1552	syam	1592	hṛ
1473	sūd	1513	styā	1553	syam	1593	lṛ
1474	sūrkṣ	1514	styai	1554	syam	1594	hṛṣ
1475	sṛ	1515	styai	1555	sraṃs	1595	hṛṣ
1476	sṛ	1516	sthag	1556	sru	1596	heṭh
1477	sṛj	1517	sthal	1557	srek	1597	heḍ
1478	sṛp	1518	sthā	1558	svaj	1598	heḍ
1479	sṛbh	1519	sthuḍ	1559	svañj	1599	heṣ
1480	sek	1520	sthūl	1560	svad	1600	hnu
1481	sev	1521	snā	1561	svan	1601	hras
1482	sai	1522	snih	1562	svap	1602	hrād
1483	so	1523	snih	1563	svap	1603	hrī
1484	skand	1524	snu	1564	svar	1604	hreṣ
1485	skambh	1525	snus	1565	svar	1605	hlag
1486	sku	1526	snuh	1566	svard	1606	hlas
1487	sku	1527	snai	1567	svād	1607	hlād
1488	skund	1528	spand	1568	svid	1608	hval
1489	skumbh	1529	sphal	1569	svid	1609	hvṛ
						1610	hve

Bibliography

Burrow, T. (1973) The Sanskrit Language. Faber and Faber.

Calvert, Watkins (1995) How to Kill a Dragon: Aspects of Indo-European Poetics. Oxford University Press.

Egenes, Thomas (1989) Introduction to Sanskrit. Motilal Banarsidass.

Huet, Gérard (07/01/2026) The Sanskrit Heritage Site [online] Available at: https://sanskrit.inria.fr › DICO › index.en.html (Accessed 17 January 2026)

Macdonell, A.A. (1927) A Sanskrit Grammar for Students. Oxford University Press.

Mayrhofer, Manfred (1992) Etymologisches Wörterbuch des Altindoarischen. Winter Verlag.

Monier, Monier-Williams (1899) A Sanskrit English Dictionary. Oxford University Press.

Ostler, Nicolas (2006) Empires of the Word. Harper Perennial.

Pokorny, Julius (1959) Indogermanisches etymologisches Wörterbuch. Francke Verlag.

Rix, Helmut (2001) Lexikon der indogermanischen Verben: die Wurzeln und ihre Primärstammbildungen. Dr. Ludwig Reichert Verlag.

Ruppel, A.M. (2017) Cambridge Introduction to Sanskrit. Cambridge University Press.

Sanskrit Word Frequency Tool [online] Available at: https://sanskritdictionary.com/frequency/ (Accessed 17 January 2026)

Whitney, W.D. (1889) Sanskrit Grammar. Harvard University Press.

Whitney, W.D. (1885) The Roots, Verb-Forms, and Primary Derivatives of the Sanskrit Language. Breitkopf and Härtel.

Wiese, Harald (2023) Sanskrit as an Indo-European Language. HASP.

Wiktionary, the free dictionary [online] Available at: https://en.wiktionary.org/wiki/ (Accessed 17 January 2026)

Alphabetical Index of Sanskrit Roots

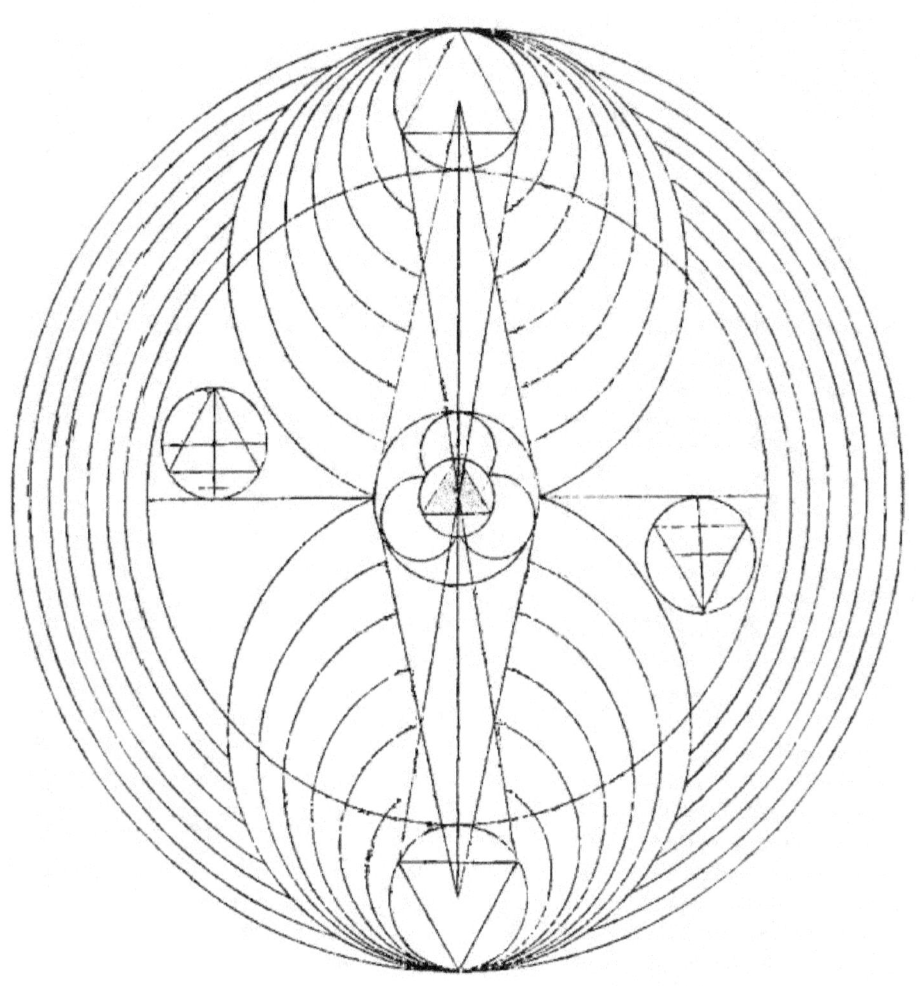

abhr	28	bādh	873	bhṛṃś	920	caṭ	388	dai	648
ad	25	bal	868	bhṛś	921	cāy	406	dakṣ	596
aḍ	18	balh	869	bhṛś	922	ceṣṭ	429	dal	603
aḍḍ	19	balh	870	bhruḍ	937	chad	433	dam	599
ag	8	baṃh	871	bhrūṇ	938	cham	435	ḍam	497
agh	9	baṇ	863	bhū	915	chand	434	ḍamb	498
ah	46	bandh	865	bhuj	913	chaṣ	436	dambh	600
aj	14	barh	866	bhuj	914	chid	437	dambh	601
ak	5	barh	867	bhūṣ	916	chṛd	442	daṃś	595
akṣ	6	beh	889	bhyas	924	chṛd	443	dān	613
akṣ	7	bhā	907	bil	875	chup	440	ḍap	496
al	39	bhaj	893	bil	876	chur	441	das	604
am	29	bhakṣ	892	bis	877	chuṭ	438	das	605
amb	30	bhal	905	biṭ	874	chuṭ	439	dās	616
aṃh	2	bhal	906	bṛh	886	ci	407	dās	617
aṃh	3	bhām	908	bṛh	887	ci	408	dāś	615
aṃh	4	bhaṇ	897	bṛh	888	cint	410	day	602
aṃś	1	bhand	899	brū	890	ciri	411	dāy	614
an	26	bhaṇḍ	898	brū	891	cit	409	de	647
añc	15	bhañj	894	buḍ	880	cīv	412	dhā	674
añc	16	bharts	900	budh	881	cīv	413	dhā	675
aṅg	12	bharts	901	budh	882	cṛt	428	dhā	676
aṅgh	13	bharv	902	bukk	878	cud	419	dhakk	669
añj	17	bhas	904	bukk	879	cuḍ	415	dham	673
aṅk	10	bhaṣ	903	bund	883	cukk	414	dhan	671
aṅk	11	bhās	909	bus	884	cul	423	dhaṇ	670
ant	27	bhaṭ	895	bust	885	culump	424	dhanv	672
anṭh	24	bhaṭ	896	cah	404	cumb	421	ḍhauk	504
āp	47	bheṣ	923	cah	405	cup	420	dhāv	677
arb	36	bhī	912	cak	382	cur	422	dhāv	678
arc	32	bhid	911	cakās	384	cūr	425	dhe	694
ard	35	bhikṣ	910	cakk	383	cūrṇ	426	dhi	679
argh	31	bhlakṣ	939	cakṣ	385	cūṣ	427	dhī	682
arh	37	bhlāś	940	cakṣ	386	cuṭ	416	dhikṣ	680
arj	33	bhlāś	941	cal	402	cuṭ	417	dhiṣ	681
arth	34	bhṛ	917	cam	396	cuṭ	418	dhor	695
arv	38	bhrāj	931	camb	397	cyu	430	dhṛ	689
as	44	bhrakṣ	927	caṇ	389	cyus	432	dhrāḍ	705
as	45	bhram	929	can	391	cyut	431	dhrai	710
aś	41	bhram	930	cañc	387	dā	608	dhrai	711
aś	42	bhraṃś	925	cand	393	dā	609	dhraj	700
aṣ	43	bhraṃś	926	caṇḍ	390	dā	610	dhraṇ	701
ās	48	bhraṇ	928	cap	394	dā	611	dhrāṅkṣ	704
aṭ	20	bhrāś	932	cap	395	dā	612	dhras	702
aṭh	23	bhrāś	933	car	398	dabh	598	dhras	703
aṭṭ	21	bhrej	934	carb	400	dad	594	dhrek	709
aṭṭ	22	bhreṣ	935	carc	399	dadh	593	dhrij	706
av	40	bhrī	936	carv	401	dagh	597	dhṛj	690
bad	864	bhṛjj	918	caṣ	403	dah	606	dhṛñj	691
bāḍ	872	bhṛṃś	919	cat	392	dah	607	dhṛṣ	692

dhṛṣ	693	dṛbh	643	ghagh	362	guṇḍ	326	i	50
dhru	707	drek	663	ghaṇṭ	365	guñj	325	īd	63
dhruv	708	dṛh	645	ghas	366	gup	332	idh	54
dhū	686	dṛp	640	ghaṭ	363	guph	333	īh	68
dhukṣ	684	dṛp	641	ghaṭṭ	364	gur	334	īj	61
dhūrv	687	dṛś	644	ghiṇṇ	367	gur	335	ikh	51
dhūś	688	dru	659	ghṛ	378	gurd	336	īkṣ	59
dhvaj	713	dru	660	ghṛ	379	gurd	337	il	56
dhvaṃs	712	druh	662	ghrā	381	gurv	338	in	53
dhvan	714	druṇ	661	ghṛṣ	380	hā	1578	iṅg	52
dhvāṅkṣ	715	du	632	ghu	368	hā	1579	īñj	62
dhvṛ	716	duh	636	ghuṇ	371	had	1573	iṅkh	60
dhyā	696	duh	637	ghuṇ	372	hal	1576	inv	55
dhyā	697	duh	638	ghuṇṇ	373	hamm	1575	īr	64
dhyai	698	dul	635	ghur	374	han	1574	īrṣy	65
dhyai	699	durv	634	ghūrṇ	376	has	1577	iṣ	57
dī	626	duṣ	633	ghūrṇ	377	haṭ	1571	iṣ	58
dī	627	dviṣ	666	ghuṣ	375	haṭh	1572	īś	66
dī	628	dviṣ	667	ghuṭ	369	heḍ	1597	īṣ	67
ḍī	502	dvṛ	668	ghuṭ	370	heḍ	1598	jabh	455
ḍī	503	dyu	683	glā	361	heṣ	1599	jāgṛ	461
dih	625	dyut	685	glah	353	heṭh	1596	jai	480
dīkṣ	629	edh	104	glai	359	hi	1580	jaj	448
dimbh	620	ej	103	glai	360	hikk	1583	jakṣ	446
dimp	619	eṣ	105	glep	356	hiṃs	1581	jakṣ	447
dinv	618	gā	316	gleṣ	358	hiṃs	1582	jal	457
dīp	630	gā	317	glev	357	hlād	1607	jalp	458
ḍip	499	gad	303	gluc	354	hlag	1605	jam	456
ḍip	500	gaḍ	299	gluñc	355	hlas	1606	jaṃs	444
ḍip	501	gaḍ	300	gṛ	345	hnu	1600	jaṃs	445
diś	623	gādh	318	gṝ	343	hṛ	1591	jan	452
diś	624	gah	315	gṝ	344	hṛ	1592	jan	453
div	621	gāh	319	grah	350	hṛ	1593	jap	454
div	622	gaj	298	granth	348	hrād	1602	jarc	462
dīv	631	gal	312	granth	349	hras	1601	jas	460
do	649	galbh	313	gras	351	hreṣ	1604	jaṣ	459
do	650	gam	304	gṛdh	346	hrī	1603	jeh	479
dṛ	639	gaṇ	301	gṛj	347	hṛṣ	1594	jeṣ	478
dṝ	646	gaṇḍ	302	gruc	352	hṛṣ	1595	jharjh	450
drā	651	garb	307	gu	320	hu	1584	jhaṣ	451
drā	652	gard	306	gu	321	hū	1590	jhaṭ	449
drā	653	garh	310	gu	322	huḍ	1585	ji	463
drāḍ	656	garh	311	guḍ	327	huḍ	1586	jim	465
drāgh	657	garj	305	gud	328	hul	1589	jinv	464
drāh	658	garv	308	gudh	329	huṇḍ	1587	jiṣ	466
drai	664	garv	309	gudh	330	hurch	1588	jīv	467
drai	665	gaveṣ	314	gudh	331	hval	1608	jñā	481
drākh	654	gep	340	guh	339	hve	1610	jṛ	474
drāṅkṣ	655	geṣ	341	guj	323	hvṛ	1609	jṝ	476
dṛbh	642	gev	342	guj	324	i	49	jṝ	477

jri	485	kas	153	klav	229	kṣmāy	269	kuṭṭ	170
jri	486	kaś	142	kleś	237	kṣmīl	270	kvaṇ	238
jri	487	kaṣ	143	klīb	234	kṣṇu	268	kvath	239
jṛmbh	475	kās	156	klīb	235	kṣu	258	lā	1157
jū	472	kāś	155	klid	230	kṣubh	263	labh	1148
juḍ	468	kaṭ	116	klind	231	kṣubh	264	lābh	1159
juḍ	469	kaṭ	117	kliś	232	kṣud	259	laḍ	1144
jūr	473	kath	131	kliś	233	kṣud	260	laḍ	1145
juṣ	471	kaṭh	118	kḷp	216	kṣudh	261	lag	1139
jut	470	katr	129	klu	236	kṣump	265	laiṅ	1189
jval	489	katth	130	kmar	208	kṣup	262	lajj	1142
jvar	488	kav	150	knas	205	kṣur	266	lakh	1138
jyā	482	kav	151	knath	204	kṣvel	272	lakṣ	1135
jyā	483	kel	194	knu	206	kṣviḍ	271	lakṣ	1136
jyut	484	kep	193	knūy	207	kū	195	lakṣ	1137
kab	134	khac	273	kṛ	209	kuc	165	lal	1152
kac	113	khac	274	kṛ	210	kuḍ	171	lamb	1149
kac	114	khac	275	kṝ	215	kud	180	lāñch	1158
kad	132	khād	288	kram	220	kūḍ	197	laṇḍ	1146
kaḍ	127	khad	281	krand	218	kūḍ	198	laṅg	1140
kaḍ	128	khai	297	krap	219	kuh	192	laṅgh	1141
kaḍḍ	133	khaj	276	krath	217	kuj	166	lap	1147
kag	112	khan	282	krī	221	kuj	167	larb	1151
kai	203	khaṇḍ	278	krīḍ	222	kūj	196	las	1156
kak	110	khañj	277	kṛp	212	kuk	164	laś	1153
kakh	111	kharb	285	kṛś	213	kul	186	laṣ	1154
kal	138	khard	284	kṛṣ	214	kumb	183	laṣ	1155
kal	139	kharj	283	kṛt	211	kumb	184	laṭ	1143
kal	140	kharv	286	krudh	224	kuṃś	188	lay	1150
kall	141	khaṣ	287	kruñc	223	kuṃś	189	lep	1188
kam	135	khaṭ	279	kruś	225	kuṇ	172	lī	1167
kamb	137	khaṭṭ	280	kṣā	249	kuṇ	173	lī	1168
kamp	136	khel	295	kṣad	242	kuñc	168	lih	1166
kaṃs	152	kheṭ	294	kṣai	267	kuṇḍ	176	likh	1160
kan	120	khid	290	kṣaj	240	kuṇḍ	177	liṅg	1161
kaṇ	119	khiṭ	289	kṣaj	241	kunth	181	liṅg	1162
kañc	115	khu	291	kṣal	248	kuṇṭh	174	lip	1163
kand	125	khuj	292	kṣam	245	kuṇṭh	175	liś	1164
kand	126	khuṇḍ	293	kṣamp	246	kup	182	liś	1165
kaṇḍ	121	khyā	296	kṣan	243	kur	185	loc	1191
kaṅk	122	kil	159	kṣap	244	kūrd	201	lok	1190
kāṅkṣ	154	kil	160	kṣar	247	kūrd	202	lū	1185
kaṇṭh	123	kīl	163	kṣi	250	kuś	187	lubh	1180
kaṇṭh	124	kīrt	162	kṣi	251	kuṣ	190	luḍ	1173
karb	148	kiṣk	158	kṣī	253	kuṣ	191	luḍ	1174
kard	147	kiṭ	157	kṣī	254	kuṭ	169	lul	1183
karj	144	kīṭ	161	kṣīb	256	kūṭ	199	lumb	1181
karṇ	145	klam	228	kṣīj	255	kūṭ	200	lumb	1182
kartr	146	kland	227	kṣip	252	kuth	179	luñc	1169
karv	149	klath	226	kṣiv	257	kuts	178	luṇṭ	1175

luṇṭ	1176	mev	1017	mur	1006	pā	781	pis	796
lunth	1178	mi	980	mūrch	1012	pac	756	piś	792
luṇṭh	1177	mī	989	murv	1007	pac	757	piṣ	793
lup	1179	mī	990	muṣ	1008	pac	758	piṭ	785
luṣ	1184	mī	991	mūṣ	1014	pad	768	plakṣ	851
lūṣ	1186	mid	982	must	1009	pai	836	plī	853
lūṣ	1187	mih	988	muṭ	1003	paiṇ	837	plih	852
luṭ	1170	mil	983	muṭ	1004	pakṣ	754	plu	854
luṭ	1171	mīl	993	nabh	725	pakṣ	755	pluṣ	855
luṭh	1172	mīm	992	nad	723	pāl	782	pluṣ	856
mā	972	miś	984	nād	734	pal	775	pluṣ	857
mā	973	miṣ	986	nah	732	pan	769	pṛ	826
mā	974	miṣ	987	nakh	719	paṇ	761	pṛ	827
mabhr	960	miśr	985	nakh	720	paṇḍ	762	pṝ	828
mac	948	mith	981	nakk	717	paṇḍ	763	pṝ	829
mad	953	mīv	994	nakṣ	718	paṇḍ	764	prā	843
mah	971	mlā	1034	nal	729	panth	770	praś	841
māh	979	mlai	1039	nal	730	pard	772	prath	842
majj	949	mlecch	1036	nam	726	parṇ	773	pṛc	830
makh	943	mleṭ	1037	nand	724	parv	774	preṅkh	848
makṣ	942	mlev	1038	naṅkh	721	paś	776	preṣ	849
mal	965	mluc	1035	nard	728	paś	777	prī	844
maṃh	970	mokṣ	1031	naś	731	paṣ	778	proth	850
man	954	mokṣ	1032	nās	736	paṣ	779	pṛṣ	832
man	955	mṛ	1018	naṭ	722	pat	765	pṛth	831
maṇ	951	mrakṣ	1033	nāth	733	pat	766	pru	845
mān	976	mṛd	1025	nay	727	paṭ	759	pruṣ	846
mand	959	mṛd	1026	nāy	735	path	767	pruṣ	847
maṇḍ	952	mṛd	1024	ned	752	paṭh	760	psā	858
maṅgh	946	mṛdh	1027	neṣ	753	pāv	783	pū	822
maṅgh	947	mṛg	1020	nī	746	pay	771	pū	823
maṅk	944	mṛj	1021	nij	738	pel	833	puḍ	802
maṅkh	945	mṛj	1022	nij	739	pes	835	puḍ	803
māṅkṣ	975	mṛj	1023	nikṣ	737	peṣ	834	pūj	824
manth	958	mṛṇ	1028	nil	742	phakk	859	pul	813
mantr	956	mṛś	1029	nīl	747	phal	861	pul	814
mantr	957	mṛṣ	1030	niṃs	743	phaṇ	860	pul	815
marb	963	mruc	1019	nind	740	phel	862	puṃs	820
marc	962	mū	1011	ninv	741	pi	784	puṇ	804
mārg	977	muc	995	niṣ	744	pī	797	puṇ	805
mārj	978	muc	996	niṣk	745	pīḍ	798	puṇḍ	807
marv	964	mud	1005	nīv	748	pīl	799	puṇṭ	806
mas	968	muh	1010	nṛt	751	piṃs	790	punth	809
maś	966	muj	997	nu	749	piṃs	791	pur	810
maṣ	967	mūl	1013	nud	750	piṇḍ	786	purv	811
mask	969	muṇ	998	okh	106	piṇḍ	787	purv	812
maṭh	950	muṇḍ	1001	olaṇḍ	108	pinv	788	puṣ	816
may	961	muṇḍ	1002	olaṇḍ	109	pinv	789	puṣ	817
me	1015	muṇṭ	999	oṇ	107	pis	794	puṣ	818
mep	1016	muṇṭh	1000	pā	780	pis	795	puṣp	819

pust	821	ri	1097	sādh	1448	śauṭ	1388	snih	1522
puṭ	800	rī	1106	sādh	1449	śav	1337	snih	1523
puth	808	ric	1100	sag	1427	ścut	1390	snu	1524
puṭṭ	801	ric	1101	sagh	1428	ścyut	1391	snuh	1526
pūy	825	riṅg	1099	sah	1444	sek	1480	snus	1525
pyā	838	riṅkh	1098	sah	1445	śel	1386	so	1483
pyai	840	riṇv	1102	sai	1482	sev	1481	spand	1528
pyāy	839	riph	1103	śak	1315	śev	1387	spardh	1531
ṛ	93	riś	1104	śak	1316	si	1452	spaś	1532
rā	1091	riṣ	1105	śākh	1343	si	1453	sphā	1536
rabh	1081	ṛj	95	sal	1442	śi	1350	sphal	1529
rac	1071	ṛṇ	98	śal	1336	śi	1351	sphar	1530
rad	1077	ṛṇ	99	śāl	1345	śī	1356	sphāy	1537
radh	1078	roḍ	1134	śāl	1346	śī	1357	sphiṭ	1538
rādh	1094	ṛph	100	śalbh	1347	śībh	1360	sphiṭṭ	1539
rādh	1095	ṛṣ	101	sam	1439	sic	1454	sphuḍ	1542
rag	1067	ṛṣ	102	sam	1440	sidh	1456	sphul	1546
rag	1068	ru	1107	śam	1331	sidh	1457	sphuṇṭ	1543
rah	1089	ruc	1108	sāmaya	1451	śīk	1358	sphuṇṭ	1544
rai	1133	rud	1116	śamb	1332	śikṣ	1359	sphur	1545
rāj	1093	rudh	1117	śamb	1333	sil	1458	sphūrj	1547
rak	1064	rudh	1118	śaṁs	1389	śil	1355	sphuṭ	1540
rakh	1066	rudh	1119	san	1436	śīl	1361	sphuṭ	1541
rākh	1092	ruh	1123	śaṇ	1326	śiñj	1352	spṛ	1533
rakṣ	1065	ruh	1124	śaṇ	1327	śiṣ	1354	spṛh	1535
ram	1082	ruj	1109	sañj	1430	śiṭ	1353	spṛś	1534
ramb	1084	rūkṣ	1125	sañj	1431	siṭ	1455	sṛ	1475
ramb	1085	ruṇṭ	1114	śaṅk	1317	sīv	1459	sṛ	1476
raṁh	1090	ruṇṭh	1115	sāntv	1450	skambh	1485	śṝ	1385
ramph	1083	rup	1120	sap	1437	skand	1484	śrā	1403
raṇ	1075	rūp	1126	śap	1329	skhad	1491	śrā	1404
raṇ	1076	ruś	1121	sarb	1441	skhal	1492	śram	1400
raṅgh	1070	ruṣ	1122	śarb	1334	sku	1486	śram	1401
rañj	1072	rūṣ	1127	śarv	1335	sku	1487	śrambh	1402
rañj	1073	rūṣ	1128	śas	1340	skumbh	1489	sraṁs	1555
raṅkh	1069	ruṭ	1110	śaś	1338	skumbh	1490	śraṇ	1396
rap	1079	ruṭ	1111	śaṣ	1339	skund	1488	śraṇ	1397
raph	1080	ruṭh	1112	śās	1348	ślāgh	1412	śraṅk	1395
ras	1087	ruṭh	1113	śās	1349	ślākh	1411	śranth	1399
ras	1088	sā	1446	sas	1443	ślaṅk	1409	śrath	1398
raṭ	1074	śā	1341	saṭ	1433	ślath	1410	sṛbh	1479
ray	1086	śā	1342	śaṭ	1319	śliṣ	1413	śṛdh	1383
ṛc	94	śabd	1330	śaṭ	1320	ślok	1414	śṛdh	1384
ṛdh	96	sabhāj	1438	śaṭh	1321	śloṇ	1415	srek	1557
ṛdh	97	sac	1429	śaṭh	1322	smi	1548	śri	1405
rebh	1132	śac	1318	śaṭh	1323	śmīl	1392	śrī	1406
rek	1129	sad	1432	śaṭh	1324	smiṭ	1549	sṛj	1477
rep	1131	śad	1328	śaṭh	1325	smṛ	1550	śroṇ	1408
reṭ	1130	śāḍ	1344	satr	1435	snā	1521	sṛp	1478
ri	1096	sādh	1447	saṭṭ	1434	snai	1527	sru	1556

śru	1407	śūl	1381	tam	518	tṛṣ	574	ukṣ	69
stai	1512	śūl	1382	taṃs	505	trup	584	umbh	82
stak	1493	śulk	1377	tan	514	truṭ	582	uñch	75
stambh	1495	śumbh	1375	tan	515	truṭ	583	und	78
stambh	1496	śun	1372	tañc	510	tsar	592	uṅkh	71
stambh	1497	śundh	1373	taṇḍ	513	tu	536	ūrd	86
stan	1494	śundh	1374	tandr	516	tubh	546	ūrj	85
sten	1509	śuṇṭh	1367	taṅg	509	tubh	547	ūrṇu	87
step	1510	śuṇṭh	1368	taṅk	508	tud	543	ūrv	88
step	1511	sur	1466	ṭaṅk	490	tud	540	uṣ	84
sthā	1518	śūr	1379	tap	517	tud	541	ūṣ	90
sthag	1516	śūr	1380	tard	521	tuḍḍ	542	uṭh	83
sthal	1517	sūrkṣ	1474	tarj	520	tuh	562	ūy	89
ṣṭhīv	1424	śuṣ	1376	tark	519	tuj	537	vā	1236
ṣṭhīv	1425	śuṭh	1365	tas	524	tuj	538	vā	1237
sthuḍ	1519	śuṭh	1366	taṭ	511	tul	558	vac	1197
sthūl	1520	suṭṭ	1463	ṭauk	494	tul	559	vac	1198
stim	1498	svad	1560	tay	523	tump	552	vad	1208
stip	1499	svād	1567	tāy	525	tump	553	vah	1235
stṝ	1506	svaj	1558	tej	565	tuṇ	544	vāh	1243
stṝ	1507	śval	1419	tep	566	tuṇḍ	545	vai	1294
stṝh	1508	śvalk	1420	tev	567	tup	548	vaj	1199
stu	1500	svan	1561	tigh	528	tup	549	vaj	1200
stu	1501	svañj	1559	tij	529	tuph	550	vakh	1193
stubh	1503	śvaṅk	1416	ṭīk	493	tuph	551	vakṣ	1192
stuc	1502	svap	1562	tik	526	tur	554	val	1220
stūp	1504	svap	1563	tik	527	tur	555	val	1221
stūp	1505	svar	1564	tīk	534	tur	556	valbh	1224
styā	1513	svar	1565	til	532	turv	557	valg	1223
styai	1514	svard	1566	till	533	tus	560	valh	1226
styai	1515	śvas	1417	tim	531	tuṣ	561	valh	1227
su	1460	śvas	1418	tip	530	tuṭ	539	valk	1222
sū	1468	ṣvaṣk	1426	ṭip	492	tvac	589	vall	1225
sū	1469	śvi	1421	tīv	535	tvakṣ	587	vam	1215
sū	1470	svid	1568	tṝ	563	ṭval	495	van	1209
sū	1471	svid	1569	tṝ	564	tvaṅg	588	van	1210
śū	1378	śvind	1423	trā	581	tvar	590	vaṇ	1205
subh	1464	śvit	1422	trai	585	tviṣ	591	vañc	1201
subh	1465	svṛ	1570	trakh	577	tyaj	568	vāñch	1239
śubh	1370	śyā	1393	traṃs	576	ubh	80	vand	1211
śubh	1371	śyai	1394	trand	578	ubh	81	vaṅgh	1196
sūc	1472	syam	1552	trap	579	ubj	79	vaṅk	1194
śuc	1362	syam	1553	tras	580	uc	72	vaṅkh	1195
śuc	1363	syam	1554	trauk	586	uch	73	vāṅkṣ	1238
śucy	1364	syand	1551	tṛd	571	udhras	76	vaṇṭ	1206
sūd	1473	taḍ	512	tṛh	575	udhras	77	vaṇṭ	1207
śudh	1369	tak	506	tṛkṣ	569	ūh	91	vap	1212
suh	1467	takṣ	507	tṛṇ	570	ūh	92	vap	1213
sukh	1461	tal	522	tṛp	572	ujjh	74	vap	1214
sukh	1462	ṭal	491	tṛp	573	ukh	70	varc	1217

vardh	1219	vlī	1314	yu	1052
varṇ	1218	vṛ	1271	yu	1053
vas	1230	vṛ	1272	yu	1054
vas	1231	vṛ	1273	yu	1055
vas	1232	vṛ	1274	yudh	1060
vaś	1228	vraj	1305	yuj	1057
vaṣ	1229	vraṇ	1306	yuj	1058
vās	1242	vraṇ	1307	yuṅg	1056
vāś	1241	vraṇ	1308	yup	1061
vask	1233	vraśc	1309	yut	1059
vast	1234	vṛdh	1282	yu	1052
vaṭ	1202	vṛh	1285	yu	1053
vaṭ	1203	vrī	1310		
vaṭh	1204	vrī	1311		
vāvṛt	1240	vrīḍ	1312		
vay	1216	vṛj	1277		
ve	1286	vṛk	1275		
veh	1293	vṛkṣ	1276		
vel	1289	vṛṇ	1278		
vel	1290	vṛṇ	1279		
ven	1288	vṛś	1283		
veṇ	1287	vṛṣ	1284		
veṣṭ	1292	vṛt	1280		
vevī	1291	vṛt	1281		
vī	1264	vruḍ	1313		
vic	1244	vuṇṭ	1270		
vid	1249	vyā	1301		
vid	1250	vyac	1295		
vid	1251	vyadh	1297		
vid	1252	vyath	1296		
vid	1253	vyay	1298		
vīḍ	1266	vyay	1299		
vīḍ	1267	vyay	1300		
viḍamb	1247	vye	1304		
viḍamb	1248	vyuṣ	1302		
vidh	1254	vyuṣ	1303		
vidh	1255	yā	1048		
vij	1245	yabh	1045		
vij	1246	yāc	1049		
vīj	1265	yaj	1042		
vil	1258	yakṣ	1040		
vil	1259	yakṣ	1041		
vip	1257	yam	1046		
vīr	1268	yantr	1044		
vīr	1269	yas	1047		
viś	1260	yat	1043		
viṣ	1261	yauṭ	1050		
viṣ	1262	yeṣ	1062		
viṣk	1263	yeṣ	1063		
vith	1256	yu	1051